RETIREMENT
PLANNING
HANDBOOK

ALLIED DUNBAR

RETIREMENT PLANNING HANDBOOK

by

D C Vessey

© Allied Dunbar Assurance plc 1994

ISBN 0 75200 0772

Published by

Longman Law, Tax and Finance
Longman Group Limited
21–27 Lamb's Conduit Street, London WC1N 3NJ

Associated Offices
Australia, Hong Kong, Malaysia, Singapore, USA

A CIP catalogue record for this book is available
from the British Library

Cover designed and illustrated by Sigmund Shalit, London

Typeset by Servis Filmsetting Ltd, Manchester
Printed and bound in Great Britain by
Biddles Ltd, Guildford and King's Lynn

Abbreviations

A and M	accumulation and maintenance
ADL	activities of daily living
APPP	appropriate personal pension plan
ARHM	Association of Retirement Housing Managers
AVC	additional voluntary contribution
COMPS	contracted-out money purchase scheme
CRAG	Charging for Residential Accommodation Guide
DSS	Department of Social Security
EC	European Community
EPP	executive pension plan
ERM	exchange rate mechanism
FIMBRA	Financial Intermediaries Managers and Brokers Regulatory Association
FOTRA	free of tax to residents abroad
FRASH	Federation of Residents Associations in Sheltered Housing (England and Wales)
FSAVC	free-standing additional voluntary contribution
FURBS	funded unapproved retirement benefit scheme
GMP	guaranteed minimum pension
HRP	home responsibilities protection
IHT	inheritance tax
IMRO	Investment Management Regulatory Organisation
LAPR	life assurance premium relief
LAUTRO	Life Assurance and Unit Trust Regulatory Organisation
NHBC	National House Building Council
NHS	National Health Service
PAYE	pay as you earn
PEP	personal equity plan
PET	potentially exempt transfer
PHI	permanent health insurance
PIA	Personal Investment Authority
PIBS	permanent interest bearing share
RPI	retail prices index
SAYE	save as you earn

SERPS	State earnings related pension scheme
SFA	Securities and Futures Authority
SHACS	Sheltered Housing Advisory and Conciliation Service
SIB	Securities and Investments Board
SRHOC	Sheltered Retirement Housing Owners Confederation (Scotland)
SRO	self-regulatory organisation
TESSA	tax exempt special savings scheme

Preface

For those living on, or just about to start living on a retirement income, Britain's departure from the Exchange Rate Mechanism must have left them wondering whether or not the sky was falling in. Although good news for businesses and those with a hefty mortgage to pay off, the subsequent reduction in interest rates to their lowest levels for over 20 years has not been good news for those living on their savings and probably led to more than one carefully packaged set of retirement plans being taken out of cold storage.

It was probably that one event which, more than anything else, suggested a rethink of the structure of this, the fifth edition of the *Allied Dunbar Retirement Planning Handbook*. It seemed appropriate that a book sponsored by a financial services company should concentrate on financial matters and leave discussion of health and leisure to those better placed to comment on them. This in no way devalues the part played by the early contributors and I am grateful to Dr Beric Wright and his colleagues for the part they played in getting the earlier editions on the map.

I have also taken the opportunity to introduce some topics which were not covered in earlier editions. Many people will, like me, be planning their own imminent retirement knowing full well that they will be sharing it with their parents or other older relatives. This inevitably means the possibility of needing outside help at some time or other and it seemed to me to be important that readers should be aware of how that help is going to be made available under the provisions of the Community Care Act.

I have set out to give the reader as broad an understanding of the various aspects of retirement planning as I can. No book of this nature can cover the whole field of, say, pensions, in complete detail; what I have tried to do is to make the reader aware of the options that are available as well as explaining some of the background behind the options.

Pensions

Pensions do require a little more detail at this point because they will be the mainstay of most people's retirement plans. The usual cry is 'why must they be so complicated?' The answer is that, in its desire to change the basis of personal taxation (lower tax rates, but fewer tax breaks), to reduce the future burden of State pensions (by decreasing the benefits in the future) and to make us all more involved in planning our own retirement (by opening up personal pensions and removing some of the restrictions on company pensions), the present Government has introduced a whole series of changes affecting State pensions, company pensions and personal pensions. There then have to be transitional arrangements for those people already in pension schemes and, in order to be seen to be fair, the old systems sometimes have to run alongside the new. The end result is a total pensions system of mind-boggling complexity which frequently runs into problems because of earlier changes and even changes before that.

I have tried to show that there is some logical structure to it all but, for specific solutions to individual problems, the reader may well have to seek personal advice—hopefully with a better understanding of the questions to ask. I am afraid there is little evidence that pensions are ever going to get simpler.

A question of sex

I have written a number of brochures and booklets in my time at Allied Dunbar and I have yet to find a good way of coping with topics that are equally relevant to both sexes. The use of 'he or she', 'him or her' and 'his or hers' just becomes irritating after a while, so I have taken the easy way out and, unless the context clearly identifies women as the subject matter, I have settled for 'he', 'his' and 'him' throughout.

Acknowledgments

Writing a book from scratch is never easy and the earlier editions proved to be a useful starting point. I am grateful to one of the original writers, Barry Bean of Ove Arup, for his suggestions on how the new edition should be structured.

I am no expert on some of the fine detail of financial planning and, in writing this book, I have learned a lot about things that have an impact on my own retirement plans. My tutors have been many and various and I extend my thanks to:

Tony Reardon (author of the *Allied Dunbar Pensions Handbook*) and Ray Dean, both of Allied Dunbar for their help on the pensions chapters.

The Swindon branch of Norwich Union for their help in providing the annuity figures in chapter 5.

Jeremy Burnett-Rae of Threadneedle Asset Management (and one of the contributors to the *Allied Dunbar Investment and Savings Handbook*) for his help on the investment chapter.

Tony Foreman (author of the *Allied Dunbar Tax Handbook*) and Bob Durham at Pannell Kerr Forster for their help on the tax chapters and the chapter on trusts.

Peter Kelly of Allied Dunbar for his help on the chapter on financial protection.

Stuart Reynolds of Allied Dunbar for his help with the chapter on wills.

Mr and Mrs Venman of Stainsbridge House Residential Home in Malmesbury, Wiltshire and Mr O'Dea of Goatacre House Nursing Home in Goatacre, Wiltshire for their kindness in showing me round their establishments and for broadening my understanding of the Community Care Act.

The mystery voices on the DSS Helpline who answered all my questions on State benefits.

Mark Davies of Allied Dunbar who read the entire manuscript to make sure the lawyers could sleep at nights.

The indefatigable duo of Jilli Smith and Silvia Saddleton at Longman Law, Tax and Finance for their ideas, patience and help during the production stage.

Finally, my apologies to all those writers who have written books or even just chapters of books for Allied Dunbar. I have bullied them all at some time or other during the last ten or so years to get their manuscripts in on time. In writing this book, I have found out, for the first time, exactly what I have been putting them through.

D C Vessey
June 1994

Contents

1 Introduction

This opening chapter looks at the structure of the book and explains why the various topics have been included. It covers the current environment in which retirement planning is being conducted, with particular emphasis on the rapidly changing world of pensions.

1.1 The structure of the book

The book is broadly in three sections. The first section (chapters 2 to 6) concentrates mainly on pension planning because that has to be the bedrock of most people's preparation for the future. However, many people may not be able to provide for all their retirement needs through their pension and so this section looks at other areas of investment as well.

The second section (chapters 7 to 12) looks at more general areas of personal financial planning. Tax is covered in this section, as are wills and trusts. There is also a chapter on retiring abroad.

The third section (chapters 13 to 15) looks more to the elderly. With an increasing number of people taking early retirement and with elderly people living longer, two generations of retired people in the same family is no longer unusual. The problem of looking after elderly people (an area where help from the public sector is looking increasingly limited) is one which may face many people planning for their own retirement. They also, of course, have to start thinking about their own old age.

Finally, chapter 16 contains a list of useful addresses and other details on where you might get further information.

1.2 The Goode committee

One of the most shocking incidents of the last few years was the Maxwell scandal. As the extent of the plundering of his employees' pension funds became clearer, it was obvious that action was needed. The Goode committee was set up to investigate the changes that were needed in order to safeguard the interests of future pensioners and the committee's recommendations will form the basis of a new Pensions Act.

As part of the investigation, Professor Goode and his colleagues spent some time investigating attitudes towards pensions. In general, they found that most people hold somewhat perverse views about an area of financial planning which offers more tax breaks than any other form of investment and which also offers the chance to enjoy a lifelong standard of living. Nevertheless, it was the generally held opinion that pensions were dull and it seems that they only lose that somewhat unwelcome aura when *something* triggers off the thought that perhaps they are not so bad after all.

The factors which adversely affected pension planning were as follows:

(1) People were apathetic and uninterested about pensions because they considered them boring and complicated.

(2) They were ignorant about pensions and assumed that the State would provide for them in their old age.

(3) They were reluctant to commit to such a long-term objective at a time when they had more pressing financial needs.

(4) They did not have a stable job environment in which to start a long-term financial commitment.

The factors which triggered more positive thoughts about retirement planning were:

(1) a realisation that they were not getting any younger;

(2) access to an occupational or personal pension scheme;

(3) a change in personal responsibilities such as marriage or parenthood;

(4) a realisation of the inadequacy of their own pension and the fact that State pensions are not likely to fill the gap.

The objective of this book is to be a further positive trigger. By and large, financial planning can never be a subject to set the pulse racing but living on the breadline after a lifetime of work doesn't seem too exciting either. Planning for our own future financial security does at least have the advantage that we will be the beneficiaries of the time we spend on it.

1.3   A time of uncertainty

This book is being written at a time of great uncertainty about the future of the Welfare State. There is a growing debate on the extent to which the State can be expected to help people at every stage of their lives. As the greatest single component of the social security budget is pensions, warning noises are being made about the extent to which anybody, particularly younger and better paid people, can look to the State for help in retirement.

At the same time, though, in its attempts to create a 'level playing field' for investment, the government is constantly reviewing the tax framework in which pensions are planned. Anybody preparing for their retirement could be forgiven for believing that in an attempt to level the pitch, the referee has, at various times throughout the match, decided to change the rules and move the goal posts. Sometimes, it is tempting to wonder whether we are still all playing the same game.

Increasing restrictions

For the pensions industry, one of life's perennial frustrations lies in the difficulty in getting the message across. Whilst the pensions legislation ushered in since 1988 has done a lot to improve flexibility and to give greater fairness to job movers, this has been achieved at the expense of reduced tax concessions. One of the most far reaching of these is the so-called 'earnings cap' which was introduced in 1989. It limits the level of pensionable income and has implications for everybody joining a pension scheme. The level of the earnings cap is technically supposed to rise each year in line with the retail prices index, but was actually frozen in 1993–94. For many company employees, the earnings cap currently means a maximum possible pension, in today's terms, of just over £51,000 a year.

Many younger people, at an early stage in their careers, may well feel that such limitations are academic and only for high flyers. They may well believe that the legislation is not intended to affect them. But it *is* intended to affect them and it always was. In his book *The View From No 11*, Nigel Lawson (the man who introduced the earnings cap) has the following to say:

> 'Although the limit sounds and is high, over the years, as earnings rise faster than prices, its significance will steadily grow'.

Most readers who are employees will be familiar with the idea of expense reporting on form P11D. This has been in place for many years and was originally introduced for 'directors and higher paid employees' earning above a certain limit. In 1972 the limit was £2,000; by 1978 it had been increased to £8,500 and there it has remained ever since. In 1979, £8,500 certainly was a high income; today, it represents about half the national average earnings. The only changes of any significance are that the volume of paperwork has mushroomed and that the words 'higher paid' have been quietly dropped. Form P11D is now part of the scenery and the earnings cap will end up being looked at in the same way.

Current legislation is designed to ensure that the tax concessions granted to pensions for many years are gradually eroded. Restrictions introduced today and aimed ostensibly at the rich are designed quite deliberately to affect everybody in time. Nobody can afford to put off planning their pension.

The book is also being written at a time of great financial uncertainty. With inflation declared effectively dead (at least for the time being) and with interest rates at their lowest level for nearly twenty years, many assumptions about retirement planning are having to be reviewed. For people with personal pension plans or anybody not cushioned by the guarantees of a company pension based on salary, the fall in interest rates has had a particularly serious effect.

The problem of ignorance

If these two uncertainties were not enough, most people planning their retirement will concede ignorance about pensions. The past ten years have probably seen more changes than the preceding seventy and the end result is a bewildering mixture of incentives and restrictions, all mixed up in a legislative tangle of rules and regulations. In a book of this nature (which is intended to be helpful) there is the danger of falling between not two but several stools. Over-complication could lead to lack of comprehension, but over-simplification could lead to it being less than comprehensive. What the author has set out to do is to inform the reader of all the options, but has not prescribed any specific solutions. Like any set of directions, it can only go so far. At a certain point, the message becomes too complicated and the only advice can be 'stop and ask the way'.

1.4   Planning your pension

This book is meant to be a practical book with suggestions on what to do and why. It is therefore not *just* a text book filled with information which has to be absorbed. However, in planning a retirement income, the text book approach cannot be ignored because there is a fair amount of information to be absorbed before the plan starts to make sense. Overall, the sequence of events is to decide what level of income you need to live on, then to find out what you can expect to get from your pension if you do nothing different, and then make plans to plug the gap. Addressing these apparently very simple points can only be done successfully if you understand some of the technical background.

First though, this part of the chapter is going to consider an overall methodology on which to base your retirement financial planning.

Step 1—How much will you need?

What this book will not do is ask you to get out the proverbial large piece of paper and to start estimating what you think you might spend on, say, clothes in fifteen years' time. What it will ask you to do is to accept that if you live comfortably on a gross salary of £X *per annum* now, the chances are that you will need in the region of £X *per annum* when you retire - in real terms that is.

Some commentators make all kinds of assumptions on where expenditure will fall and normally state that you won't have the costs of being at work. True - but while you are at work, you don't have the costs of more leisure time. By and large, the safest assumption to make is that you currently live quite well on your current take home pay and the same level of income should be your target for when you retire.

However, the one area where you will save is that, once retired, you will not be contributing to a pension plan and your national insurance contributions will either be relatively small or nothing at all. In order to have a target to aim at, we will take 'in the region of' as meaning 85 per cent of your current gross salary in real terms. By and large, taking into account the reduction in pension and national insurance contributions, your net salary should end up as more or less the same.

Somebody on a gross salary of £30,000 *per annum* today, therefore, will be aiming for the equivalent of £25,000 *per annum* at retirement.

Step 2—How much will you get?

The pension you can expect will come from at least one, usually two and often all three of the following sources:

(1)   State pension.
(2)   Company pension.
(3)   Personal pension.

Chapters 2 to 4 look at each of these in turn and each chapter includes a section on how you can find out what you are likely to get from each of these sources.

For the purpose of this chapter, we will assume that our individual on £30,000 *per annum* will get a State pension of £7,000 *per annum* in today's terms and that his company pension will provide him with half his final salary. As he has no idea what his final salary is going to be, his only way forward is to assume that his current salary will keep pace with inflation, ie he can anticipate a pension in today's terms of £15,000 *per annum*.

He is therefore looking forward to a total pension, in today's terms, of £22,000, but would like £25,000 to be comfortable.

Step 3—How do you make up the difference?

This is the area where we have to start making assumptions. In order to provide a source of income, he will have to take into account a number of factors.

How long will he need the income for? Let's assume that each man feels he has a reasonable expectation of living until he is 85. If he hopes to retire at 60, he has to provide his missing income for 25 years.

Assuming that his investments can earn interest at five per cent, he will need a lump sum of 14 × his required income to provide the income. To get an additional income of £3,000 a year for 25 years, he will need a lump sum of £42,000.

The factors for other timescales over which the income may be needed (based on a net interest rate of five per cent) are:

Years	15	20	25	30	35
Factor	10	12½	14	15	16

When will he need the income? The further away the point is, the more time he has to prepare. However, because of inflation, he will need a larger sum than £42,000 because he will need a larger income than £3,000.

Let us assume our individual is 45 now (ie he has 15 years to go to retirement) and that he believes that over the 15 years inflation will average five per cent. How much bigger than £3,000 will his income need to be?

The income he needs at age 60 under these assumptions is twice what he thought it was (2.07 times bigger to be precise). The factors for various other timescales and rates of inflation are as follows:

Years	5	10	15	20
Inflation				
1%	1.05	1.10	1.16	1.22
2%	1.10	1.22	1.34	1.48
5%	1.28	1.63	2.07	2.65
10%	1.61	2.59	4.17	6.73

Consequently, and under the assumptions of timescale, interest rates and inflation he has made, the lump sum he actually needs at retirement to make up his pension shortfall is £84,000.

Purists will no doubt find fault with the accuracy of the model and the impracticality of guessing what interest rates and inflation might be over the next 40 years. But it is not meant to be accurate; it's meant to provide a basis for working out what kind of gap may be emerging. It is little more than a pointer to the fact that something needs to be done, although the purist's views are a clear indication that the situation has to be reviewed on a regular basis.

For a man with 15 years to go to retirement, the figures *will* be crude, but he will at least have 15 years in which to take constant corrective action. A man with two years to go will begin to get a very much more precise idea of his needs, but very little time in which to plug any gaps.

This will always be one of the fundamental problems in pension planning, but the rather crude approach outlined above does at least provide some basis for an action. The essential point is that estimates of your future pension can be obtained and this has to be the first step in your retirement planning.

As to making up the difference, the first choice has to be *improving* your pension because that will be the most tax-efficient way of making up the shortfall. Chapters 2 to 4 are largely devoted to the ways in which you can improve the various types of pension you may be entitled to. This has to be the first step in any review of our retirement plans because of the tax breaks attached to pension plans.

Step 4—Are there any tweaks to the system?

There is one aspect of pension legislation that helps to solve some of the problems. Although, under the circumstances, it is not surprising that few people understand the details of their pension arrangements, it is also true that most do not understand the flexibility of their actual pension when they come to take it. With the State pension, it is true that there are few choices, (but there are *some*), but with company pensions, and even more so with personal pensions, the choices become almost bewildering. Once again, the time factor doesn't help us. Anybody enquiring about a pension due in 15 years' time is likely to be given a figure. Anybody enquiring about the pension they can expect when they retire in six months' time, could find themselves with dozens of options.

Pensions tend to be seen as simply 'an income for life' over which we have little control. The reality is that, although once we have made certain decisions about our pension we are stuck with them, we have considerable flexibility over when we make those decisions and over what the decisions involve.

Chapter 5 looks at this topic in much more detail.

Time is the problem

The further we are from the event, when time is on our side, the less likely we are to tackle the problem. 'There's plenty of time yet' we say, and then tend to ignore the fact that there *is* plenty of time. Later on, when the problem is more obvious, time is against us.

But is it a real problem? After all, the man in our example was only £3,000 *per annum* short. He was, but in our example, he was going to qualify for a company pension equal to half his salary. To obtain that, he may have had to have been in his company pension scheme for 20 years. Many people won't achieve that.

And he is 'only' £3,000 short because, for him, the £7,000 a year from the State represents almost a quarter of his requirements. But that is a fixed amount. If he earned double his current income, he might still only qualify for a State pension of £7,000 a year leaving him with a shortfall of £14,000 a year at retirement. And, although the State pension will help, he won't be able to draw it until he is 65.

The key message is that it is never really too early to start planning a pension because it can be so difficult to catch up later on. Within 15 years of retirement, you should be fully committed to maximising your pension. The other investments that can help you to make up your retirement income shortfall can probably be looked at over a shorter timescale although, as you begin to get a clearer idea of your retirement needs, ten years before retirement is not too late to start thinking about supplementing your pension.

Chapter 6 looks at these other investments in more detail. It looks at the range of investments suitable for the short-to-medium term (two to five years) and for the longer term (five or more years) and suggests an overall investment strategy. We have not gone into too much detail on the technical features of each investment. The essential thing is for you to decide what your needs are, what your tax position is and what type of investor you are. Armed with that knowledge about yourself, you can then assess what type of investments you should consider.

For anybody approaching retirement, the choice of investment has an added twist in that our tax position could change literally overnight. One minute we could be enjoying the salary and opportunities of a higher rate tax payer; the next we could be living on a pension and perhaps only paying tax at the basic rate. This merely means taking a little more care when selecting investments as we approach retirement. One that is recommended because of its benefits to higher rate tax payers may be less attractive at a later time.

1.5   Other financial planning

Protecting your finances

Whilst pension planning, and looking at the broad range of additional investments, will provide the fundamental basis of an income in retirement, there are other aspects of financial planning that cannot be ignored. Providing the total level of financial resources to see us through retirement can be difficult enough without our plans being torpedoed by death, ill health or accident along the way.

Most important is the area of financial protection, the best known, of course, being life assurance. Many forms of pension plan include an element of life cover, but that is not a good reason for not having additional life cover. Chapter 7 looks at the various forms of life cover and suggests an approach for deciding how much you may need. Although we have tried as far as possible to avoid sexist undertones (the book is addressed to 'he' and 'him' to avoid the tedious 'he or she'), this is one area where women, particularly married women, have to take notice. Regardless of European diktat, women live longer than men (about four years more on average) and our relative maturities at a younger age show up in the fact that women tend to marry men four or five years older than themselves. Put these two statistics together, and you end up with the fact that the average married woman will be a widow for the last eight or nine years of her life. To flesh out these statistics, the census figures clearly show that of the population aged over 65, widows outnumber widowers by about ten to one.

Illness cover, too, is becoming increasingly a part of personal financial planning. It comes in two different forms: permanent health insurance (PHI) which provides an income during a period of illness or disability and the so-called 'dread disease' or 'critical illness' plans which provide a lump sum on diagnosis of one of a range of conditions. Both have their place in a retirement planning programme.

Taxation

Taxation is covered in two chapters. Chapter 8 is on income tax and capital gains tax and Chapter 9 on inheritance tax. Once again, the book will take a practical approach and will look at those tax matters which are of particular interest to people planning for retirement. Specifically with income tax, it will cover the year of retirement and the taxation of pensions.

It is, of course, difficult to show clear demarcation lines between all these chapters. The choice of investments (covered in Chapter 6) will to some extent be governed by, and can sometimes affect, your tax position.

Wills and trusts

Chapter 10 is devoted to wills and there is no apology for including a chapter on this allegedly familiar subject. The facts are that the majority of people do not make a will for reasons best known to themselves. Part of the reason could, of course, be cost and some people will shy away from paying a solicitor to advise them on this really essential aspect of financial planning. It is true that solicitors charge for the service but, during 'Will Week '93' one solicitor went on record as saying that he earned far more from sorting out badly drafted wills than he would ever have earned from drafting them properly in the first place—had he been asked.

A badly drafted will (or, worse still, no will at all) more or less guarantees that your family will remember you in a way that you may not have intended. Couple that with the fact that a correctly drafted will can save inheritance tax and there are virtually no reasons why this particular task should be avoided.

Chapter 11 looks at another area of financial planning which is often overlooked and that is trusts. Trusts have been with us in one form or another since the time of the Crusades. They are a more specialist form of financial planning but they can have a part to play in even the most routine circumstances. There has always been a slight air of 'tax evasion' about them, but don't let the misdeeds of the few lead you away from a method of financial planning which has been of benefit to many more people.

Finally in this part of the book, chapter 12 looks at the specific issues facing people who decide to spend all or part of their time after retirement living abroad.

1.6   Beyond retirement

One of the great sociological/biological developments of the last 50 years has been the shifting balance of the population. This has been due in no small way to the improvements in medical sciences which have given all of us a higher life expectancy than has been enjoyed in the past. The result has been a quite marked increase in the population of people in their 80s and is often referred to as the 'demographic time bomb'.

Unfortunately, increased life expectancy hasn't gone in hand-in-hand with any noticeable increase in physical or mental ability. We may be living longer but, for many people, it means an increased period of physical or mental frailty. This in turn has meant an increased demand for State help and, just as in the areas of pensions, the State is giving us advance notice that it cannot continue to provide this level of help and that we must increasingly fend for ourselves.

This will increasingly affect the provision of residential and nursing home care and the effects will be felt not only by those elderly people who need the care, but also their children—who will tend more and more to be facing the twin problems of financing their own retirement and caring for their elderly parents.

The final chapters of the book are therefore devoted to the financial implications of living in retirement. Chapter 13 looks at the range of State benefits that are available to people of pensionable age and how they interact with their State pension. It is not always the case that you should draw your State pension as soon as you are able to and this chapter looks at some of these circumstances.

Chapters 14 and 15 look at the range of benefits that are available to elderly people, either through the State or through local government, with chapter 15 being concerned mainly with the problems to be faced when the time comes to move to residential or nursing home care. Anybody with elderly parents or other relatives would do well to acquaint themselves with the broad provisions of the Community Care Act and this is also covered in chapter 15.

1.7   A world of change

The final point to make about everything in this book is that nothing stays the same for long. Any book concerned with matters of finance, tax and the occasional bit of law has to be read in the knowledge that it starts being out of date almost from the moment it goes to print. In addition, there is the broader world of economic reality, in which inflation changes and interest rates go up and down, and your own micro-economic world in which your personal circumstances change. Your retirement planning can never be a once-and-for-all activity; it must be a series of plans which are constantly reviewed as you change and as the world around you changes.

The only constant factors about retirement planning are that it is never too early to start and that it is probably already later than you think.

2 Your State pension

This chapter is concerned with the first stage of getting your pension priorities in order and looks at what you can expect from the State schemes.

Pension provision by the State is in something of a state of flux; and that is putting it mildly. It has been undergoing regular change over the last twenty years and the announcements in the November 1993 Budget on the equalisation of State pension ages more or less guarantee that it will be undergoing constant change for the next twenty as well.

There are regular indications from Government sources that the right to a basic retirement pension is one of the planks of the Welfare State but as the value of this particular plank continues to erode in relation to earnings, it would be wise not to regard your State benefits as anything more than a relatively minor part of your future plans.

This chapter looks at State pensions under the following headings:

(1) The State scheme
(2) National insurance contributions
(3) Contributory pension—the basic 'old age pension'
(4) The State earnings related pension scheme (SERPS)
(5) Graduated pension
(6) Non-contributory pension
(7) How to find out what you will get
(8) Contracting-out of SERPS
(9) Taking benefits
(10) The complexity of State pensions
(11) Changes on the way.

Your options on the way you may actually take your State pension and the interaction between State pensions and other benefits are covered in chapter 13.

2.1 The State scheme

The State provides two types of basic old age retirement pension through the social security system: contributory and non-contributory. The contributory pension may be paid from State pension age. It is not possible to take benefits early though it is possible to take them late (see 2.9.1). The non-contributory pension (which is only available in special cases) is paid from the age of 80.

Both types of pensions are for weekly amounts; no part of the benefits may be taken as a lump sum.

There is also an 'age addition' paid to everyone over the age of 80.

In addition to these pensions, you may also qualify for an 'additional pension'. This will either be under the State Earnings Related Pensions Scheme (SERPS) or the old graduated pension scheme (or both). Both these additional pensions are calculated according to the contributions you have made. The graduated pension is funded by contributions paid between 6 April 1961 and 5 April 1975. SERPS is funded by certain classes of national insurance contributions made from 6 April 1978. If you paid contributions under both schemes you will receive two additional pensions.

2.2 National insurance contributions

National insurance contributions are paid under four 'classes'.

Class 1 contributions are paid by employees as a percentage of their 'band earnings'. These are earnings between a lower limit and an upper limit. No contributions are paid on earnings above the upper limit; no contributions at all are paid if an individual earns less than the lower limit.

Class 1 contributions are also paid by employers. These are called 'secondary contributions' (those paid by employees are called 'primary contributions'). Secondary contributions are also a percentage of earnings, but there is no upper limit.

Employers are also liable for Class 1A contributions where a company car is available for private use.

Class 2 contributions are payable by self-employed individuals unless their earnings are below a certain level and they have applied for a certificate of exemption.

Class 4 contributions are also paid by the self-employed as a percentage of a band of their schedule D earnings.

Class 3 contributions are a type of voluntary contribution paid by people who are neither employed nor self-employed (eg retired but below State retirement age) in order to secure the full benefits under the State retirement pension.

Only Classes 1, 2 and 3 count towards the old age pension (or towards any other social security benefit for that matter).

In addition to actually paying contributions, Class 1 contributions (and sometimes Class 3 contributions) may be 'credited' to you. This means that you are regarded as having paid the contributions, even though you haven't. You will be credited with contributions:

(1)   while you are claiming Unemployment Benefit and certain other benefits (see chapter 13);
(2)   while undergoing full-time education or training;
(3)   when you reach 60 (if male); or
(4)   when your marriage ends (if female).

2.3   Contributory pension—the basic 'old age pension'

This is normally paid from the age of 65 for men or 60 for women, although it is possible to defer the pension (see 2.9.1). A State retirement age of 65 for both men and women is to be introduced over the period 2010–2020 (see 2.11.1).

A man may only claim if he has paid sufficient national insurance contributions. A woman may claim either on the record of her own or her husband's contributions. If your contributions are not enough for the full pension, you may get a reduced pension.

2.3.1   The conditions

The qualifying conditions for a contributory pension are not at all straightforward and not particularly easy to understand. They combine the number of national insurance contributions you have paid or been credited with, the number of years during which you have built up a minimum record of contributions (referred to as the number of 'qualifying years') and the number of years that have elapsed since you were 16 (referred to as your 'working life').

The overall effect is that you will qualify for a full pension if you have a record of national insurance contributions covering 90 per cent of your working life. If you have less than the required number of qualifying years, you will receive a reduced pension—provided that your contribution record contains at least one quarter of the required number of qualifying years.

All this makes it extremely difficult to keep track of your pension, but the DSS will come to your aid. If for any year, your contributions are insufficient, they will write to ask you if you want to make (voluntary) Class

3 contributions to preserve your record (and they will tell you how much you have to pay). It is normally worthwhile paying these contributions in order to ensure that you get your full pension.

2.3.2 Married women

The basic State pension is paid at two rates: one rate is for a single person, the other higher rate is for a married couple. If you are a married woman, you can qualify for a pension as follows:

(1)   If you have paid enough national insurance contributions at the full rate, you can get a basic pension in the same way as a man or single woman. You will get this at age 60 provided you have paid or been credited with full rate contributions for 39 qualifying years.

(2)   Alternatively, you can receive a basic pension based on your husband's contributions if he is receiving his pension, you are over age 60 and you can be treated as having retired.

The pension that you receive will normally be the higher of the two pensions described above (there are more details on this in chapter 13).

Reduced rate national insurance contributions

Up to 6 April 1977, married women who were employed had the choice of paying either a reduced rate of national insurance contributions or of paying at the full rate. If you are still paying contributions at the reduced rate, you will not qualify for the full retirement pension and you will not qualify for SERPS. However, you will usually be able to get a pension on the basis of your husband's contributions though this will be less than the full single person's pension.

However, there are certain other benefits that you will not qualify for and the trend is slowly to encourage people to move to paying full contributions. Since October 1989, the rules are such that low earners (ie married women earning between £65 and £75 per week depending on whether or not they are contributing into SERPS) may actually be paying less in national insurance contributions at the full rate than they would if paying at the reduced rate.

2.3.3 Home responsibilities protection

If you are not working or your earnings are too low, you do not have to pay national insurance contributions. However, you will receive credits if you do not work because of home responsibilities. This is called home responsibilities protection (HRP) and protects your rights to a basic retirement pension if you:

(1)   receive child benefit (see 13.2.3) for a child under 16; or

(2)   receive income support (see 14.2) so that you can stay at home and look after a sick or elderly person; or

(3)   look after a sick or elderly person receiving attendance allowance or disability living allowance (see 14.7.2).

The benefit operates by allowing you to deduct the number of years during which you meet these conditions from the number of qualifying years (down to a minimum of 20).

HRP is available to both men and women but a married woman will not be eligible for HRP if she is paying national insurance contributions at the reduced rate.

2.4   State earnings related pension scheme (SERPS)

On 6 April 1978, the present State pension scheme started. It consists of two pensions—a basic pension and an earnings related additional pension (SERPS). At the time, employers with an occupational pension scheme providing pensions on a 'defined benefit' basis (see 3.1.1) could 'contract out' of SERPS. Employees who are contracted-out on this basis will receive the basic pension from the State and an additional earnings-related pension from their occupational scheme.

In 1988, it became possible to contract out of SERPS on what is called a 'money purchase basis' through either an occupational pension scheme set up by the employer or through a personal pension plan specially set up for the purpose. Those employees who are contracted-out in this way will receive:

(1)   the basic pension from the State; and

(2)   a reduced additional pension (ie SERPS) for those years for which they were not contracted-out; and

(3)   a so-called 'protected rights' pension based on the contributions made to the money purchase scheme while they were contracted-out.

The reduction in additional pension due to contracting-out is called the 'contracted-out deduction'. Contracting-out is covered in more detail in 2.8.

Self-employed people, however, are entitled only to the basic pension, not the earnings related pension (their national insurance contributions are substantially lower than those paid by and on behalf of an employed person).

The other group of people who do not qualify for SERPS are those married women who pay national insurance contributions at the reduced rate.

2.4.1 Objective of the earnings related State pension

The single person's basic pension was originally set at around 25 per cent of the national average earnings. It now stands at about 19 per cent, a result of increasing it each year in line with increases in the retail prices index rather than the national average earnings index, as applied before 1979. The original objective of SERPS was to increase the general level of the State pension for single persons by a further 25 per cent of national average earnings over a period of 20 years starting from April 1978.

The Social Security Act 1986, however, brought about major changes to SERPS. These changes will result in a reduction in SERPS, mainly for people retiring in the next century. The 1986 Act has also had a major impact on occupational schemes as it is now simpler for employers to set up pension schemes to contract out of SERPS and it is also possible for individuals to contract out of SERPS through the use of personal pension schemes.

2.4.2 Qualifying conditions

SERPS is paid as part of the State pension. The qualifying conditions are therefore the same as those for the basic pension, namely that the individual:

(1)   has reached State retirement age; and
(2)   has retired from regular employment; and
(3)   satisfies the contribution conditions.

The actual amount of SERPS that you will receive will depend on the level of contributions that you have made while in regular employment. It will also (following the Social Security Act 1986) depend on the year in which you reach State retirement age. A pension based wholly on the old rules will be 25 per cent of the average of your best 20 years' earnings (limited, of course, to 'band earnings', not your full salary). A pension based wholly on the new rules will be 20 per cent of the average of your lifetime's earnings.

(1)   If you reach State retirement age in 1998–99 or earlier, your pension will be based on the original rules.
(2)   If you retire in 2009–10 or later, your pension will be based on the new rules for earnings since 6 April 1988 and the old rules for any earnings between 6 April 1978 and 5 April 1988.
(3)   If you retire between these dates, your pension will be calculated on a sliding scale between the old and new rules.

2.5   Graduated pension

This scheme existed between April 1961 and April 1975. People who were employed during this period bought 'units' at the rate of one for every £7.50 of weekly earnings for a man, or £9.00 for a woman, subject to an upper limit (which varied between £15 and £62 a week). An employer was allowed to 'contract out' employees if they were provided with an equivalent occupational pension; such employees will receive a smaller graduated pension as they will have accumulated fewer units.

Each unit buys an amount of weekly pension. This amount is uplifted each year by the rate of inflation. The highest number of units and the maximum weekly pension (at 1994–95 rates) they will provide is as follows:

	Maximum *units*	*1994–95 pension* *per week*
Men	86	£6.43
Women	72	£5.39
	Contracted-out	
Men	48	£3.59
Women	40	£2.99

2.6   Non-contributory pension

If you cannot claim a contributory old age pension at all, you can claim a non-contributory pension from the age of 80 (for men and women). The non-contributory pension is sometimes called the 'old person's pension'. This pension is also payable to someone who *does* qualify for a contributory pension but one that is lower than a non-contributory pension. This could apply to anyone who receives a contributory pension of less than 60 per cent of the full contributory pension.

2.6.1   The qualifying conditions

To qualify for a non-contributory pension you must satisfy two conditions:

(1)   You must not be receiving either a contributory pension or any other social security benefit of a higher amount. For this purpose you ignore any earnings-related pension, graduated pension or guaranteed minimum pension (see 2.8.3).

(2)   You must be 'ordinarily resident' in the United Kingdom (see 12.3.1) and you must have lived in the United Kingdom for at least 10 of the 20 years up to your 80th birthday.

If you are already receiving other social security benefits when you reach 80, this pension will make little difference to you, as the other benefits will be reduced by the amount of pension you receive. However, if you are of independent means, the pension will make a difference as it is not affected by the amount of other income. This could be of benefit, for example, to someone who settled in the United Kingdom in their 60s.

2.7 How to find out what you will get

The results of the various changes over recent years means that your State pension could be a confused amalgam of various payments. You could qualify for one or more of:

(1) The basic State pension.
(2) The graduated pension.
(3) SERPS (and this could be a mixture of the old and new rules)

It will be very helpful for you to use the retirement pensions forecast service operated by the Department of Social Security. You should ask for Form BR19 (available from any office of the DSS) and send it to the relevant office in Newcastle-upon-Tyne. The form asks for some basic information and, in return, you will get a full forecast of the State pensions you qualify for. In addition, there are a small range of useful 'what if?' options. You can, for example, get an idea of the impact on your retirement pension of stopping work before State retirement age or working on beyond it.

Overall, a State pension is unlikely to be adequate for anybody earning over the national average. Even with the benefit of SERPS, it is still likely to fall well short of the benefits provided by a good company or personal pension scheme. In addition, the State scheme does not allow any part of the benefits to be taken as a lump sum, there are no life assurance benefits and there is no provision for early retirement.

The major advantage of the State scheme is the degree of inflation proofing provided.

By and large, there is not a tremendous amount you can do to improve your benefits under the State scheme. What you can do, of course, is to make sure that you qualify for the maximum benefits you are entitled to by making sure that your contribution record is up to date. However, it's not all cut and dried. You get no tax relief on national insurance contributions and (provided you are eligible to do so) you might feel it better to invest the missed contributions into a personal pension scheme where you do get tax relief.

This is an option, but don't forget that it is not just the State pension that is determined by your contributions record. Other benefits (principally widow's benefits) depend on the national insurance contributions you have paid and it could be a false economy to look for alternative methods of saving.

The reverse argument may apply, however, when it comes to SERPS.

2.8   Contracting-out of SERPS

Because of the likely future costs of providing an earnings related pension, the Government took two decisions:

(1)   They reduced the ultimate benefits of SERPS. This will start to take effect on those people reaching State retirement age in 1999–2000 and will take full effect on those people retiring in 2009–10.

(2)   They introduced incentives to encourage people to leave SERPS and make their own arrangements.

It is only possible to leave SERPS if either you or your employer makes appropriate provision to replace the SERPS benefits with a suitable, approved alternative. To encourage this, individuals and employers who 'contract out' in this way receive benefits in the form of reduced national insurance contributions or a direct payment into individual personal pension plans.

There are currently three ways in which you can contract out of SERPS:

(1)   membership of an appropriate personal pension plan (APPP);

(2)   membership of a contracted-out money purchase pension scheme (COMPS);

(3)   membership of an occupational scheme providing a guaranteed minimum pension (GMP).

2.8.1   Appropriate personal pension plans (APPP)

These require no employer involvement at all. In order to contract out, you take out a personal pension plan with a pension provider of your choice (eg a life assurance company). You and your pension provider must complete a Joint Notice (Form APP1) which is submitted to the DSS. You can use only one APPP to contract out at any time and you must contract out for at least one complete tax year.

Once the Joint Notice is accepted by the DSS, payments are made, normally once a year, directly by the DSS to the pension provider. These payments, called 'protected rights' contributions, consist of a national insurance rebate, an element of tax relief on your share of the rebate and, for those who are 30 or over at the beginning of the tax year, a payment equal to one per cent of band earnings. Both you and your employer continue to pay the full rate of national insurance contributions.

The protected rights contributions *must* be used to provide a pension at State retirement age, or a widow(er)'s or dependant's pension or a lump sum on death. The value of these benefits is not guaranteed and to find out what you might expect to get, you will have to ask your pension provider (see 4.3).

2.8.2 Contracted-out money purchase schemes (COMPS)

These are occupational pension plans where the employer takes the initial decision to contract out, although the employer may allow individuals the choice of whether to contract out or not.

Both you and your employer pay a reduced rate of national insurance contribution but this saving is balanced by the protected rights contributions which your employer must ensure are paid into the pension scheme on a monthly basis. Normally, both you and your employer will contribute your respective shares of the protected rights contributions.

Unlike APPPs, there is no extra payment for employees aged 30 or over and the protected rights contributions do not automatically include an element of tax relief (although where you are obliged by your employer to pay your share of the protected rights contributions you will effectively receive full tax relief on this part of the contributions). The protected rights contributions must be used to provide benefits in the same way as those provided by an APPP. As with an APPP, the value of benefits is not guaranteed.

2.8.3 Guaranteed minimum pensions (GMP)

This method of contracting-out involves an occupational pension scheme which provides a guaranteed minimum level of pension equivalent to that provided by SERPS. Both you and your employer benefit from a reduced level of national insurance contribution but your employer has to be prepared to provide the pension scheme with sufficient funds to enable it to meet the guarantee (but see 2.11.3).

2.8.4 Contracting-in or contracting-out?

If you contract out using an APPP or a COMPS, you must consider whether the benefits provided by the protected rights contributions will exceed the likely benefits from SERPS. A protected rights scheme is a money purchase scheme ie the benefits which emerge are dependent almost entirely on the size of the fund built up; there is no guarantee that the benefits will exceed SERPS and this is almost certainly the case for older people.

In general, contracting-out will be of benefit to younger people with older persons likely to benefit more from SERPS. The cut-off ages depend on future investment performance but, for those contracting-out using an APPP, the ages for 1993-94 are approximately 49 for males and 43 for females. For those contracting-out using a COMPS, the ages are approximately 46 for males and 39 for females.

To help you decide whether or not it is in your interests to contract out, the DSS provide a forecasting service specifically for the additional pension. This can be obtained by applying on the form contained in leaflet NP38.

2.8.5 Contracting back into SERPS

If you are approaching the pivotal age when contracting-out ceases to be attractive you should consider informing the DSS that you no longer wish to be contracted out. This is done by sending a completed form APP 2 to the DSS. If you are a member of a COMPS, you will have to approach your pension scheme trustees to find out your options, which might include switching into a 'not contracted-out' category of membership whilst remaining in the scheme.

There are proposals that could change this position (see 2.11.2).

2.9   Taking benefits

2.9.1 Taking benefits late

Although you cannot take your State pension early, it is possible for you to defer taking your pension if you wish either to continue working or simply put off taking your retirement benefits. Your pension will be increased when you finally retire. You can only defer drawing your retirement pension for five years after you reach State retirement age.

The State pension increases at a weekly rate equivalent to an overall increase of about 7.5 per cent for each full year that it is not claimed. If you defer for the full five years, your pension will be increased by around 35 per cent (in addition, of course, to any increases introduced automatically through indexation). There are more details on deferring State pensions in section 13.3.1.

2.9.2 Contracted-out benefits

If you have contracted-out of SERPS through an occupational scheme providing a guaranteed minimum pension (GMP), the amount of additional pension you would have been entitled to under SERPS will be reduced by an amount equal to the GMP. This deduction is called the 'contracted-out deduction'.

If you have contracted out of SERPS through a protected rights scheme then, in this case also, you will not be getting any SERPS benefits for the years during which you have not been paying contributions. The protected rights scheme itself will provide a pension at State retirement age and, in order to calculate the contracted-out deduction, the DSS will assume that this pension is equal to the GMP.

If at State retirement age, the pension you actually get is *less* than GMP, then the overall additional pension you get will be less than you would have got under SERPS. The DSS will not, of course, make up any shortfall, but neither will they be entitled to a refund if you get a better pension

2.9.3 Widows, widowers and the divorced

A woman may claim a State retirement pension either on her own records or on her husband's. A widowed or divorced woman may claim on her former husband's records for the longer of:

(1) the period in which she was married to him; or
(2) the period from the start of her working life to the date of her husband's death or the date of their divorce.

A widower or divorced man may claim on the basis of his wife's standard-rate contributions (reduced-rate contributions do not qualify) on the same basis as a widow.

Widows' benefits

The basic position is that, at age 60, a widow can retire and start to draw the State retirement pension which will be based on her own contribution record and/or her late husband's contribution record. In the meantime, she will receive a widow's pension which will be based on her age either at the time of her husband's death or when her youngest child ceases to be dependent upon her. If this age is less than 45, she will receive no widow's pension at all and her retirement benefit at age 60 will depend entirely on her own contributions.

It is not essential to make a final decision at age 60; it can be put off or changed at any time up to age 65.

Widows' benefits are covered in more detail in chapter 13.

Widowers' benefits

A widower who is not entitled to a full basic pension may be able to improve it by taking into account his late wife's standard rate contributions.

Under the original rules, a widower may claim any SERPS based on his late wife's contributions provided:

(1)   both he and his wife had reached pensionable age before she died; and

(2)   he had retired from regular employment.

The maximum SERPS a widower may inherit was such that, when added to his own SERPS entitlement, it does not exceed the maximum SERPS an individual would be entitled to based on his own maximum contributions.

Since SERPS was modified, the amount of SERPS which a widower may inherit from his late wife will be 50 per cent of that calculated on the original basis, if she dies after 5 April 2000.

2.10   The complexity of State pensions

From the foregoing, you will gather that State pensions are not straightforward. The actual pension you can receive and the circumstances under which you are entitled to receive it can vary considerably and the DSS have published a whole range of leaflets and booklets to explain the different sets of circumstances that apply. If you wish to pursue any particular area in any detail, a good starting point is booklet FB2 available from any office of the DSS (or by post from the Benefits Agency distribution centre—see chapter 16). This leaflet is entitled *Which Benefit?—A Guide to Social Security and NHS Benefits* and gives a broad outline of all the benefits that are available. It also gives details of the individual leaflets that can be obtained from the DSS to explain any particular point in more detail.

If you wish to explore State retirement benefits in more detail, leaflet FB 6 gives a good overview; booklet NP 46 provides considerably more information.

2.11   Changes on the way

One of the problems in producing a book on financial matters, particularly one which depends to any extent on government policy, is that things never stay the same for long. Towards the end of 1993, three changes were put forward which will have an impact on the retirement plans of a large number of people (though it is by no means certain that all the proposals will come to fruition).

2.11.1   The equalisation of State retirement age

As part of the Budget announcement in November 1993, the Government introduced an equalised State retirement age of 65 for both men and women. This is to be phased in over a ten year period between 2010 and 2020. It will have no effect on women who were aged 44 or older at the time of the announcement.

It will be implemented by adding an extra month to the State retirement age for a woman born in April 1950, an extra two months for a woman born in May 1950 and so on. A woman born in April 1950 will therefore have a State retirement age of 60 years and one month, whereas a woman born in April 1953 will have a State retirement age of 63 and one month. Any woman born in April 1955 or later will have a State retirement age of 65.

To offset the impact, the Government announced its intention to improve home responsibilities protection (see 2.3.3) by increasing the number of years over which it may be claimed and by extending the scheme to cover SERPS as well as basic pension benefits. There are also to be changes to the escalation rate if a State pension is deferred (see 13.3.1).

2.11.2 Contracting back into SERPS

One of the reasons for encouraging people to withdraw from SERPS was to reduce the cost to future Governments of providing an income related pension. The idea of the rebate (see 2.8.1) was to persuade as many people as possible to withdraw but a *level* rebate is not attractive to older people who find it advantageous to contract back into SERPS.

The Government have introduced the idea of an age related rebate which will make it more likely that older people will not find it so attractive to rejoin SERPS. At the time of preparing this book, the idea is still at the discussion stage.

2.11.3 The removal of GMP

Another proposal put forward by the Government, at the end of 1993, is to look at alternatives to the guaranteed minimum pension (GMP) which is described in 2.8.3. The GMP is designed to ensure that it is impossible for anyone who contracts out of SERPS in this way to be worse off than if they had stayed in. It is therefore a complex calculation and the Government is anxious to simplify it. One option being discussed is to replace it with a form of protected rights scheme, similar to APPPs or COMPS. This would mean that everybody contracted out of SERPS would have at least part of their pension based on a money purchase scheme, regardless of the rules of their own company scheme.

At the time of preparing this book, no firm decisions had been made.

Useful reading matter

The following social security booklets will contain more details on the State benefits covered in this chapter. They can be obtained from your local DSS office or direct from the Benefits Agency distribution centre (the address is in chapter 16).

FB 2—Which benefit? A guide to Social Security and NHS benefits

FB 6—Retiring? Your pension and other benefits

NP 45—A guide to Widow's Benefits

NP 46—A guide to Retirement Pensions

3 Improving your company pension

Having found out what your State pension is likely to be, you may well start wondering what you can do to improve your company scheme. If the curse of modern pensions' legislation is its Byzantine complexity, the other side of the coin is that this complexity is due in no small way to the choices we have. Hand in hand with this has to go the fact that, although the Government may be trimming back on the tax benefits in an attempt to create a level playing field for long-term investment, the legislation is providing more means to protect our retirement and is also offering some people (particularly the early leaver) a much fairer deal.

Despite these changes, some dated concepts are still very much a part of the world of company pensions, the principal one perhaps being the need to work for up to 40 years with the same employer in order to obtain the maximum allowable pension. Given the increasing improbability, in today's world, of such a cosy, long-term relationship, the need to make complementary arrangements is of growing importance. This chapter looks at the following topics:

(1)   The structure of company schemes
(2)   Finding out what you will get
(3)   Maximum benefits
(4)   Maximum pensions
(5)   Maximum cash lump sums
(6)   Special rules for company directors
(7)   The framework for improvement
(8)   Topping-up company schemes
(9)   Additional voluntary contributions (AVCs)
(10) Free-standing additional voluntary contributions (FSAVCs)
(11) Executive pension plans
(12) Funded unapproved retirement benefit schemes (FURBS)
(13) Leaving your company scheme
(14) Changing your job.

3.1   The structure of company schemes

A company pension scheme may be contributory or non-contributory. Contributory means that both you and your employer make contributions to the fund; non-contributory means that only your employer makes contributions.

Typically, you may be contributing about five per cent of your salary to a contributory scheme. The employer will usually contribute a sum between five and ten per cent of your salary, but this is simply a convenient mathematical device for funding the pension scheme. You generally have no right to the *money* in the pension scheme but you do have rights to the *benefits* provided by the scheme.

The type of scheme will either be a final salary scheme or a money purchase scheme and it is important to understand the difference between the two.

3.1.1   Final salary schemes

If you are in a final salary scheme, your pension will be defined as a percentage of your final salary at or around retirement, eg 1/60th or 1/80th of your final salary for each year of service to retirement.

This type of scheme (which is sometimes known as a 'defined benefit scheme') involves your employer in an open-ended liability because the ultimate benefit will be based on your future earnings, which are unknown, making it difficult to quantify the future cost.

Final salary schemes can either be 'contracted-in' or 'contracted-out' (see 2.8).

3.1.2   Money purchase schemes

You may be a member of a money purchase scheme, also known as a 'defined contribution scheme'. With this kind of scheme, the benefits will not be related to your salary at retirement, but will depend upon the size of the fund built up when you come to take the benefits. This in turn will depend on:

(1)   The contributions paid into the scheme by your employer on your behalf.

(2)   Any additional contributions which you make yourself.

(3)   The investment growth on all the contributions.

An occupational money purchase scheme gives your employer rather more control over the costs to him. For example, your employer may be paying a percentage of your salary or a contribution which may vary from year to year depending on his profits.

Although the benefits of a money purchase scheme are not related to your salary, the *maximum* benefits that you may receive from either type of scheme *are* related to your 'final salary'.

3.1.3 What is 'final salary'?

In many calculations on pensions, 'final salary' is mentioned and this has no precise definition. The general rule is that final salary is either:

(1)   the highest annual salary out of the last five years before retirement age; or
(2)   the average of any salary paid over three consecutive years out of the last twelve.

If you are a controlling director (see 3.6.1), only the latter option may be used.

The taxable value of benefits-in-kind (eg, company car or free accommodation) may also be included as part of your salary. The value of share option schemes and termination payments is excluded. The Revenue is, however, fairly generous when it comes to determining final salary. For example, it is possible to build in a rate of inflation to previous years' salaries for the purposes of determining your final salary. This is called 'dynamisation' (see 3.4.2).

3.1.4 The main benefits

What you can expect from your pension scheme depends first on the rules laid down by the Inland Revenue and second on the rules of the scheme itself. You may not necessarily get all the benefits that your company pension scheme can provide and the maximum benefits provided by your company scheme may be less than those allowed by the Inland Revenue.

Lifetime income

The principal benefit is a lifetime income payable, on a guaranteed basis, from the moment you retire until the day you die. This will usually be expressed as a percentage of your final salary when you retire but your particular pension scheme may have variations in it. For example, it may be a fixed pension or there may be provision for it to increase at an annual rate which will compensate you in some way for the effects of inflation. There may be provisions for this lifetime income to continue after your death if you die within a very short time of retiring.

Lump sum

Your company pension scheme may also provide you with the facility to take a tax-free cash lump sum when you retire. This will also generally be expressed as a percentage of your final salary. However, you cannot enjoy the maximum benefits of both a lump sum and a lifetime income; if you take the cash lump sum, then your lifetime income will be correspondingly reduced.

Widow's/widower's pension

Your scheme may also provide for a pension to be paid to your widow or widower. As with your own pension, the level of income payable is dependent on your salary (but this time at the date of your death).

The maximum widow's/widower's pension is two-thirds of your own maximum pension.

Life assurance

Many pension schemes also provide life assurance while you are actually employed. This is called 'death in service benefit' and will usually be expressed as a multiple of your current salary, up to a maximum of four times salary (see 7.3.3).

3.2   Finding out what you will get

The Social Security Act 1985 introduced rights for employees regarding their retirement benefits. It requires pension scheme trustees to provide information about the scheme and its benefits (including its investment policy and finances) to current members, early leavers and also prospective members.

In addition, you have the right to ask for certain information about the benefits being provided in your own case. Your company must supply this information within two months though they have the right to refuse this request if it is less than twelve months since you last received such information. In practice, most companies will arrange for some kind of annual statement to be sent out to employees and this will give you a good deal of useful information.

You will normally find the pension you can expect to receive at your normal retirement age (ie that of your company which may well be lower than State pension age) and you may also get the value of the cash lump sum you may withdraw at that time. The quoted pension will probably be based on your current salary (ie it will not assume any increase in salary between the date of the statement and your normal retirement date) which in turn will enable you to work out what percentage of your final salary you can expect to be drawing when you retire (the percentage will not change as it is based on the number of years' service to normal retirement date). That percentage is often enough to get most people thinking about what they can do to improve the situation.

If your pension is a money purchase scheme, then the rules are a little tougher. Every twelve months, your company must supply you with information on the amount of money paid in contributions in the preceding twelve months and must also tell you (in the case of a COMPS— see 2.8.2) how much has been paid into your scheme by the DSS.

Finally, it is also possible that you have a pension arrangement with a previous employer which will pay you some benefits in the future. If you feel that this applies to you but are not sure what your entitlement will be, you may be able to find out details of your 'missing' pension through the Pension Schemes Registry. The address is in chapter 16.

3.3 Maximum benefits

The maximum benefits available to an employee or director from a pension scheme normally depend on your years of service with your employer and your salary at or around retirement. There is, however, a distinction between what the Inland Revenue permits and what a particular pension scheme might provide; a pension scheme may provide benefits well below the maximum permitted by the Inland Revenue. The following sections lay out what the Inland Revenue limits are, how they depend on the date you joined your current scheme and describe the overall framework in which improvements to your pension can be planned.

3.3.1 The basic position

Most people will be familiar with the underlying Inland Revenue rule on maximum benefits that can be achieved through a company scheme. Provided you have the necessary years of service in your company scheme, you may retire on a pension of up to two-thirds of your final salary. Part of this pension may be commuted into a tax-free cash lump sum that may not exceed one and a half times your final salary.

This, broadly, is the situation that existed up to 1987 and, for people who joined their current employer's occupational scheme before then, those are the simple rules which still apply.

The first ripples to disturb the mirror-like calm of this simple situation came in 1987. The Government introduced new rules for high earners which limited the maximum tax-free cash lump sum to £150,000. Somebody with a final salary of, say, £300,000, would still be able to qualify for a pension of £200,000, but the lump sum would be restricted to £150,000 and not £450,000. This limit may be altered at any time in the future by Treasury order, although it has remained unchanged so far.

The next, and rather more substantial ripple, came in 1989 with the introduction of the 'earnings cap'. This put a limit on the earnings that could be pensioned and still enjoy the tax benefits of an approved pension scheme. The limit for 1994–95 is £76,800 which means a pension (in today's terms) of no more than £51,200 and a maximum tax-free cash lump sum of £115,200, regardless of what your salary is. Once again, this restriction is ostensibly aimed at high earners but, as increases in the cap are linked to increases in the retail prices index rather than average earnings, it will affect more and more people as time goes by. There are more details about the earnings cap in 3.12.1

The question of which rules affect you is determined by the date on which you joined your current employer's scheme.

(1)   If your current scheme was established before 17 March 1987, and you joined it before that date, (referred to throughout this chapter as a 'pre-1987 member'), you are covered by the old rules with no effective limits to your pension or tax-free lump sum.

(2)   If your current scheme was established before 14 March 1989 and you joined it after 17 March 1987 but before 1 June 1989, (referred to as a '1987–1989 member'), your maximum tax–free cash is limited to £150,000.

(3)   If you joined your current scheme on or after 1 June 1989, or if you joined a scheme set up on or after 14 March 1989 (referred to as a 'post-1989 member'), you will be affected by the earnings cap.

This means that anybody changing jobs in the future, or joining an occupational scheme for the first time, will have his pension benefits affected by the earnings cap.

Regardless of what your maximum allowable benefits are, Inland Revenue rules require that you have to belong to your employer's scheme for a minimum period of time before you qualify for the maximum benefits. The rule that most people are familiar with (the 40 year rule) does not always apply and the precise minimum period depends, once again, on the date you first joined your current scheme. The following sections (3.4 and 3.5) contain the details.

3.4   Maximum pensions

3.4.1   The basic position

The Inland Revenue will always permit a pension benefit of up to 1/60th of final salary for each year of service (this is known as the '60ths scale' or 'straight 60ths') so that a maximum pension of two-thirds of final salary is obtained only after completing 40 years' service with the employer—an unlikely event for most people. It is still possible, however, for you to receive the maximum pension of two-thirds of final salary in a shorter timescale (if permitted by the rules of your scheme) depending on when you joined your scheme.

Pre-1987 members

The two-thirds maximum pension is permitted if at least ten years' service has been completed with the employer at normal retirement date. In arriving at the maximum pension obtainable it is necessary to include a restriction to take account of additional pensions arising from any voluntary contributions (see 3.9 and 3.10) and any 'retained benefits' (see 3.4.3).

1987–1989 members and post-1989 members

For people joining schemes on or after 17 March 1987, the maximum pension is 1/30th of final salary for each year of service. The two-thirds maximum is therefore permitted only on completion of at least 20 years' service with an employer at normal retirement date.

There is a further restriction on post-1989 members who are also controlling directors (see 3.6.4).

3.4.2 Dynamised or indexed final remuneration

Final salary may be re-calculated as a notional figure (known as 'dynamised final remuneration' or 'indexed final remuneration') by increasing the actual salary earned in a particular year by the increase in the retail prices index between the end of the year in question and normal retirement date. The result is to produce a pension which is related to the salary which an employee would have received had his previous years' salaries kept pace with the cost of living.

Dynamisation, however, may not be used:

(1)   to increase the tax free lump sum (see below) payable to a pre-1987 member unless the pension is increased to the same proportionate extent, ie dynamisation must be justified by an increase to the overall entitlement to benefits;

(2)   to increase the final salary of a 1987–1989 member used to calculate the tax-free lump sum beyond £100,000;

(3)   to increase the final salary of a post-1989 member beyond the value of the 'earnings cap' as at the date of retirement.

3.4.3 Retained pension benefits

It may well be that you have other pension entitlements in addition to those being provided by your current employer. For example, you may have a deferred pension from a previous employer or you may have built up a personal pension plan through previous self employment. If your current benefits are to be calculated on the 'straight 60ths' scale, then (unless you are a controlling director—see 3.6.4) you need not take any retained benefits into account. However, if your pension is to be improved under any of the methods described above, then any retained benefits will be taken into account.

3.5 Maximum cash lump sums

In the same way that pensions can be improved up to the maximum level laid down by the Inland Revenue, so can cash lump sums.

3.5.1 The basic position

Most pension schemes allow an employee to give up part of his pension on retirement for a tax-free cash lump sum. Inland Revenue rules lay down that the maximum tax-free lump sum that can be provided for any employee is 1½ times his final salary after completing 40 years' service at normal retirement date: this represents 3/80ths of his final salary for each year of service.

Pre-1987 members

Pre-1987 members can obtain the maximum lump sum after 20 years' service with the same employer but *only* if the rules of the pension scheme itself allow lump sum benefits to be built up over 20 years.

1987–1989 members

It is possible to provide the maximum lump sum cash after 20 years (up to a maximum of £150,000) but only if the scheme provides the maximum approvable pension benefits on the accelerated scale for pensions, ie 1/30th of final salary for each year of service. This means that both benefits must be uplifted in the same way; it is not possible to uplift the lump sum in isolation. If the rules of your scheme are such that the pension provided is between 1/60th and 1/30th of final salary for each year of service, an enhanced cash lump sum may be payable according to a laid down formula.

Post-1989 members

The maximum lump sum is the greater of:

(1)   3/80ths of final salary (capped at £76,800 in 1994–95—see 3.12.1) for each year of service, and

(2) the pension multiplied by 2.25. 'Pension' is the amount before commutation or any reduction in favour of widows/dependants and is calculated on the basis on which it will actually be paid, eg in monthly instalments, increasing in payment at five per cent *per annum* compound (see 5.3 for details on the various ways in which pensions may be taken).

3.6 Special rules for company directors

The Inland Revenue regards company directors, particularly controlling directors, as a special category for whom membership of a company pension scheme has certain restrictions. Directors of investment companies are in a particularly poor position. The company itself may not be able to set up a pension scheme if the membership includes controlling directors and such directors are prohibited from contributing to personal pension schemes.

3.6.1 The definition of controlling director

There are two definitions and they depend on the date that you joined your company scheme.

(1) If you joined your scheme on or after 1 December 1987, you will be treated as a controlling director if, at any time after 16 March 1987 and within ten years of retirement or leaving pensionable service, you have been a director of the company and able to control, either directly or indirectly, 20 per cent or more of the company's ordinary share capital.

In arriving at the degree of control you exercise, the shareholdings of your 'associates' will be taken into account; 'associates' in this context includes relations and partners, trustees of settlements where you are the settlor etc. All the shareholdings are added together and, if they exceed 20 per cent, you will be a controlling director even if you do not own or control any share capital yourself.

(2) If you joined your scheme before 1 December 1987, then you will be regarded as a controlling director if, at that date, you were a director who either alone or along with your wife and minor children controlled 20 per cent or more of the voting rights of the company. This 20 per cent will also include any rights held by the trustees of a settlement of which you or your wife were settlors.

The definition in (1) applies to all members for the purposes of the certificates needed for controlling directors wishing to transfer benefits to a personal pension plan (see 3.14.3).

3.6.2   Restrictions on all controlling directors

Final salary

The definition of final salary (see 3.1.3) and dynamised final remuneration (see 3.4.2) must be averaged over a period of three consecutive years.

Maximum contributions

For schemes set up before August 1993, the maximum contributions payable by a controlling director have been reduced as a percentage of earnings. The old, higher levels remain in place for existing schemes but, if contributions are increased, the new, lower basis must be used from then on.

However, maximum contributions under the old basis, although initially higher for any given age, remained level. Maximum contributions under the new basis, although initially lower for a given age, increase with age and so, at some point, it *may* be beneficial for a person with an existing plan on the old scale to move over to the new scale so as to take advantage of the higher percentages. However, it is not entirely straightforward as the existing plan fund value is taken into account and this may reduce future contributions.

3.6.3   Restrictions on pre-1987 and 1987–1989 members

Normal retirement date

The earliest normal retirement date is 60 for both men and women. However, there are a number of occupations where a reasonable case can be put to the Inland Revenue for a lower retirement age. It is never automatic; each case has to be argued on its merits. Also, if accepted, it will probably be that you will have to take the benefits at the agreed date ie it will not be possible to defer them.

Benefits on late retirement

If you delay taking your pension benefits beyond your normal retirement date, you will get no additional credit up to age 70 though you will get some credit if you defer your retirement date beyond age 70 (see 5.7.6).

3.6.4   Retained benefits

With the exception of post-1989 members, all benefits from retirement annuity contracts or personal pension plans must be taken into account when calculating the maximum benefits from a company scheme or executive pension plan.

For post-1989 members, there is no need to take account of any benefits from such schemes set up during earlier periods of self employment or with a previous employer *unless* your benefits under your current scheme are being provided in a shorter timescale (see 3.4.1). Benefits from any personal pension schemes relating to your current employment must always be taken into account and will be treated as if they were benefits from your occupational scheme.

3.7   The framework for improvement

Having taken the first step of finding out what pension you are likely to receive from your employer's occupational scheme, you will now be able to see to what extent you can improve it. However, there is an important distinction to be drawn between the limits laid down by the Inland Revenue and the rules of your own company scheme. The Inland Revenue lay down the maximum benefits that may be taken from a company scheme and the timescale over which these benefits may accrue. The rules of your own scheme cannot exceed these limits, but they do not have to meet them.

Consequently, there are two principal reasons why you may not qualify for the maximum pension to which you are entitled:

(1)   You may not have achieved sufficient years of service with your employer when the time comes for you to retire. This means that you will not qualify for the maximum pension allowed by the rules of your company scheme.

(2)   The maximum benefits allowed by the rules of your company scheme may be less than the maximum benefits allowed by the Inland Revenue.

For example, you may belong to a company scheme that is based on the 60ths rule ie you have to complete 40 years service to achieve a maximum pension. The Inland Revenue rules, however, permit you to take a maximum two-thirds pension after only 20 years. There is nothing to prevent you from retiring at any time to suit yourself but the trustees of your company scheme are not obliged to start paying you a pension until you reach the normal retirement age of your company scheme.

Even if they do agree to pay you a pension, it may not be the maximum (because you will not have worked the required number of years) and the rules of your scheme may also provide for an early retirement penalty which would reduce your pension still further.

It is the interplay between the Inland Revenue rules and the specific rules of your own company scheme that establish the basic structure of the problem you are trying to solve. If you wish to retire at a certain age on full pension, what are the maximum benefits the Inland Revenue will allow you to take, what are the maximum benefits provided by your company scheme and how do you plug the gap?

There are also other benefits allowable by the Inland Revenue rules which are not necessarily contained in your company scheme. Your company scheme may provide you with a fixed pension whereas Inland Revenue rules allow you to take one which is index-linked. Your company scheme may not have the benefit of a dependant's pension. Finally, your company benefits may be related to your basic salary and take no account of other forms of remuneration such as bonuses, company car, private medical insurance contributions and other fringe benefits all of which can be included in the definition of 'salary' (or, more correctly, your 'total remuneration').

Consequently, in drawing up plans to improve your company pension, you can look at it, not just from the point of view of increasing the amount of your pension, but also increasing the overall level of benefits and perhaps also of taking benefit at an earlier age. As the next sections will show, there are a number of options for you to rectify the situation either in conjunction with your employer or completely privately.

3.8   Topping-up company schemes

There are essentially four ways in which you can improve your company benefits:

(1)   Additional voluntary contributions (AVCs)
(2)   Free standing additional voluntary contributions (FSAVCs)
(3)   Executive pension plans
(4)   Funded unapproved retirement benefit schemes (FURBS).

3.9   Additional voluntary contributions (AVCs)

The Inland Revenue will allow you to contribute up to 15 per cent of your total remuneration into a pension scheme. If you are already paying, say, five per cent to your company scheme, then you may pay the balance (ten per cent) into a supplementary scheme. However, the earlier point about basic salary versus total remuneration (see 3.1.3) may be valid here. If your employer pays a percentage of your *basic salary* into the pension scheme, you are free to pay the balance of 15 per cent of your *total remuneration* into an AVC scheme ie you can include the 'shortfall' on your employer's contributions.

You have a choice of investing AVCs through either your employer's scheme ('in-house' AVCs) or through a free standing scheme (see 3.10). The general rule for an in-house AVC scheme is that it runs parallel to a company scheme. The whole of your contributions will be deducted from your pay before tax which means that you get tax relief at the highest rate you pay. Its whole purpose is to improve on the benefits provided by your company scheme up to the level of benefits allowable by the Inland Revenue rules (although AVCs started after 8 April 1987 may only provide a pension; no part of the benefits may be taken as a lump sum).

3.10   Free-standing additional voluntary contributions (FSAVCs).

These were introduced on 26 October 1987. They are an entirely personal form of retirement plan and will not normally require any involvement on the part of your employer. They may be arranged through a range of pension providers which includes insurance companies, banks, building societies and unit trusts. You have total freedom of choice when selecting your pension provider.

An FSAVC scheme has the following characteristics:

(1)   It can be used to provide income in retirement only, not tax-free lump sums.

(2)   Contributions are subject to the normal limits. The maximum contributions you may pay must not exceed 15 per cent of your salary (including any personal contributions which your employer may require you to pay under an occupational scheme or under a separate executive pension plan). Contributions paid by post-1989 members will also be subject to the earnings cap (see 3.12.1).

(3)   Benefits will also be subject to the normal limits applying under occupational schemes.

(4)   The scheme is completely separate from your employer's occupational scheme. When benefits become payable, eg on retirement, the trustees of your employer's scheme will inform your pension provider of the maximum benefits permitted under Inland Revenue rules, and the amount being provided under the employer's scheme. The balance may be provided by the free standing scheme. If there is a surplus when benefits become payable, it will be returned to you minus a tax charge (see below).

(5)   You pay contributions net of basic rate tax (similar to the basis on which you would obtain tax relief on mortgage interest payments). Any higher rate tax relief will be obtained through your tax return.

3.10.1   Over provision

If the combination of benefits under the main occupational scheme and your free-standing scheme provides excessive benefits, the surplus arises under the free-standing scheme, ie the main scheme benefits are not reduced. Your pension provider is obliged by law to deduct tax at 35 per cent (not 25 per cent) from the surplus fund and this tax cannot be recovered even if you are a non-taxpayer at the time. If you are a higher rate tax payer, further tax at 15 per cent is payable on the grossed up amount.

For example, if the fund had a surplus of £1,000, the scheme administrator would return £650 to you (ie £1,000 less 35 per cent). This would represent a gross payment of £867 (ie £650 grossed up at the basic rate of 25 per cent) but, if you are a basic rate taxpayer, no further tax would be payable. If you are a higher rate taxpayer, you would face a further liability of 15 per cent of the grossed up amount (ie 15 per cent of £867 = £130).

3.10.2   Contribution levels

One of the benefits of a free standing scheme is that it is entirely personal to you and will not involve your employer at all. If you plan to take early retirement but are not keen to let your employer in on your plans, there is nothing to prevent you from setting up a free standing scheme to provide the funds.

However, you will probably want to know how much could be contributed to the free-standing scheme to top up the overall benefits to the Inland Revenue maximum. An indication of the scope for AVCs can be provided by the main scheme trustees or by the pension provider who runs the free-standing AVC.

If you want to contribute £2,400 *per annum* or more, you have to give your pension provider information about the main scheme and any retained benefits. Your pension provider will then test for the possibility of over provision: if this is likely, your pension provider will tell you what your maximum contributions can be to ensure that overall benefits do not exceed Inland Revenue limits.

If you intend contributing less than £2,400 *per annum*, the pension provider does not have to carry out an initial check (but will do so should your contributions exceed £2,400 *per annum* at any time in the future).

3.10.3   Benefits at retirement

One disadvantage of a free-standing AVC scheme is the inability to take any of the emerging benefits in the form of a tax-free lump sum and this is often a deterrent to some people. In practice, though, this problem may be overcome by looking at the combined benefits emerging from the free-standing scheme and your other pension arrangements.

Your first step should be to enquire about the rules of your company scheme. The rules of occupational schemes will often contain powers of augmentation allowing the trustees to increase the tax-free lump sum (and other benefits) up to the maximum permitted by the Inland Revenue. You could, therefore, take increased cash from your occupational scheme, leaving a lower income from that scheme which would be topped-up by the pension from your free-standing scheme. Post-1989 members may also be able to benefit from the '2.25 times pension' rule (see 3.5.1).

There are more details on the options open to you when taking your pension in Chapter 5 (see particularly 5.2).

3.11 Executive pension plans

Another way of supplementing your pension benefits is to ask for your employer's co-operation in setting up an executive pension plan (EPP) for you. This is a separate plan, ie it is not part of the group scheme, but it would be possible for your employer to pay the contributions to the plan on your behalf and to subtract them from your gross salary.

However, if your benefits are to be topped-up by means of a separate executive pension plan, your employer *must* contribute at least 10 per cent of the total costs. If your employer is unwilling to bear any additional expenditure, his contribution can be made by your giving up part of your salary voluntarily.

There is no need for the EPP to mirror the group scheme and this offers some other benefits. The Inland Revenue permits categories of employees to have (effectively) two normal retirement dates. A director or executive could, for example, be a member of a group pension scheme with a normal retirement age of 65 (when the majority of employees will retire), and also be a member of an executive pension plan arranged specially for him with a retirement age of 60. For the purpose of deciding the maximum approvable benefits under the executive pension plan, the benefits payable under the main scheme at the earlier retirement age have to be assessed.

The precise way in which the EPP can be used to top up your group scheme will, of course, depend on the day you joined the main scheme.

3.11.1 The range of additional benefits

By combining an executive pension plan with a group pension scheme, one or more of the following benefits could emerge:

(1)   A full two-thirds pension at an earlier age.
(2)   Increases in dependants' benefits.
(3)   A pension increased in line with increases in the cost of living.
(4)   Increases in the tax-free lump sum up to the maximum permitted.
(5)   More flexibility in the event of leaving service. If you leave your company, your benefits (often in the form of an individual policy) can be transferred to your new employer (and even if it is not transferred, it will continue to benefit from future investment growth).
(6)   Improved death in service protection (life assurance).
(7)   The use of dynamised final remuneration.
(8)   Improved benefits on early retirement.
(9)   Greater control over the investment medium in which your contributions are invested and greater privacy over your retirement provisions.
(10) Items which are not normally pensioned, eg bonus, commission, are more easily handled under an executive pension plan.

3.12   Funded unapproved retirement benefit schemes (FURBS)

3.12.1   The earnings cap

The 1989 Finance Act introduced the concept of the earnings cap. This puts a level on the salary that can be pensioned and applies to all post-1989 members.

The intention of the Government was to limit the amount of pension that could be built up with the full benefits of tax relief. The level was originally set at £60,000 and was index-linked to rises in the cost of living. However, indexation is not guaranteed and may be suspended by the Government (as it was in 1993–94 when the cap stood at £75,000).

Realistically, the number of people currently caught out by the cap is not high and it only applies to people who joined their company scheme since 1989. However, by linking annual rises to prices rather than annual earnings, and by reserving the right to suspend even this limited index-linking, the cap is steadily being reduced in real value compared to average earnings. Higher paid people moving jobs and developing their careers could well expect their salary to grow in excess of the rate of increase in average earnings and, for them, the earnings cap could soon become a bar to adequate pension provision.

For example, if we assume that inflation really is beaten and stays at two per cent *per annum*, the cap could rise to just under £94,000 in ten years time (assuming the Government does not freeze the cap in the meantime).

Somebody earning £30,000 today would need an annual salary increase of around 12 per cent *per annum* to hit problems in ten years' time. If that rate of salary increase seems over-optimistic, salary increases of just over 8.5 per cent *per annum* would see him hit problems in 15 years' time.

3.12.2 The introduction of FURBS

Fortunately, the Government realised the dangers and introduced the concept of unapproved schemes at the same time as the earnings cap. Employers are now able to set up unapproved schemes where it is recognised that the benefits under an approved scheme are not sufficiently attractive to recruit and retain key staff. This will then allow the employer to:

(1) provide additional lump sums on retirement;
(2) offer a pension greater than the normal maximum of two-thirds of final salary;
(3) provide a full two-thirds pension where the normal rules would not allow it;
(4) provide lump sums or pensions on earnings above the earnings cap.

3.12.3 Funded or unfunded?

If your employer wishes to provide additional benefits for you under an unapproved scheme, he has a choice in the way these benefits are provided. The benefits will either be paid at retirement on a 'pay as you go' basis (the unfunded method) or out of money set aside in advance to meet the future benefits (the funded method).

Most people will probably prefer the far greater security of the funded method where money is set aside each year by the employer and earmarked specifically for the individual member. The arrangements can be incorporated into a contract of employment and, once paid, the money cannot normally be reclaimed as a result of the employer being taken over or going into liquidation.

3.12.4 The tax position

The following is an overall summary of the tax implications of unapproved schemes:

(1) The contributions paid by your employer are treated as an expense against profits and will normally qualify for tax relief in the same way as for approved schemes.
(2) Contributions paid by your employer are regarded as income in your hands and are treated as a benefit in kind; the full amount of contributions paid will be reported on your annual P11D. Alternatively, provided you are not a director, your employer may pay this tax for you as part of your total remuneration package in

which case the contributions will not appear on your P11D.

(3)   You cannot pay any contributions yourself as this could have adverse consequences on your tax position.

(4)   At retirement, the fund is paid to the trustees who in turn will pay it to you as a lump sum. You may then reinvest the lump sum to provide a regular income if you prefer. As the funds will usually already have been taxed on their income and capital gains, this lump sum is entirely tax-free. However, if your FURBS was established after 30 November 1993 and the income and capital gains have not been subject to UK tax (eg an offshore scheme), the lump sum will be taxed at your top rate of tax.

(5)   In the event of your death before retirement, a lump sum could be paid to your dependants. As with approved schemes, this will be free of inheritance tax.

In exchange for a tax regime that is less advantageous than under an approved scheme, there is no limit to the benefits that can be provided by a FURBS.

3.13   Leaving your company scheme

From 6 April 1988, it has been possible for you to leave your employer's scheme if you wish and it is no longer possible for employers to make entry into the pension scheme a condition of employment. Generally speaking, however, if you are a member of a company scheme, you are going to be better off remaining a member. This is particularly true of a final salary scheme as it is hard to imagine any private pension arrangements offering the level of guarantee that is inherent in a final salary scheme.

If you leave your company scheme, you will have two options:

(1)   to make no private provisions at all and rely on State pension benefits; or

(2)   to take out a personal pension plan.

It is possible that your employer might be prepared to contribute to your personal pension plan as he will not be contributing on your behalf to the occupational pension scheme that you have left. However, your employer is under no obligation to do this and could refuse to allow you back into the company pension scheme at a later stage.

3.13.1   Should you leave?

The factors that you should consider will vary according to your personal circumstances and the benefits provided by the company scheme, but, in general, you should take care to note the following points:

(1)   If you take out a personal pension plan, will your employer contribute to it?

(2)   What benefits will you be giving up if you leave? Scheme benefits can vary enormously (for example, they could include life assurance and long-term sickness benefits) and it might be difficult to replace these by taking out a personal pension plan.

(3)   Is your company pension scheme contributory or non-contributory?

(4)   Does the company scheme provide benefits on a final salary basis (which offers you certain guarantees about the level of your pension) or on a money purchase basis (which will be the same basis as a personal pension plan)?

(5)   Are the transfer values offered attractive?

(6)   If you leave, can you rejoin?

The older you are, the more attractive the final salary guarantees become so, overall, you should think *very* carefully before leaving your company scheme and take competent financial advice before you do. It would be hard, for example, to think of many reasons why it would be sensible to leave a non-contributory scheme and, even if you belong to a contributory scheme, you will still be giving up your employer's contributions.

However, if after considering the matter carefully, you decide to leave your company scheme then your best solution is to take out a personal pension plan. These are described in more detail in chapter 4.

3.14 Changing your job

For people planning their retirement, a change of job could be the last thing on their minds. However, nothing in life is certain and a change of employer, either voluntary or otherwise, clearly cannot be ruled out. Although changing your job in itself is hardly likely to improve your pension, there are a number of options open to you to make sure that your future pension is not jeopardised.

Until 1975, many pension schemes provided nothing for the job mover whether he was dismissed for misconduct, was made redundant, or left of his own accord. Since then, the position has changed dramatically. The Social Security Act 1973 significantly altered the benefits of early leavers with effect from 6 April 1975, and the subsequent Acts of 1985, 1986 and 1990 have made further improvements. The position now, for people who leave their company scheme after 1 January 1991, is that company schemes have to provide benefits at or after normal retirement date and (in the case of final salary schemes) must revalue preserved pensions in line with increases in the retail price index up to a maximum of five per cent *per annum*.

The options normally available to employees are set out below, although some of the options may not be available, either as a result of the preservation requirements under the Act or because the employer's pension scheme does not provide some of the options. In basic terms, you have the choice between leaving your current pension where it is and taking the transfer value and investing it in an alternative pension arrangement.

The options are as follows:

(1)   A deferred pension (sometimes known as preserved, paid up or frozen pensions) may be provided by your current scheme, payable when you reach the normal retirement age of the scheme you are leaving, although early and late retirement options will be permitted.

(2)   A cash transfer from your current scheme may be used to purchase a deferred annuity from an insurance company which issues so-called 'Section 32 annuities' (sometimes called 'buy-out plans').

(3)   A cash transfer from your current scheme may be paid into a personal pension plan.

(4)   A cash transfer from your current scheme may be paid to your new employer's pension scheme.

(5)   The assignment of an executive pension plan by the trustees of the original scheme.

3.14.1   Deferred pension

A deferred pension is generally limited to a proportion of your total final remuneration at the date of leaving your employment. The deferred pension must be revalued in line with the cost of living between the date of leaving and normal retirement age, subject to a maximum of five per cent *per annum*. Part of the pension may be exchanged for a lump sum on reaching normal retirement date. The maximum lump sum is calculated on the same basis as for early retirement (see 5.7.5).

3.14.2   Section 32 annuity

Rather than providing deferred benefits under the scheme as above, the trustees may effectively transfer the benefits by purchasing (from an insurance company chosen by you) a deferred annuity in your name. A series of such annuities may be purchased (not necessarily from the same insurers) allowing benefits to be taken in stages.

The maximum pension and the maximum tax-free cash lump sum permitted by the Inland Revenue will be endorsed on the policy issued by the insurer. These benefits may be increased between the date on which the transfer is made and the date of retirement in line with increases in the retail prices index subject to a maximum of five per cent *per annum*. One of the specific benefits of a Section 32 annuity is that if part of your current scheme consists of a guaranteed minimum pension (see 2.8.3) then the GMP element is transferred into the annuity.

The Section 32 annuity itself may include an open market option (see 5.4) and power to surrender the policy and transfer it to a new scheme, including a personal pension scheme.

Benefits (pension and tax-free cash lump sum) may be taken from age 50 onwards, (but not later than age 75), regardless of whether or not you have retired or are continuing to work. Also, the cash lump sum entitlement may be increased each year in line with movements in the retail prices index between the date of leaving and the date of drawing benefits.

3.14.3 Personal pension plans

An individual leaving his employer's scheme also has the option of transferring his benefits into a personal pension plan. Although a personal pension plan is generally only available to the self-employed or to those in non-pensionable employment, there is an exception: an individual who is in a pension scheme can take out a personal pension plan which is funded by the transfer from another scheme.

This new option may be more flexible than the Section 32 annuity described above because the transferred benefits will be subject to the personal pension legislation allowing you to pay future contributions if you have 'net relevant earnings' (see 4.7.2).

However, before benefits may be transferred to a personal pension plan, the trustees of your original company scheme must provide certificates as required in Inland Revenue regulations, as follows:

(1) A controlling director's/high earner's certificate

This certificate is required in respect of anybody who is a controlling director (see 3.6.1) or was a high earner (defined, in 1994–95, as anybody earning £76,800 or more ie the same level as the earnings cap), at any time during the ten years prior to the date in which the transfer value is applied for. The certificate must confirm that the transfer value does not exceed the cash equivalent of the maximum benefit that could have been paid under the rules of the transferring scheme.

(2) A cash sum certificate

This certificate is required in respect of anybody who is a controlling director or high earner (as defined above) or who is over age

45 at the date that a right to a transfer value is applied for. This certificate must state the maximum cash lump sum payable under the transferring scheme at normal retirement date based on salary and service at the date of leaving.

3.14.4 Transfer values into your new scheme

When you leave one employment to take up another employment, your benefits under the original pension scheme may be transferred to the new pension scheme provided your new employer's scheme is willing and able to accept a transfer value. Alternatively, as described above, the trustees may pay the transfer value to an insurance company of your choice to buy a Section 32 annuity or a personal pension plan (and there is nothing to prevent you having the transfer value divided up between both of these alternatives). However, it is not possible for the transfer value to be paid direct to you.

If your new employer's scheme is a money purchase scheme, there will not be a great deal to discuss; the transfer value will simply be the start of your retirement fund with your new employer. If it is a final salary scheme, the position is more complicated as the transfer value will be credited to you in the form of 'added years' service' with your new employer's scheme. There is no hard and fast rule on how many added years you should get; it could be a matter for negotiation with your new employer.

Right to a transfer value

If you leave your company scheme, you have a right to a transfer value if you had been in the scheme long enough to qualify for benefits—normally two years. There is no right to a transfer value if you are already receiving a pension from your current scheme or if you have less than one year to go before reaching the previous scheme's normal retirement age.

You also have the right to a transfer value if you left a scheme after 1 January 1986; at the time of preparing this book, there is a proposal from the Government that this right should be extended to anybody who has left a company scheme in the past.

3.14.5 Assignment of an executive pension plan

If you had set up an executive pension plan as part of your retirement arrangements with your previous employer, it is possible for the policy to be assigned to a new employer. However, this will be regarded by the Inland Revenue as a new scheme set up by the new employer in order to bring the maximum benefits into line with your new company scheme, which would mean that it will be restricted by the earnings cap.

There are two further options:

(1)   The trustees of the original scheme could assign the executive pension plan to you personally; or

(2)   The policy may continue to be held by the trustees and will participate in any future growth.

Both of these options will keep the plan under the existing rules which means that benefits may not be affected by the earnings cap.

3.14.6   What about your AVCs?

If you leave your company, the in-house AVCs are regarded as part of your contributions. They may be included as part of the transfer value or as part of the deferred pension.

In contrast, free-standing AVCs are completely portable and can be taken with you, regardless of what happens to the rest of your pension contributions.

3.14.7   To defer or transfer?

There is no simple answer to this question. Your first step must be to find out what deferred pension you can expect and then to find out what benefits your transfer value might provide through the other options. Part of the problem is getting a fix on the underlying value of any transfer value you are offered. There is no standard method of calculating transfer values and, although the trustees are supposed to offer you a transfer value that is fair and reasonable, opinions may vary as to exactly what *is* fair and reasonable.

It is a decision that needs careful thought and competent advice; your future pension is a vital part of your long-term financial security and it is an area which should be covered in any negotiations with a potential employer as part of your overall remuneration package. If you decide to move to a new scheme, you will then be affected by the earnings cap (even if you were previously unaffected by it) and this needs to be taken into account in any discussions with a future employer, ie you may wish to discuss a FURBS.

4 Improving your personal pension

Personal pension plans have had a significant impact on the world of pensions since they were first introduced in 1988. Replacing the older self-employed retirement annuities, they now provide a means of contracting out of SERPS, topping up a company scheme or providing the basic retirement needs for the self-employed or those whose job does not provide a pension. As with company schemes, the rules are not particularly straightforward but the recent relaxations made to the maximum level of contributions make it increasingly easy to provide a high level of retirement income.

This chapter looks at both types of personal pension scheme under the following headings:

(1) Personal pension plans and retirement annuities
(2) What type of plan?
(3) Finding out what you will get
(4) The framework for improvement
(5) Limits on benefits
(6) Maximising contributions
(7) Earnings
(8) Maximum contributions
(9) Carry forward/ carry back facilities
(10) Investment strategy.

4.1 Personal pension plans and retirement annuities

Background

Retirement annuities were, at one time, the means by which the self-employed provided for their retirement. The term 'self-employed retirement annuity' is, however, misleading as it suggests that eligibility was confined to one group: in fact, employed people in non-pensionable employment have also taken out these contracts in the past.

From 1 July 1988, personal pension plans came into being and no new retirement annuities were available from that date. However, retirement annuities taken out before 1 July 1988 may still be maintained and may even accept increases in contributions (provided that the contract itself is able to take increased contributions). Some people may well have one of each type of plan.

The basic rules of eligibility remain unchanged; if you are self-employed or employed by a company that does not have an occupational pension scheme, you may build up your own pension through a personal pension plan.

The benefits

Three types of benefit may be provided by both types of pension scheme:

(1)   A pension at retirement with provision for taking part of the benefits as a tax-free cash lump sum.
(2)   A pension for the wife (or husband) of the planholder or for any one or more dependants of the planholder.
(3)   A lump sum on the death of the planholder before age 75. The lump sum can be paid in instalments to provide income for dependants.

The principal differences between the two types of scheme are the limits on benefits (see 4.5) and the limits on contributions (see 4.8).

4.2   What type of plan?

Personal pension schemes are issued by pension providers, usually an insurance company but increasingly through banks and building societies. There are a number of different basic structures of plan but the broad division is between with-profits plans and unit-linked plans.

4.2.1   With-profits policies

Many pension plans on the market fall into this category and are issued by traditional life offices. The policy will be either:

(1)   a 'pure endowment' where a guaranteed capital sum will be payable on retirement, converted into an annuity at an annuity rate that may be guaranteed in the policy; or
(2)   a deferred annuity with a guaranteed annuity payable on retirement, possibly with a guaranteed cash option.

If you are investing in a conventional with-profits policy, you may well have been offered a 'projected capital fund per £1,000 of annual contribution' made up of three elements:

(1)   A minimum guaranteed amount payable at retirement age.
(2)   An additional sum, which is not guaranteed, and which will depend on the actual results achieved over the full investment period. This additional sum (known as a 'reversionary bonus') is normally expressed as a percentage of the minimum guaranteed amount in (1) and will usually benefit from a compounding effect.
(3)   A final additional amount (known as a 'terminal bonus') which will depend on economic and financial conditions prevailing at the time of retirement.

Once a reversionary bonus has been declared by the insurance company, it cannot subsequently be removed even if future investment results fail to match expectations.

In recent years, there has been a general reduction in reversionary bonuses and more emphasis on terminal bonuses. There is no guarantee with terminal bonuses, however, as these are discretionary payments depending upon investment conditions when the policy matures.

4.2.2   Unit-linked policies

The 1970s saw an upsurge of insurance companies offering policies on unit-linked principles. The unit-linked route has become so popular that companies which traditionally marketed only with-profits policies now also offer unit-linked policies.

Under a unit-linked policy, you are able to choose the investment sector in which you would like your contributions to be invested and you may switch between sectors from time to time. The contributions paid are used to buy units in one or more of the chosen funds and the value of the units at any time is dependent on the value of the underlying investments in the funds.

On retirement, the units are encashed and the proceeds are used to purchase an annuity. No bonuses are declared and the value of units is not guaranteed.

4.3   Finding out what you will get

Personal pension schemes are money purchase schemes. The final benefits you can expect will depend on the size of the fund built up and this, in turn, will depend on the amount of money you have paid in and investment performance over the period. In this way, they are no different in structure from occupational money purchase schemes except that, unlike company schemes, the benefits you can take out are not restricted by final salary. However, there are restrictions on the amount of money you can pay into these schemes (see 4.8).

At retirement, the fund built up is used to provide a pension and this will depend on your age and sex and on long-term interest rates generally available at the time (see below). You may also take a proportion of the fund in tax-free cash (see 4.5) with a corresponding reduction in pension.

4.3.1 Getting a quotation

The only source of information about the likely benefits from any personal scheme is your pension provider and you should ask them to give you an illustrative quotation of what the benefits are likely to be. There are, however, two points to bear in mind if you intend to compare these quotations with the quotation received when you first started contributing to your pension (especially so if it was before 1988).

(1)   The basis on which projections of benefits are made is more rigorously controlled.
(2)   The annuity rate you were originally quoted may no longer be relevant.

4.3.2 The projection of benefits

With quotations in general, the position before 1988 was very fluid. Companies were free to use more or less any basis of future investment return which they considered reasonable and this frequently led to some quite remarkable projections of future fund values (the so-called 'telephone number' projections). It was also difficult to compare quotations from different companies because each used its own specific charging structure to arrive at the final estimates.

This all changed after 1 July 1988 following the implementation of the Financial Services Act. The Life Assurance and Unit Trust Regulatory Organisation (LAUTRO) ruled that all future projections were to be based on standard assumptions of charges, expense deductions and future investment return.

More recently, the bases of future investment returns have been set lower. In 1988, it was agreed that quotations could be based on two rates of investment return—8.5 per cent and 13 per cent *per annum*. With effect from 1 November 1993, these rates were reduced to six per cent and 12 per cent (with similar reductions being made to assumed rates of change in average earnings and retail prices). The overall impact is a reduction in the size of projected funds with a more marked impact on future funds where contributions are index-linked.

There was a further change in 1994 which required companies (from January 1995) to issue projections that were based on their own charges so that quotations can be compared.

4.3.3 Annuity rates

In addition, there has been a marked change in the pensions that the funds will generate. In providing you with a pension for life, the company actuary has to invest those funds where he can be sure of obtaining a known rate of income for a substantial number of years and where he knows the capital will be safe. The only form of investment that meets these requirements is long-dated Government gilt-edged securities (see 6.3.4). Consequently, when quoting future annuity rates to you, your insurance company will have based their quotation on the yields on long-dated gilts.

Since the United Kingdom left the ERM in September 1992, interest rates have fallen to their lowest level for 20 years with a knock-on effect on the yields of all gilt-edged securities. The overall result is lower annuity rates, ie lower pensions for every £1,000 of fund.

To complicate the position even further, when quoting annuity rates a long time in the future, the company may make assumptions on what yields on long-term Government securities may be in the future. As you get closer to your actual retirement date, the more realistic the annuity rate is likely to be.

The overall impact on quotations of the reduced rates of assumed future investment return together with a real reduction in annuity rates has been quite severe. It is therefore no bad thing to get an up-to-date quotation. The assumed rates of growth are, of course, just that; there is no reason to believe that your pension provider will not achieve a better return (or a worse return for that matter). However, the rates that LAUTRO require to be used in quotations have been lowered in order not to give false expectations after a decade of relatively high inflation and rapid stock market growth.

4.4   The framework for improvement

The size of the fund from which benefits are taken is limited, but only to the extent that the contributions going in are limited. There are also limits on when the benefits may be taken and the size of the tax-free cash lump sum. These limits are dependent on the type of personal pension scheme involved and the date it was taken out.

However, as personal pension schemes have no limit on the eventual fund that may be built up, so the facility for pensions improvement is far greater. If the fund itself enjoys high growth over the period, there is no limit on the level of the pension that may be taken at retirement. Consequently, the opportunity open to people with personal pension schemes is for them to contribute the maximum they are allowed.

4.5 Limits on benefits

There are limits on when benefits may be taken and also in the way the tax-free cash lump sum is calculated. The limits differ between retirement annuities and personal pension plans.

4.5.1 Retirement annuities

The limits are as follows:

(1) Benefits must be taken between ages 60 and 75 (or earlier, if you work in a specialised occupation (see 4.5.3)).

(2) The tax-free cash lump sum is limited to three times the annuity remaining after the cash lump sum has been taken. It will immediately be seen that the calculation cannot be done by the layman but your insurance company will do the figures for you. In carrying out the calculations, the Inland Revenue rules allow the lump sum to be calculated on the most favourable terms, ie on the basis of the highest possible annuity even if you do not actually choose that form of annuity (there are more details in 5.3 on the various ways in which annuities may be taken).

(3) On plans taken out on or after 17 March 1987, the cash sum is limited to £150,000.

(4) If, at retirement, the plan is converted into a personal pension plan under the open market option (see 5.4), the limits below will apply.

4.5.2 Personal pension plans

The limits are as follows:

(1) Benefits may be taken between ages 50 and 75 (or earlier, if you work in a specialised occupation—see below).

(2) 25 per cent of the fund may be taken in cash.

(3) If any part of the fund is due to protected rights contributions (see 2.8.1), the tax-free cash will be reduced accordingly.

4.5.3 Lower retirement ages for specialised occupations

The Inland Revenue permits a pension age lower than age 50 (under personal pension plans) and lower than age 60 (under retirement annuity contracts) in the cases of certain specialised occupations where early retirement is customary. Anybody in one of these occupations has the option of paying contributions into a personal pension scheme which will provide benefits to commence at the earlier pension age allowable. If the individual's job changes to one which would not fall into the definition of a specialised occupation, he will have to stop paying contributions to the original contract and divert future contributions to a new contract which will specify the normal range of pension ages from 50 to 75.

If a new, lower retirement age is agreed for any particular specialised occupation, it would be possible for an ex-member of that occupation to take the benefits at the lower age, provided he was able to show that he was a member of that occupation at the time he took out the contract.

4.6   Maximising contributions

Maximum contributions are governed by two factors. There is an overall limit in place which applies to your 'net relevant earnings' (see below). These earnings are carefully defined and it may be possible for you to increase the amount you may contribute to a personal pension scheme by calculating your net relevant earnings more accurately.

The second factor relates both to your age (which stipulates the maximum percentage of your 'net relevant earnings' that you may contribute) and also to an upper monetary limit which may apply to personal pension plans (but not retirement annuities).

The following sections will look in more detail at the following topics:

(1)   Earnings
(2)   Maximum contributions
(3)   Carry forward/carry back facilities
(4)   Investment strategy.

4.7   Earnings

4.7.1   Relevant earnings

It is necessary to have 'relevant earnings' to be eligible to pay contributions to a personal pension plan or retirement annuity. The relevant earnings for an employee or director taxed under Schedule E would be his actual earnings during the fiscal year beginning on 6 April and ending on 5 April.

For self-employed people, relevant earnings for the year of assessment will usually be based on the earnings in the accounting year which ended in the previous fiscal year. This preceding year basis of assessment under Schedule D, however, may not apply in the closing years of the business. (The preceding year basis is to be replaced with the simpler 'current year' basis. For people currently on Schedule D, the new basis will come fully into effect for the tax year 1997–98—see 8.3.1.)

4.7.2   Net relevant earnings

Although it is necessary to have relevant earnings to be eligible to pay contributions to a personal pension plan or retirement annuity, the tax efficiency of the arrangement depends on having 'net relevant earnings'. The contributions which you may pay are calculated with reference to your net relevant earnings.

'Net relevant earnings' means the amount of relevant earnings less business expenses including any deductions in respect of losses or capital allowances. Personal charges such as maintenance payments, charitable covenants and non-business interest do not reduce net relevant earnings.

Contributions to both types of personal pension scheme, although requiring to be deducted from earnings in order to arrive at total income for tax purposes, are not deductible for the purposes of arriving at net relevant earnings.

4.7.3   Schedule E taxpayers

If you are in non-pensionable employment taxed under Schedule E, you will normally have no deductions to make from your relevant earnings: your gross earnings from your employment will be your net relevant earnings and all deductions (such as tax, national insurance contributions, maintenance payments, covenants and interest) whether or not allowable for tax, are ignored.

If you are a member of an approved personal pension scheme, any contributions made by your employer are not chargeable to income tax.

4.7.4   Schedule D taxpayers

If you are self-employed and taxed under Schedule D, you will have to make the following deductions from your gross profits in order to arrive at your net relevant earnings:

(1)   all expenses incurred in earning the profits, such as rent, rates, business interest, employees' salaries, etc;
(2)   losses, whether:
    (a)   incurred in the current tax year; or
    (b)   incurred in a previous tax year and carried forward to set against profits in the current tax year; or
    (c)   incurred in a previous tax year, relieved against other income, and not yet deducted from net relevant earnings;
(3)   capital allowances.

Personal mortgage interest and covenants to charity can be ignored.

4.8   Maximum contributions

The maximum contributions differ for retirement annuities and personal pension plans.

4.8.1   Retirement annuities

Contributions (as a percentage of net relevant earnings) which may be made to retirement annuity contracts for tax years 1987–88 and onwards are:

Age on 6 April	Maximum contributions
Up to 50	17.5 per cent
51 to 55	20 per cent
56 to 60	22.5 per cent
61 to 74	27.5 per cent

All the above figures are inclusive of any contributions for life assurance (see 7.3.3) and waiver of contribution benefit (see 7.5.3). Part of any lump sum life assurance benefit could instead be taken as a pension for dependants.

4.8.2   Personal pension plans

The maximum contributions which may be made to a personal pension plan, from the tax year 1989–90 onwards, are the lower of a percentage of net relevant earnings and a monetary limit, as shown in Table 4.1 opposite. Up to five per cent of net relevant earnings for life assurance are included in the maximum contributions in Table 4.1, as is the cost of waiver of contribution benefit. Part of any lump sum life assurance benefit may be taken instead as a pension for dependants.

Where a personal pension scheme is used for contracting-out purposes (see 2.8.1), the contributions paid by the DSS are payable in addition to the maximum contributions,

The monetary limits shown in Table 4.1 are the relevant percentage of the earnings cap, ie personal pension plans carry the same restrictions as occupational schemes. For the tax year 1988–89 there was no monetary limit and the maximum contributions were the same as for retirement annuity contracts.

4.8.3   Personal pension plans versus retirement annuities

Many people who contribute to existing retirement annuities also wish to take advantage of the higher contribution limits available under personal pension plans. However, special conditions apply in these circumstances.

Table 4.1—Maximum contributions to personal pension plans

Age on 6 April	Maximum contribution	1989–90 £	1990–91 £	Monetary Limit 1991–92 £	1992–93 £	1993–94 £	1994–95 £
up to 35	17.5%	10,500	11,340	12,495	13,125	13,125	13,440
36 to 45	20.0%	12,000	12,960	14,280	15,000	15,000	15,360
46 to 50	25.0%	15,000	16,200	17,850	18,750	18,750	19,200
51 to 55	30.0%	18,000	19,440	21,420	22,500	22,500	23,040
56 to 60	35.0%	21,000	22,680	24,990	26,250	26,250	26,880
61 to 74	40.0%	24,000	25,920	28,560	30,000	30,000	30,720
Maximum contributions for life assurance		3,000	3,240	3,570	3,750	3,750	3,840

The maximum amount that may be paid to a personal pension plan includes any contributions being paid to a retirement annuity contract; if the latter is to continue this may mean that no contributions can be paid to the personal pension plan.

4.9 Carry forward/carry back facilities

It is possible to take advantage of two facilities to maximise your pension contributions and obtain the best possible tax advantages on those contributions. These two facilities are generally referred to as 'carry forward of unused relief' and 'carry back provisions'.

4.9.1 Carry forward of unused relief

This allows you to pay a higher contribution than you would normally be able to in the *current* year in order to catch up for missed contributions in *previous* years. If you do pay higher than normal contributions then, if you are contributing to a retirement annuity, the Inspector of Taxes will automatically refer back over the previous six years to discover any unused reliefs which can be carried forward to soak up the excess contributions. If you are contributing to a personal pension plan, you will have to make an election on form PP42.

Tax relief, however, will always be against the *current* year; there is no impact on tax paid in previous years. Also, tax relief is only available up to the level of tax payable on earned income for the current year, ie there is no tax relief on contributions in excess of the level of taxable earnings. For Schedule E employees, the position is slightly better. Their contributions are paid net of basic rate tax and must not exceed their net relevant earnings for the current year (which will generally be higher than their taxable earned income because of personal allowances, mortgage interest relief, etc).

4.9.2 Carry back provisions

A contribution (or part of a contribution) may be carried back to the tax year preceding the year of payment regardless of whether there are relevant earnings in the year of payment. If there were no net relevant earnings in the preceding year, the contribution may be carried back one further year.

The contribution will be taxed as if it had been paid in the year to which it is carried back. The contributions allowed for that year will be the normal maximum for that year plus any unused reliefs for the previous six years as described in 4.9.1.

Consequently, a contribution paid in 1994–95, and carried back to 1993–94, would be allowed against your income tax bill for 1993–94. It could also include an amount relating to missed contributions carried forward from 1987–88 (if the plan were a personal pension plan, the limits would be those for retirement annuities as personal pension plans did not come into existence until April 1988).

If you are a Schedule E employee, only your own personal contributions may be carried back, ie there is no facility for any contributions being made by your employer to be carried back.

4.10 Investment strategy

The fact that there is no limit on the size of the fund built up at retirement means that your eventual retirement income could depend to no small extent on investment growth over the period. As most personal pension schemes give you a choice of investment fund, you are in a position to do something about it.

However, the guidelines in Chapter 6 are relevant here. Although you may regard your retirement fund as a long-term investment, it ceases to be such as you get to within, say, five years of your retirement date, particularly if your plan does not have the facility to take benefits over a number of years.

The important point to bear in mind is that your pension fund is a source of guaranteed income for the rest of your life. Although you may be able to take some risks with your choice of investment area over the long term, as you get closer to retirement, your pension plan becomes more a source of guaranteed long-term income than a short-term investment opportunity. There may come a time when you have to regard it as a short-term investment and move to a fixed interest fund. That may give rise to some 'if only' thoughts if the stock market subsequently enjoys an unexpected surge but that is better than having alternative 'if only' thoughts if the stock market suffers an unexpected fall.

If you are tempted to hang on until the last minute, remind yourself about October 1987. And if you think that it can't happen again, remind yourself about the oil crisis of 1974.

5 Taking your pension

When the time comes for you to take the benefits of your pension plans (which may not necessarily mean that you actually have to retire), the complexity of pension plans does not diminish. Once again, you may be faced with a wide range of options, a further indication of the flexibility you have in tailoring your pension to your actual needs. It is here, too, that the differences between those in occupational schemes and those in personal pension schemes start to blur.

This chapter covers the following topics:

(1)   What is an annuity?
(2)   Pension versus cash lump sum
(3)   Types of annuity
(4)   The open market option
(5)   Dealing with low annuity rates
(6)   Impaired lives
(7)   Company pensions
(8)   Personal pension schemes
(9)   Staggered vesting
(10) Summary.

5.1   What is an annuity?

An annuity is the purchase of a lifetime income in exchange for a lump sum payment. In many ways, it can be looked at as the reverse of a life assurance policy where, in return for the payment of a regular series of premiums (which depend on the age and sex of the policyholder), a lump sum will be paid on death. An annuity reverses that by agreeing to pay, in exchange for a lump sum, a regular series of payments (which will be determined by the age and sex of the annuitants) until the death of the annuitant.

Annuities for older lives will be higher than for younger people (because the insurance company will assume that fewer payments will be made) and will usually be lower for females (as women have a life expectancy of between four and five years longer than a man of the same age). However, in the name of equal opportunity, annuity rates are now tending to move towards being the same for both sexes, though men have not yet been given the opportunity to enjoy the extra four or five years.

For the purposes of this chapter, there are two principal types of annuity:

(1)   Compulsory purchase annuities
(2)   Purchased life annuities.

A compulsory purchase annuity is, as its name suggests, an annuity purchased under compulsion. The funds built up under an approved pension plan, after the cash lump sum has been deducted, *must* be invested in a compulsory purchase annuity. If the cash lump sum is not taken, the whole fund must be invested in a compulsory purchase annuity.

Unapproved plans (see 3.12) do not have this restriction; the whole fund may usually be taken as tax-free cash.

A purchased life annuity, on the other hand, is an annuity which you would purchase if you had a choice in the matter. If you had a sum of money available (the tax-free cash lump sum from your pension, for example) and you had decided that you wished to invest it in an annuity, then you would invest in a purchased life annuity.

The difference between the two types of annuity lies in the way they are taxed. With the compulsory purchase annuity, the *whole* of the income is taxed as income. With the purchased life annuity, part of each payment is regarded as a return of capital with the *balance* being regarded as income and therefore taxable.

As an example, a fund of £100,000 invested in a compulsory purchase annuity could provide, for a man aged 60, an income of £9,736 *per annum*. If this was subject to tax at 25 per cent, it would leave a net income of £7,302 *per annum*.

If the fund were taken in the form of a tax-free cash lump sum of £25,000 plus a reduced net income of £5,474, the cash of £25,000 could be used to buy a purchased life annuity which would provide a net income of £2,121. The combination of the two net annuities would be £7,595, an increase in net income of £293 *per annum*.

Consequently, if you have decided that you wish to use your *entire* pension fund to provide you with an annuity, then the best approach is to take the largest amount of cash you can out of your fund and use the cash to buy a separate purchased life annuity rather than leaving the whole fund to be used to provide you with a compulsory purchase annuity.

5.2   Pension versus cash lump sum

The general suggestion to people at retirement is always to take the cash lump sum because this then gives them greater flexibility in the way they use their retirement benefits. Even if you are in the position where you need the maximum possible income from your pension, it may still make sense to take the cash lump sum and re-invest the proceeds into a purchased life annuity.

This is certainly true of money purchase schemes but you should consider your overall options more carefully if your occupational pension scheme is a final salary scheme. Under these circumstances, your pension is guaranteed (in that it will be a fixed percentage of your final salary), it will probably guarantee a pension for your spouse if you die first and may well benefit from increases in the future (see 5.7.7). If you take the cash lump sum, you will be reducing this guaranteed pension in return for the option of perhaps buying a purchased life annuity on the open market. At a time of low annuity rates, you will need to make quite sure that your replacement income is not inferior to the pension you are giving up out of your final salary scheme. The position is eased if you have a supplementary pension plan (see 5.7.4).

5.3   Types of annuity

If you are in an occupational scheme that provides you with a pension based on your final salary then, if you take the pension that is offered to you, you will probably find that you have very little choice in the type of pension you may draw (as the form of the pension will probably be laid down in the scheme rules). In every other set of circumstances (eg money purchase company schemes, FSAVC schemes, personal pension schemes, and so on), you may have considerable flexibility in the way you take your pension. Even people in final salary schemes can give themselves the flexibility if they wish, because they are not obliged to take the pension offered to them by their company scheme (see 5.4).

The following are the various types of annuity that are available:

Single life versus joint life

The annuity can either be chosen for the life of one person or can be a lower annuity which will last for the lifetime of two people.

Frequency of payment

The amount will depend on the frequency of payment. Payments can be made monthly, quarterly, half yearly or annually.

In advance versus in arrear

Annuities can either be paid at the start of the period of frequency or at the end (monthly in advance, annually in arrear and so on).

For example, if you choose a quarterly annuity payable in advance, you would receive your first payment immediately and your second payment in three months' time. If the annuity were payable in arrear, you would receive your first payment in three months' time.

Level versus escalating

You may choose a level pension or one which increases each year at a predetermined rate of compound interest. Typical examples are annuities which escalate at three per cent, five per cent or eight and a half per cent.

It is also possible to choose annuities linked to rises in the retail prices index.

Term of annuity

You may choose between an annuity which is paid for life or one that is paid for a guaranteed number of years, even if death occurs in the mean-time. With a purchased life annuity, you have the further choice of a temporary annuity (one that is paid for a fixed term of years) or a deferred annuity (one that does not start to be paid until the end of a fixed term of years).

5.3.1 The impact of choice

For a given age and a given purchase price, the highest type of annuity is a level, single life annuity, paid for life with no guarantees on early death and paid annually in arrear. For a man aged 60, with a fund of £100,000 invested in a compulsory purchase annuity, he could draw an income of £7,302 a year after basic rate tax.[1]

The following list gives an idea of the impact of the various options on the level of annual net income.

(1) Variation of frequency of payments made in arrear

Annually	*Half-yearly*	*Quarterly*	*Monthly*
£7,302	£7,123	£7,037	£6,980

(2) Comparison of annuity paid in arrear with one paid in advance

Annually in arrear	*Annually in advance*
£7,302	£6,635

[1] All the annuity figures in this chapter were obtained from the same source and were prepared on 27 January 1994.

(3)   Comparison of level annuity with initial payments from an escalating annuity

Level	*3 per cent*	*5 per cent*	*8.5 per cent*
£7,302	£5,606	£4,548	£2,966

(4)   Comparison of lifetime annuity with annuities with minimum payment periods

Lifetime	*5 year*	*10 year*
£7,302	£7,169	£7,082

(5)   Comparison of single life annuity with joint life annuity (wife five years younger).

Single life	*Joint life*
£7,302	£6,126

From all the foregoing, you will see that the level of annuity can vary enormously depending on exactly what you want to achieve. The above figures merely give an indication of the scale of change between simple options; the impact of several options working together can be even more dramatic. For example, a joint life annuity, escalating at five per cent, payable monthly in advance would be £3,192 compared to the £7,302 achieved on a more straightforward basis.

The range of choice is clearly very wide and there are further options which are not immediately apparent. For example, it may seem automatic for a married man to choose a joint life annuity. This will mean that, in return for a lower overall annuity, there will at least be the guarantee of an annuity for his wife if he dies before her. However, his wife might die first in which case he will have given up the higher single person's annuity for nothing. A better result *might* be obtained by taking a single life annuity (on the husband) and using part of the income to pay for a life assurance policy (on the husband's life) so that, in the event of the husband's death, his wife can use the proceeds to buy a single life annuity for herself.

The message is to use this flexibility in the best way you can. You have to do some very careful analysis of the type of income you want from your pension and then to make your decision. The important point is that, once you have made your decision and started to draw your pension, you cannot change your mind at a later date.

Consequently, it is absolutely vital that you consider exactly what type of pension you want and get a range of quotations from different companies. That is the final element of flexibility open to you and it is called the open market option.

5.4 The open market option

Pension plans usually permit an 'open market option' where the accumulated fund can be transferred, when the benefits are being taken, to another insurance company. You will normally wish to do this if another insurance company offers better annuity rates than those of your original pension provider. You may occasionally incur a penalty if the monies are transferred to another insurance company and, if you use the services of a specialised service, you may have to pay a fee for the pensions 'search'. Generally speaking, the advantages of getting a higher pension usually outweigh these costs.

Personal pension schemes arranged through banks, building societies and unit trusts are not allowed to provide pension benefits on retirement directly. The underlying funds (after the tax-free cash has been paid) have to be transferred to an insurance company which then provides the annuity.

5.5 Dealing with low annuity rates

In chapter 4, we covered the impact of low interest rates on the yields on long-dated Government securities. With these rates at their lowest for many years, there are some who would argue that conventional annuities are now poor value for money. Clearly, timing is everything and some people may be tempted to delay taking their pension in the hope that things may improve (which they will to some extent because they will be getting steadily older and thereby automatically moving towards a better annuity rate). However, this approach has two major faults. In the first place, you are not getting any income at all in the meantime and, in the second place, there is no guarantee that interest rates are going to move up significantly in the short term.

One way out of this dilemma is to recognise that long-term yields may not recover substantially in the immediate future and to consider alternative forms of annuity. There are some more specialised forms of annuities where the income is not related to the yield on long-dated gilts but is instead linked to the future performance of an underlying investment. These include with-profits annuities and unit-linked annuities.

5.5.1 With-profits annuities

The annual pension is based on the performance of the underlying fund. The percentage chosen initially is based on anticipated bonuses (eg eight per cent *per annum*) but the future income will depend on the value of the underlying fund. If this were to grow steadily over the years, the bonuses would also grow and hence the annual income.

Some companies will offer you a guaranteed minimum level of annual bonus; others will not and you will have to take whatever level of bonus is declared.

The risks are those of any long-term asset-backed investment; there is no guarantee that the value of funds will continue to rise (by their very nature, there will be some years when values will fall) and the value of bonuses will also fluctuate. The basic argument in favour of such annuities is that they are unlikely initially to be much poorer than conventional annuities when yields are low (but they do not look initially so attractive when conventional yields are high).

5.5.2   Unit-linked annuities

These are similar to with-profits annuities but the annual income is taken by encashing a fixed percentage of units (as unit-linked plans do not declare bonuses). The number of units that are encashed each year is calculated by dividing the total number of units by the expected number of payments according to the annuitant's life expectancy. Once again, provided that unit growth is consistent over the longer term, this type of annuity can provide a secure and rising income. Nevertheless, the risks are there.

The most important point to make about these alternative annuities is that they are not for the faint hearted. They do involve some risk (principally that of falling values over the shorter term) and, if you are more comfortable with an annuity that is guaranteed, then you should stick with a conventional annuity. If, however, you have other sources of income in retirement that could make up any shortfall in the lean years, and if you believe yourself to be in reasonably good health, then the alternative forms of annuity could prove to be a suitable long-term choice, particularly at a time when the yields from conventional annuities are low.

5.5.3   Index-linked annuities

A final type of annuity that is an alternative to the more conventional forms is the fully index-linked annuity. Conventional indexation is typically RPI or five per cent, whichever is the lower. A fully indexed annuity will be adjusted in accordance with movements in RPI regardless of what inflation will be in the future. When inflation was at high levels, such annuities provided a very low level of income in the early years but, with inflation at very low levels, the annuities on offer are not so different from the more conventional forms of indexed annuities. Consequently, the loss in the early years will not be so great and you have the assurance that the income you start with will remain the same in real terms for the rest of your life.

5.6   Impaired lives

Just as there are specialised forms of annuity for those people who can take a long-term view of their retirement, there are also specialised annuities for those people who have a medical condition that is sufficiently serious as to affect their normal life expectancy. Such annuities will increase the level of income as the annuitant's life span is shorter. There are no clear guidelines; each case is treated on its own merits though it is perhaps worth emphasising that the annuity will be based strictly on life expectancy and not quality of life.

This clearly is a very difficult and specialised area and advice should be sought from one of the specialist annuity offices.

5.7   Company pensions

In this section, the options open to you are covered as follows:

(1)   The overall position
(2)   Options on retirement
(3)   The impact of other plans
(4)   Benefits from supplementary schemes
(5)   Early retirement
(6)   Late retirement
(7)   Pension increases in retirement.

5.7.1   The overall position

When the time comes for you to retire from your company, you could be faced with a range of pension plans:

(1)   There will be the pension from your current occupational scheme, which will be either a final salary scheme or a money purchase scheme.
(2)   You may have augmented your company scheme with additional voluntary contributions.
(3)   You may have the benefits of a separate executive pension plan.
(4)   You may have set up a separate free standing additional voluntary contributions scheme.
(5)   You may have deferred pensions from previous periods of employment.
(6)   You may have a personal pension scheme as a result of previous self-employment or employment with a company that did not provide you with a company pension.
(7)   As a controlling director, you may have a personal pension scheme relating to your current employment or to previous employment.

(8)   You may have been contracted out of SERPS at some time through a protected rights plan.

On top of all that, you may be retiring earlier or later than the normal retirement date laid down by your current scheme.

5.7.2   Options on retirement

The maximum pension benefits you may take will be laid down by the Inland Revenue rules and the way these may be taken will depend in part on when you joined your company scheme (see 3.3). In practice, however, the benefits you can take are more likely to be determined by the rules of your company scheme.

You will have to decide whether or not to take the cash lump sum (and, if so, what to do with it) and you will also have to decide whether to take the pension being offered to you by your company scheme or whether to try your luck on the open market.

On reaching normal retirement date, it is normally possible (depending on the rules of your company scheme) to:

(1)   take all the benefits, ie tax-free cash lump sum and pension;
(2)   defer all the benefits;
(3)   take the tax-free cash lump sum and defer the pension (or *vice versa*).

In respect of post-1989 members, the benefits may only be taken at actual retirement date (ie it is not possible to take the benefits if you intend working on beyond normal retirement date). Also, option (2) is of limited value because the maximum approvable pension is not increased beyond normal retirement date (see 5.7.6) and option (3) is not permitted.

The fact that post-1989 members have certain restrictions on the way they can take benefits indicates that the overall position is not straightforward and depends on the date you joined your current scheme. This, of course, gives rise to questions about the level of benefits which may be provided for people who move to new schemes or join other schemes to provide additional benefits. The broad intention is that members of a company scheme who remain with the same employer (or who effectively remain members of the same scheme) should not be adversely affected by any changes introduced by the legislation.

This is the general line taken by the Revenue, ie that a pre-1987 member should not normally be restricted by the changes which apply to 1987–1989 members and that the restrictions introduced for post-1989 members should not apply to the other two classes.

However, it is not all one way traffic. There may be circumstances where it would be *better* for a pre-1987 member to receive the benefits applicable to a post-1989 member. If you are in this position, then you should ask the trustees of the scheme to see if they are prepared to allow your benefits to be augmented.

If you are a 1987–1989 member, you can opt to be classed as a post-1989 member if the results are beneficial to you. There is no requirement to ask the trustees for permission; you have the right to make that decision by law.

5.7.3 The impact of other plans

Protected rights plans

Your company pension will not be affected by any protected rights benefits (which, in any event, cannot be taken until you reach State retirement age).

Personal pension schemes and retained benefits

Your pension will not normally be affected by any personal pension plan you may have taken out in the past. Also, if your pension is based on the 'straight 60ths' scale (see 3.4.1), you will not have to take into account any retained benefits (ie deferred pensions) from earlier employments. However, if you have been building up your company pension under one of the enhancement methods, then your total pension from your company scheme plus any retained benefits must not exceed two-thirds of your final salary.

Similar rules apply to controlling directors (see 3.6.4).

5.7.4 Benefits from supplementary schemes

If you are contributing to an additional voluntary contribution scheme to augment your company scheme, the benefits will probably follow the normal maximum limit of your company scheme, ie there may be an overall limit to the benefits you can draw. It would also usually be the case that the benefits of both schemes have to be taken at the same time.

If you are contributing to a supplementary money purchase scheme, the problem of whether people in a final salary scheme should take the tax-free cash (see 5.2) is largely solved. Under these circumstances, you can draw the full pension from your final salary scheme and use the fund built up from the supplementary plan to provide the tax-free cash.

Free standing AVC schemes

If you are contributing to a free-standing scheme, it will be completely separate from your employer's scheme. However, when benefits become payable, the trustees of both schemes will liaise to ensure that you do not receive more than the maximum allowable benefits under Inland Revenue rules. The benefits from your company scheme will always be topped up by the benefits from your FSAVC fund; if there is a surplus on your FSAVC fund, the excess will be returned to you, less a tax charge (see 3.10.1).

Although FSAVCs may not be commuted to a cash lump sum, the pension provided may (for post-1989 members) be used in the '2.25 × pension before commutation' calculation to increase the tax-free lump sum provided by your employer's scheme (see 3.5.1). However, if your employer's scheme is a final salary scheme, it may not necessarily be in your best interests to take any cash from it.

As your supplementary scheme is a money purchase scheme, you are able to take advantage of the open market option.

5.7.5   Early retirement

You can take an immediate pension and cash lump sum from age 50 if your employment is terminated or if you retire early. This age is reduced to 45 for women provided they are within 10 years of their normal retirement date and provided they are in a scheme which was approved before November 1991.

You will not, of course, get the benefit of any State pension until you reach State retirement age. Some occupational schemes make good this shortfall by paying a 'bridging pension' which is paid until State retirement age.

Pre-1987 members and 1987–1989 members

Maximum benefits on early retirement can be calculated in accordance with the following formulae:

$$\frac{N}{NS} \times P \text{ or } \frac{N}{NS} \times LS$$

'N' is the number of years of service which have been completed to the point of early retirement (maximum 40).

'NS' is the number of years which could have been completed from the date of joining service to normal retirement date.

'P' and 'LS' are the maximum pension and tax-free lump sum you would have been entitled to had you retired at your normal retirement date but based on your final remuneration at the date of your early retirement.

These are the overall limits and include the value of any retained benefits which must be deducted from the value of P and LS before doing the calculation.

Post-1989 members

The maximum benefit is 1/30th of final remuneration for each year of service completed up to the date of early retirement. For example, if you have completed 20 years' service, a maximum pension of two-thirds of final remuneration may be provided from age 50 onwards (this is one set of circumstances where it could be advisable for a pre-1987 member to request the benefits of post-1989 membership).

Early retirement through ill health

If for reasons of physical or mental incapacity you are unable to follow your normal employment or have your earning capacity impaired, you can take early retirement. The maximum benefits are those based on your years of service had you reached your normal retirement date, but will be based on your final salary at the date you are required to take early retirement.

If your incapacity is such that your expectation of life is very much shorter than normal (ie measured in months rather than years), you may be able to exchange the whole of your early retirement pension for an immediate cash lump sum. However, this lump sum will not be totally tax-free.

Money purchase schemes

In general terms, the early retirement pension limits as described above do not apply. The permitted maximum is the same as that on early retirement through ill health, ie based on potential service to normal retirement age and final salary at the date of early retirement.

Transfers to a personal pension plan

If you leave your employer's scheme as a result of early retirement, you also have the option of transferring the benefits into a personal pension plan. Although a personal pension plan is generally only available to the self-employed or for those in non-pensionable employment, there is an exception in that an individual who is in a pension scheme, can take out a personal pension plan which is funded by the transfer from another scheme.

This will allow you to take part in the process known as 'staggered vesting' (see 5.9).

If you have contracted out of SERPS (see 2.8), then any part of your pension that results from protected rights must be taken at State retirement age and so would not be available to you before then.

5.7.6 Late retirement

Except for post-1989 members (who receive no additional benefits at all from working on after normal retirement age), you can be provided with additional benefits up to the maximum which would apply if your actual retirement date were your normal retirement date.

1987–1989 members will also receive a credit for extra years worked. If you will have achieved 40 years' service or more at normal retirement date, you can increase the pension to a maximum of 45/60ths of final salary (and the cash lump sum to 135/80ths). If you will have worked less than 40 years' service at your normal retirement date, the increased pension that you would receive at your actual retirement date will be calculated on an actuarial basis.

Controlling directors

If you defer drawing benefits beyond your normal retirement date, the limits on your pension and tax-free cash up to age 70 are exactly the same as those that would have applied had you retired at your normal retirement date, ie you get no benefit for working up to age 70.

If you defer your retirement beyond age 70, you have two options for increasing your benefits:

(1)   Your benefits, based on your years of service and final remuneration at age 70, can be increased by the greater of an actuarial increase (ie one that takes into account your age) or an increase in the retail prices index.

(2)   Your benefits can be based on your years of service and final remuneration at your normal retirement date. Provided you will have at least 40 years' service at age 70, you can receive an extra 1/60th of final remuneration for each year you work beyond age 70 up to a maximum of 45/60ths.

If you are a pre-1987 or 1987–1989 member, and you have the option to take the tax-free cash and defer your pension, the position is slightly different. If you take the cash before age 70, the maximum residual pension may only be increased by reference to RPI up to age 70. After age 70, it may be increased by the greater of an actuarial increase or an increase related to RPI.

5.7.7 Pension increases in retirement

Many schemes allow the escalation of pensions in payment. These are normally limited to a fixed percentage, say three per cent or five per cent *per annum* compound, while other schemes provide increases on a discretionary basis from time to time. Following the Social Security Act 1990, the trend is to provide escalation of pensions in payment at five per cent *per annum*, or the rate of increase in the retail prices index, whichever is less.

It is also possible for your employer to increase a pension in payment up to the level of the maximum approvable pension which would have been payable at retirement, subsequently increased in line with RPI. If you retired before 31 August 1991, this maximum approvable pension need not take into account any pension commuted for a cash lump sum.

5.8   Personal pension schemes

5.8.1   Income in retirement

The purpose of a personal pension scheme is to provide an income in retirement commencing (in the case of a retirement annuity) at any time between the ages of 60 and 75 or (in the case of a personal pension plan) between the ages of 50 and 75. An annuity can be drawn regardless of whether or not you are working and it is possible to stagger the benefits over that period by having a series of schemes with different retirement ages (see 5.9).

The facility to take benefits under a personal pension plan from age 50 compared with age 60 under a retirement annuity is attractive, but not a sufficient reason for stopping contributions to a retirement annuity in favour of a personal pension scheme. Most people simply will not have the opportunity to build up sufficient funds to provide a worthwhile income at age 50.

5.8.2   Lump sums

Up to 25 per cent of the fund accumulated in a personal pension plan may be taken as a tax-free lump sum.

Retirement annuities have a different treatment; the tax-free lump sum is restricted to three times the remaining annual pension after the cash has been taken. The Inland Revenue allows this calculation to be done on the most favourable basis (ie to base the calculation on the highest possible annuity) whilst at the same time allowing the annuity *after* the lump sum has been taken to be calculated on a different basis.

Although more complicated, this method usually provides more tax-free cash. However, that is not a hard and fast rule and, at a time of low annuity rates, it could be that the 25 per cent rule under the personal pension plan legislation gives a more favourable result.

5.8.3 The open market option

Both personal pension plans and retirement annuities are able to take advantage of the open market option. If this is done with a retirement annuity, then the fund is transferred to a personal pension plan under which the tax-free cash will be limited to 25 per cent of the fund. Under certain circumstances, therefore, (eg at a time of low annuity rates), it could prove beneficial to transfer the retirement annuity to a personal pension plan, using the open market option, in order to release more tax-free cash.

5.9   Staggered vesting

Personal pension plans may be taken out so as to provide a retirement income between ages 50 and 75. There is no requirement to stop working when the pension starts and there is no rule which says that all the benefits must be taken at one time. Personal pension plans are therefore frequently set up as a series of individual contracts which can be used to provide retirement benefits at any time during the age 50 to 75 period.

This leads to the concept of what has come to be known as 'staggered vesting'. Rather than take the full lump sum/annuity benefits at one point in time, the benefits can be taken gradually over a number of years. This is also becoming an approach for those people taking early retirement from an occupational pension scheme or those with a retirement annuity who wish to use the open market option. In both cases, they have the chance to move to a personal pension plan and take the benefits over a period of time.

However, as with everything else in life, there are some negative aspects which need to be kept in mind.

The positives

(1)   Staggered vesting enables retirement income to be built up at the required rate and, by only drawing benefits when they are needed, ensures that the residual segments of the plan continue to enjoy the benefit of tax-free growth.

(2)   Taking benefits in later years means that you get the added advantage of improving annuity rates as you will be getting older.

(3)   Staggered vesting is also a way of using the full flexibility of annuities. Just as you can take the benefits in a series of 'mini-pensions', you can also vary your choice of annuity as each slice is taken up. You may decide, for example, that the first part of your pension should be a level, joint life annuity paid monthly in advance. Later on, your need for immediate income could be less urgent, so the

second phase could be an escalating, single life annuity paid half yearly in arrear. And so on.

(4)   Any residual funds which have not yet been used to provide an annuity would form part of your estate if you died, ie they are a form of life assurance.

The negatives

(1)   If you take your annuity in segments, you must take your tax-free lump sum in segments as well. For some people, the lump sum is an important part of their plans for their retirement.

(2)   If you defer part of your pension, then you do not have the benefit of it. For example, using the figures in 5.1 as a starting point, delaying the annuity until age 65 would lift it from a net £7,302 to £8,220. However, you would not have had the benefit of the £7,302 for five years so you would have over £36,000 of income to make up. The same principle holds true in staggered vesting.

(3)   Staggered vesting makes use of the fact that as you get older, the annuity rate increases. It does, but as you now have a money purchase scheme, any gains on this side of the equation could be wiped out by poor investment performance over the period or lower interest rates when you come to take the next segment of your annuity.

(4)   Each new annuity is a new contract with its own level of charges, so a multiple arrangement can be more expensive than a single arrangement.

(5)   Employees may be able to transfer their company scheme into a personal pension plan if they take early retirement. However, if you are in a final salary scheme, this will mean giving up the safety of a guaranteed pension. If you are in a money purchase scheme (or if you are contributing to a supplementary scheme) then the case for considering staggered vesting is stronger.

(6)   Staggered vesting arrangements do not always provide the same level of security to widows as that provided by an occupational scheme. If you transfer to a staggered vesting scheme, you will have to consider how best to provide these other benefits.

(7)   Staggered vesting means that you do not make a once-and-for-all decision but, on the other hand, it also means that you have to watch overall investment performance and interest rates to make sure you do not lose out in the future.

Overall, staggered vesting is a more complex arrangement and you have to balance the simplicity of a straightforward arrangement against the flexibility and possibly higher benefits from a staggered arrangement. If you opt for a staggered arrangement, it is perhaps best to review your overall strategy on an annual basis (rather than taking one of the packaged deals that may be on offer).

5.10   Summary

When the time comes to take your pension, regardless of whether you are in a company scheme or a personal scheme, there may well be a considerable number of options open to you. The most important thing is to give yourself plenty of time when deciding which options to take. This is one of those occasions when there are no fixed rules; everybody's situation will be different and will need a different solution. Consequently, this is one time when the best advice is 'stop and ask the way'. There are a number of organisations who specialise in helping people through the annuity maze and the fee charged could prove to be a very worthwhile investment.

6 Investments

There have been many books written on investment; there have been whole books written on specific types of investment. A single chapter in a book of this nature cannot pretend to do anything other than provide an overview. However, this book has a purpose and that is to give you some suggestions as part of your overall retirement planning.

Consequently, the starting point is to assume that you have analysed your pension arrangements and done what you feel is necessary to maximise your future pension (because that is probably going to be the most important investment of all). This chapter will look at the range of investments available to you either because there is a shortfall in your pension income and you will have to make up the difference from your savings or because you have some spare capital and you want to invest it in a safe(ish) way.

The chapter covers the following topics:

(1) Introduction
(2) Short-term investment
(3) Tax efficient short-term investment
(4) Long-term investment
(5) Pooled investments
(6) Personal equity plans (PEPs)
(7) Other tax efficient investments
(8) Offshore investments
(9) Regular savings
(10) An overall strategy
(11) The home as an investment.

It is not the purpose of this book to have detailed descriptions of the various types of investment. Its purpose is to describe the general range of available types of investment with emphasis on the features which make them suitable for people planning their retirement. Further details on all of the investments in this chapter can be found in the *Allied Dunbar Investment and Savings Handbook*.

6.1   Introduction

Before looking at specific investments, this section covers some aspects of the overall background to this chapter, under the following headings:

(1)   The overall approach
(2)   Investment criteria
(3)   The four elements of investment
(4)   Asset-backed investment versus inflation
(5)   The comfort factor
(6)   Investor protection.

6.1.1   The overall approach

For our purposes, investment relates to the money which you are putting on one side now because you have decided that you do not need it for immediate purposes. It is impossible to say how much should go into any one particular type of investment as each portfolio will be arranged to suit individual circumstances. However, most people will probably be uneasy about locking up all their money in long-term investment and will necessarily feel more comfortable with some of it where it can be used in an emergency.

The overall objective is directed towards your long-term capital (defined here as capital you do not need for five years or more). Before you get to that point, you need to set aside a sum of money that can be used in an emergency and you may also feel more comfortable if some of your money was generally available in no more than five years' time.

As a general truism, the shorter the term, the more your money should be placed where it has no chance of losing its value in terms of pound notes. The longer the term, the more your money should be placed where it has less chance of losing its value in terms of its purchasing power.

6.1.2   Investment criteria

The *Allied Dunbar Investment and Savings Handbook* suggests that there are a few simple criteria to be borne in mind when considering investments.

Diversification

The first maxim for practically every investor should be diversification which reduces risks by spreading them. Diversification can be achieved by investing in varying kinds of investments but can also be achieved within a particular class of investment (eg through 'pooled' investments such as unit trusts).

Balance

Every investor should, as far as possible, have a balanced portfolio. Part of his capital should be earmarked for security and invested in, for example, building society or bank deposits. However, investors should also look for a measure of capital appreciation as a hedge against inflation so a part of his capital should be invested in equity type investments which tend to give higher long-term returns on average. The precise balance will depend on the individual circumstances and inclinations of the particular investor.

Getting advice

The investor should be willing to look for advice. There is a range of people, some acting for individual companies, others acting independently, who will provide a service which, if well performed, is a valuable one and for which they quite properly require remuneration. There has been a lot of comment on commission versus fees; of far more importance is the need to find somebody you can deal with and whose opinions you respect.

Taxation

The general rule is that your investment policy should not be dictated by tax considerations alone. Clearly, you should take advantage of all the tax benefits you can, but the investment decision should come first, not the tax benefit. There is no guarantee that an investment with tax benefits will produce a better return than an investment which has no tax benefits at all. Not only may these other investments have compensating benefits (eg better capital appreciation) but future tax legislation could alter or even nullify tax benefits that are now available; yet another reason for a policy for diversification.

6.1.3 The four elements of investment

Capital and income

Two basic elements of an investment are capital and income. At one end of the scale, the capital remains constant while the income produced may vary (for example, bank and building society deposits); at the other end, there are non-income-producing assets (such as works of art) where no income is produced but the capital value fluctuates.

Inflation

An essential third element in evaluating investments is inflation. The current view is that inflation is officially 'dead' which, on analysis, would seem to mean that it has been around two per cent for just over two years.

People with not particularly long memories will recall inflation at ten times that level and everybody has to take account that the reduction in inflation has brought other ills in its wake such as unemployment. A future administration might feel that unemployment is not a 'price worth paying' and any investor with an eye on retirement has to be ready for this. At the time this book was in the final stages of preparation, the Deputy Governor of the Bank of England suggested in a speech that, whilst much had been achieved, the view that the war against inflation had been won was 'an illusion, and a dangerous one at that'.

Time

The fourth investment dimension is the time factor. Within a long-term trend, there are likely to be many short-term fluctuations, caused by myriad factors. When to buy and when to sell are therefore difficult decisions for the investor which can be offset to some extent by investing in pooled investments where the more difficult decisions are taken for you.

6.1.4   Asset-backed investment versus inflation

One of the longest running surveys in the United Kingdom is the BZW Equity Gilt Study which monitors the performance of various investments back as far as 1918. Despite all the bad news of the last 80 years (including the Second World War and the catastrophic impact of the oil price rise in the early 70s), investment in equities with the income reinvested has produced the best overall return and one that has provided the best hedge against inflation. Of course, there will always be periods when interest rates are high and provide a better short-term bet. However, the trend has been for interest rates not to remain high for very long and you have the problem of deciding when to get back in to the equity market. As one investment guru put it 'the best way to get in, is to be in'.

6.1.5   The comfort factor

Comfort has a great deal to do with investment choice. There are literally thousands of different investments, but the ones that are likely to be the best for you are the ones that you understand and that you feel comfortable with. However, that is not a reason for excessive caution or for sitting back once you have made your investment decisions. There is a relationship between risk and reward and some of your long-term capital should be placed where it has a higher risk of short-term falls. However, there are various ways of doing that, some more comfortable than others.

Comfort also has a lot to do with the balance of a portfolio. Anybody with only £5,000 spare capital would only feel comfortable if they put it in a deposit account if it represented their entire capital. By the same token, anybody with £50,000 to invest ought to be feeling uncomfortable if they took the same cautious approach and equally uncomfortable if they invested the whole amount in equities. For them, there is a balance between the two but the precise mix of investments is a purely personal decision and one that the individual feels relaxed about.

6.1.6 Investor protection

Outside the range of deposits offered by banks and building societies, other types of investment will generally fall under the area of supervision of the Securities and Investments Board (SIB). It was widespread concern following the collapse of several investment firms in the early 1980s which led to the enactment of the Financial Services Act 1986 and the setting up of the SIB. Today, with very few exceptions (such as the Bank of England and members of Lloyd's), any person or organisation giving investment advice or carrying on investment business in the United Kingdom must be authorised to do so under the terms of the Financial Services Act; to do otherwise would be a criminal offence. The SIB maintains a central register of all such authorised people and organisations.

Investor protection is now provided through a series of self-regulatory organisations (SROs) each of which is responsible to the SIB for ensuring that the firms authorised by them to conduct investment business do so in a tightly controlled way.

(1)   The Securities and Futures Authority (SFA) regulates the activities of those who deal in securities (ie shares), futures and options.
(2)   The Investment Management Regulatory Organisation (IMRO) regulates the managers of investments including the managers and trustees of collective investment schemes such as unit trusts and investment trusts.
(3)   The Life Assurance and Unit Trust Regulatory Organisation (LAUTRO) regulates the marketing activities of life companies, and collective investment scheme managers.
(4)   The Financial Intermediaries Managers and Brokers Regulatory Association (FIMBRA) regulates the many independent intermediaries who advise on life assurance, pensions, collective investment schemes and other investments.

It is anticipated that LAUTRO and FIMBRA may merge to form the Personal Investment Authority (PIA).

All SROs are required to ensure that their member organisations follow the basic principles laid down by the SIB (and there are compliance and monitoring procedures in place backed up by disciplinary powers, including powers of expulsion against those who fail to meet the required standards). Amongst these requirements is a responsibility to obtain information about customers before giving advice on specific investments. Consequently, when seeking advice from any source, you must be prepared to give your adviser a good deal of information about your financial circumstances in order that he can help you make an informed judgement about the suitability of specific investments.

The one area of investment which is not covered by the Financial Services Act is residential housing because that will frequently involve a mortgage. All forms of borrowing are covered by the Consumer Credit Act and the monitoring of firms offering credit is handled by local trading standards officers under the overall guidance of the Office of Fair Trading.

6.2   Short-term investment

For the purposes of this book, short-term investment covers anything invested for up to five years. Within the market for short-term capital investment, there is a whole range of types of investment. Some offer fixed rates of interest, some have variable rates. In most cases, the interest is taxed at source; in others it is paid gross.

For the majority of people, the most obvious home for their short-term capital is a bank or building society deposit. However, there are alternatives which could be worth keeping an eye on.

The following are covered in this section:

(1)   Bank and building society accounts
(2)   National savings
(3)   Other forms of deposit
(4)   Guaranteed income bonds.

Although the security of these sorts of investments is generally taken for granted, there is some statutory protection in that most providers will either be an approved institution under the Banking Act 1987 (under the terms of which 75 per cent of individual deposits up to £20,000 are safeguarded) or are covered by the Building Societies Act 1988 (under the terms of which 80 per cent of deposits up to £20,000 are safeguarded).

Safeguards for life assurance-based guaranteed income bonds are provided by the Policyholders Protection Act 1975.

Most bank and building society deposits and most National Savings products fall into the definition of 'narrower range' investments under the Trustee Investments Act 1961 (see 11.6.1).

Throughout these early sections, the distinction will be drawn between those interest-bearing investments which pay interest net of tax and those which pay interest gross. With most of them, interest will be paid net of tax but, in the majority of cases, non-taxpayers can apply to have it paid gross. Form R85 (available from banks and building societies) should be completed in respect of each account earning interest; interest will then be paid gross. As soon as the individual's total income rises over the tax threshold, the accounts must be de-certified.

Parents or guardians can make similar application for children under 16. The certification automatically expires at age 16; the account-holder must then re-apply on his own behalf.

6.2.1 Bank and building society accounts

For money that you need in a hurry, a popular place is a bank or building society. You have the choice of current accounts or deposit accounts. With building societies, there is a growing emergence of postal accounts which tend to offer slightly higher rates of interest. It really does pay to keep on top of these rates because they do change and some institutions are not in any hurry to tell you that your particular type of account is no longer paying the best rate.

There are various publications (of which *Moneyfacts* is probably the best) which will keep you up to date on rate changes. At the end of 1993, the rates of interest being quoted on a £5,000 instant access building society deposit ranged from one per cent to 6.4 per cent. It pays to shop around if up to £270 a year can be earned simply by writing a couple of letters.

Interest is generally paid net of tax (but see 6.2.3) although a number of banks and building societies have offshore branches ('offshore' being defined as the Isle of Man and the Channel Islands). Interest on these accounts is paid gross.

A few building societies offer special accounts to people over 55 (some reduce this to 50; others raise it to 60). The rates of interest are not nec-essarily better, but there are occasional add-on features such as shopping discounts and so on.

6.2.2 National Savings

National Savings accounts

National Savings provide two types of account—the ordinary account and the investment account. Interest on both of these is paid gross. The interest on ordinary accounts is low, but the first £70 of interest is tax-free, which makes a limited investment in this account of interest to higher rate taxpayers.

National Savings income bonds

Interest is paid gross on a monthly basis. There is a loss of part of the interest if any withdrawals are made in year one. Subsequent withdrawals are allowed (subject to three months' notice), but at least £2,000 must be left deposited.

These bonds are generally of interest to those non-taxpayers who can tie up £2,000 for at least 12 months.

First option bonds

These are a lump sum savings vehicle where the interest rate is guaranteed for one year at a time. On the anniversary, the net interest is capitalised and the whole amount can be withdrawn or reinvested for a further year.

No interest is paid on any money withdrawn in the first year; withdrawals during the second and subsequent years accrue interest at half the stated rate, unless the withdrawal is made on the anniversary date.

Premium bonds

They can be bought and sold at any time and qualify for a prize after they have been held for one clear calendar month (so the best time to buy them is towards the end of the month). The maximum holding is £20,000. Prizes are free of income tax and capital gains tax.

According to National Savings, your holding should be at least £1,250 if you are to have an average chance of winning a prize in any one year; the maximum holding puts you in line to win, on average, 16 prizes a year.

6.2.3   Other forms of deposits

Fixed rate accounts

A number of organisations offer fixed rate accounts where the rate of interest is determined by the size of the deposit and the time period (which usually ranges from one to seven years although some banks and building societies offer accounts for one, three and six months).

Interest is paid net, except for interest on deposits of £50,000 or more (known as 'qualifying time deposits') which is paid gross. The frequency of interest varies with individual accounts. Some is paid monthly but the majority pay annually or at maturity.

Some banks and building societies offer offshore fixed rate accounts. They also offer what are called 'money market term deposits' though the minimum level of deposit is usually very high, eg in excess of £50,000. Interest on both these types of account is paid gross.

Escalator bonds

A limited number of building societies offer escalator bonds (also known as 'rising bonds'). These are fixed term investments where the initial rate of interest is fixed and guaranteed to increase each year of the term. The interest is always paid net of tax.

Retail co-operative society fixed term deposits

A small number of UK retail co-operative societies offer fixed term deposits. The interest on these is paid gross. The societies which offer these fixed term deposits are members of the Co-operative Deposit Protection Scheme which has been approved by the Treasury in accordance with the Banking Act 1987.

6.2.4 Guaranteed income bonds

These are issued from time to time by various insurance companies. In return for a lump sum investment, the insurance company guarantees a monthly or yearly income with a full return of capital at the end of the term. The income is paid net of basic rate tax but is not reclaimable by non-taxpayers. Higher rate taxpayers may have an additional liability to tax when the bond matures.

6.2.5 Summary

By and large, all of these investments can play a part in anybody's financial planning (though some may feel the uncertainty of premium bonds is something they can do without). Your choice will depend on personal preference but it always pays to shop around for the best rates.

6.3 Tax efficient short-term investments

For investments where you are prepared to put your capital on one side for up to five years, the range of options increases. All the investments mentioned in 6.2 are valid here but committing funds for longer periods of time should only be done where you can obtain some additional benefits, eg guarantees or tax incentives (you can also get the benefit of regular savings which are covered in more detail in 6.9).

However, these guarantees and tax benefits do require some level of commitment and so, with the exception of gilt-edged securities, all the investments in this section only provide the full benefits if they are held for the full term. Also, only gilts and guaranteed equity bonds offer any scope for capital growth.

The following investments are covered:

(1)   National Savings
(2)   TESSAs
(3)   Guaranteed equity bonds
(4)   Gilt-edged securities.

6.3.1   National Savings

National Savings certificates

These are guaranteed by the Government. A number of issues have been made. An issue can be withdrawn at any time. The maximum holding varies from issue to issue. No interest is payable but the certificates are redeemed for a higher value than the original purchase price. The full benefit is gained only if the certificates are held for five years.

The gain is totally tax-free which makes them attractive for higher rate taxpayers. Holdings should be reviewed from time to time, particularly if interest rates are rising (in which case, it might be more beneficial to surrender an issue early and invest in a new issue).

Index-linked certificates

These are designed to provide inflation proofing. The current issue (March 1994) guarantees a rate of return equal to rises in the retail prices index over a five year term plus an additional rate of interest which equates to three per cent *per annum* over the five year term. All gains are free of income tax and capital gains tax which make them attractive to higher rate taxpayers.

There is, of course, a theory that, as the Government is giving the guarantees, the active marketing of index-linked investments (see also 6.3.4) is a sure sign that the Government is confident that inflation is going to stay down. Index-linked investments should therefore perhaps be seen as a hedge against inflation returning at some point in the future.

Capital bonds

These accrue interest which is capitalised on each anniversary of the purchase. The interest is taxable and must be declared. The capitalised interest accrues at an increasing rate—the full benefit requires a bond to be held for five years. The capital can, however, be withdrawn in whole or in part at any time.

Capital bonds could be suitable for people who pay little or no income tax and who can tie up funds for five years. However, their overall attraction depends on the level of interest rates generally available; they could become unattractive if interest rates start to move up.

Pensioners' guaranteed income bonds

These were introduced in the early part of 1994. They are available to people aged 65 or over. Up to £20,000 may be invested (doubled for joint holdings) and this is used to provide a regular monthly income guaranteed for five years. The income is taxable but is paid gross.

The money invested may be withdrawn without penalty at the fifth anniversary; earlier withdrawals require 60 days' notice and no interest is payable during the period of notice.

6.3.2 TESSAs

TESSAs (Tax Exempt Special Savings Accounts) are offered by a range of banks and building societies. You may invest up to £9,000 through an initial deposit of up to £3,000, followed by three further annual deposits of up to £1,800 with a final payment of up to £600 (but see 6.9).

Interest accrues during the five year period net of basic rate tax. At the end of the five years, a bonus equal to the amount of basic rate tax deducted is added back into the TESSA, ie it effectively becomes a tax-free investment.

Interest added to a TESSA does not count towards 'total income' for the purposes of the higher age-related personal allowance (see 8.4.2).

During the five year period, the net interest can be withdrawn without affecting the tax exempt status of the account but, if any *capital* is withdrawn, the right to the tax bonus is lost. If you run a TESSA for, say, four years and then close it, any remaining accrued interest will be taxed in the year of closure even if it actually arose in earlier years.

TESSAs are therefore best seen as a five-year investment with tax-free interest. The rates of interest are variable (though a small number of building societies offer fixed rate TESSAs). You may only own one TESSA at a time but you may switch it to another bank or building society to get a better rate (though this may involve you in a transfer fee).

6.3.3 Guaranteed equity bonds

These are investments which combine a guarantee of return of capital at the maturity date with the opportunity to benefit in stockmarket growth (usually related to movements in the FTSE-100 Index) over the period. There are a variety of ways in which you can benefit from this growth, and you should read the promotional literature to decide which one you feel most comfortable with. Some bonds, for example, measure the movement in the index over the full five years; others 'lock-in' gains on a regular basis, usually annually.

A point to make is that it is not strictly an asset-backed investment. The return is related to movements in the Index, and is only indirectly related to the performance of the constituent companies. Dividends are not usually taken into account.

Many of these bonds operate as a term deposit where the relevant gain in the FTSE-100 Index is credited to the bond as interest. This interest is paid net of tax. Basic rate taxpayers pay no further tax, but higher rate taxpayers will face an additional liability in the year of maturity if the maturity value exceeds the original investment.

6.3.4 Gilt-edged securities

Gilt-edged securities represent borrowings by the British Government and are guaranteed to be repaid in full (at 'par') at maturity (the redemption date). The period to run to redemption is used to classify them as follows:

(1)   'Shorts'—less than 5 years to redemption
(2)   'Mediums'—5 to 15 years
(3)   'Longs'—over 15 years
(4)   'Undated'—stocks with no fixed redemption date.

Shorts and mediums are the gilts of most interest to people planning for retirement.

The year of redemption may be precisely defined (eg Treasury 8¾% 1997) or lie within a range (eg Gas 3% 1990–95). The precise date of redemption varies from stock to stock, but will be the anniversary of its date of original issue. That is also the reference point for the half yearly payments of interest. The amount of interest paid is determined by the 'coupon', for example, £100 of Gas 3% 1990–95 will pay £3 *per annum* each year until redemption.

Interest is paid net of tax except in the case of War Loan 3½% and any stock bought at a post office or direct from the National Stocks and Bonds Office. Gilts are exempt from capital gains tax. People living abroad are exempt from all UK taxes on a range of gilts (see 12.7) known as the FOTRA stocks (Free Of Tax to Residents Abroad).

Gilts are guaranteed to be redeemed at par at the redemption date, ie £100 of nominal stock will be bought back by the Government for £100. In the meantime, the price will vary according to the coupon and the general level of interest rates. Prices decrease as interest rates rise and increase as interest rates fall but will always converge eventually towards the par value at redemption.

The return from gilts is, therefore, a combination of two factors: the rate of interest paid and the rise (or fall) in value between the date of purchase and the date of redemption. This total return is called the redemption yield and, in very broad terms, the redemption yield will tend to follow interest rates generally available.

At a time when interest rates are high, locking in to a high coupon gilt (ie one with a coupon more or less equal to outside interest rates) can:

(1)   guarantee a high level of income until redemption (should interest rates fall in the meantime); and

(2)   hold out the prospect of a tax-free capital gain should interest rates fall between the date of purchase and the date of redemption.

Index-linked gilts

These have been available since 1981. The redemption value and annual income are linked to changes in the retail price index. The income from index-linked stocks is relatively low as the main advantage is through the inflation proofing given to the capital (provided it is held to maturity). The income payments increase every six months to reflect changes in the retail price index.

6.3.5   Summary

These medium term investments certainly have a part to play in planning for retirement. National Savings and TESSAs have the attraction of tax-free gains, guaranteed equity bonds offer the chance of matching stock-market growth and gilts offer a known level of income with the guarantee of repayment of capital, often with a tax-free gain thrown in.

The downside is that they require a committed term of investment to get the *full* benefits and, if you are close to retirement, you need to assess what your tax position might be at the end of the term to make sure they are still as attractive.

You also need to remember that they will all differ in their response if interest rates start to move up again. Holdings of National Savings certif-icates could start to look unattractive, TESSAs will benefit, gilts will fall and, although guaranteed equity bonds in themselves will not be affected, they could lose their attraction if the interest rate increase is sufficient to rattle the Stock Market.

Even investments with guarantees and tax benefits have to be watched and managed.

6.4   Long-term investment

6.4.1   Introduction

'Long-term' in the context of this chapter means over five years, but not more than ten. Investment planning more than ten years in advance starts to lose some credibility. Far too much can happen over a ten-year period to make forecasting anything other than a qualified guess. Even our plans to retire at a given age may be overtaken by events.

Long-term investing is appropriate to the riskier forms of investment which carry far greater potential for protecting the real value of our money. Most of this money should usually be invested in real assets such as stocks and shares or property. Gilt-edged securities can play a part in this type of portfolio, but it must be accepted that the guarantees inherent in gilts (the guaranteed income and repayment value) do mean sacrificing much of the potential for growth. A gain of 25 per cent could be quite difficult to achieve via a gilt-edged security; gains of 25 per cent, even 2,500 per cent, are a fact of life in the stockmarket.

Investment in assets can either be done by direct investment in the asset itself (eg by the buying of ordinary shares in a specific company through a stockbroker) or through one of the 'pooled' investments which seek to reduce the risks by diversification. Pooled investments have grown rapidly in recent years and this growth was fuelled by the introduction of personal equity plans (PEPs) which add the benefits of tax incentives to asset-backed investment.

Direct investment is clearly more risky because you are committing funds based on your judgement of an individual organisation. It is also, it must be said, a more troublesome form of investment because you will be required to deal with all the paperwork of scrip issues, bonus issues, take-over bids and so on. Investment in individual companies is covered here for the sake of completeness but, on the basis that we are covering retirement planning, it is not recommended for the average investor. If you feel you must invest in a specific company, try and do it through a PEP. As well as getting the tax benefits, most of the paperwork will be done for you.

6.4.2   Individual investments

The principal types of individual investment suitable for the long-term are those securities created when bodies such as the Government or individual publicly quoted companies wish to raise money. They can do this either by borrowing the money from you (which usually carries with it some kind of guarantee) or by inviting you to share in the fortunes of their organisation (which rarely implies any kind of guarantee at all). Investments with guarantees will generally have less opportunity for capital growth; those without guarantees offer the opportunity for unlimited capital growth (and also total loss).

This section looks at investment through borrowings and by direct investment in company ordinary shares.

6.4.3 Public sector stocks

These include gilt-edged securities. Examples of other bodies entitled to borrow are certain of the Co-operative Retail Societies, the Agricultural Mortgage Corporation and the Port of London Authority.

6.4.4 Listed company fixed interest securities

Fixed interest stocks are also a form of borrowing, with one exception. There are three main types.

Debenture stocks

These are secured loans and represent the most secure form of investment in a company (although, of course, companies can vary in their creditworthiness). If the company defaults, debenture holders obtain rights over the company's property or assets.

Loan stocks

These are unsecured obligations. If the company fails to meet its obligations, loan stockholders are in the same position as other unsecured creditors but rank higher than ordinary shareholders.

Preference shares

These are not borrowings but part of the share capital of the company. Preference shareholders are entitled to a fixed dividend in advance of any dividends paid to ordinary shareholders and, if the company is wound up, rank ahead of ordinary shareholders up to the nominal value of their capital.

Convertibles

Convertible stocks are a special form of loan stock or preference shares which carry the further right to convert into a stated number of ordinary shares of the company on a stated date.

Income and taxation

Dated debentures, dated loan stocks and redeemable preference shares carry a stated rate of interest for a specified number of years. However, under certain circumstances (for example, if general interest rates fall substantially below the coupon) companies may have the right to repay before the stated redemption date.

Interest on debentures and loan stocks is paid after deduction of basic rate tax. Dividends on preference shares are paid under the 'imputation' system (see below).

6.4.5   Permanent interest bearing shares (PIBS)

Permanent interest bearing shares are issued by certain building societies. They are traded in the same way as ordinary shares on the Stock Market. They have a fixed rate of interest (the coupon) but no fixed redemption date. The interest is paid net of tax at the basic rate.

PIBS are similar to gilts in that they pay a known rate of interest. The capital value is subject to change in the same way (ie market prices will rise as interest rates fall) but is more dependent on supply and demand. Their lack of redemption date makes them a riskier option particularly for investment at a time when interest rates are low.

6.4.6   Ordinary shares

These are a company's risk capital. The investor hopes to get a reasonable and rising dividend and a rising share price, but there is no guarantee of this. If the company does less well than expected, the share price may fall; if the company fails, the investor could lose his whole investment. Ordinary shares are therefore only suitable for investors who are prepared to accept a certain level of risk and who are prepared to follow the fortunes of their chosen company. The company's fortunes could be affected by any number of factors that you might not foresee and they are generally most suitable for the active investor who follows the market closely.

The selling of shares is a chargeable event for the purposes of capital gains tax, although gains can be reduced by the impact of indexation (see 8.6.1).

The imputation system

Dividend income is paid to investors after deduction of a tax credit (at the rate of 20 per cent). Non-taxpayers may reclaim this tax credit. The liability of basic rate taxpayers is fully satisfied by this tax credit, even though they may be paying tax at 25 per cent on the rest of their income. Higher rate taxpayers will face a further tax liability of 20 per cent on the gross dividend to bring their total liability up to 40 per cent.

6.5   Pooled investments

Pooled investments offer the safer route for the would-be stockmarket investor by giving him the opportunity to invest in a range of company shares. This then means that the poor performance of one or two shares need not have a significant impact on the overall portfolio (though, by the same token, you will not get the full benefit of a couple of star performers). A portfolio of shares should normally be more rewarding than any equally risky individual shareholding.

The other attraction is that the underlying investments are being looked after by professional fund managers. There are no guarantees about stockmarket investment but the individual investor simply cannot have rapid access to the world-wide body of information which is now an integral part of investment. Fund managers are not infallible and their decisions may in the end come down to informed judgement but their judgement stands a better chance of being correct due to the information at their disposal. Furthermore, economies of scale allow them to take opportunities which may not be practicable for individual investors (eg dealings on foreign exchanges).

The range of pooled investments is simply enormous and it is now possible to invest in a general or specific way, across sectors, across markets and across the world.

There are three main types of pooled investment:

(1) Unit trusts
(2) Investment trusts
(3) Single premium bonds.

6.5.1 Unit trusts

Unit trusts are a form of pooled investment where the value of units is a direct reflection of the value of the underlying assets. The investment powers of unit trusts are regulated by the Securities and Investments Board (SIB); a trust is not able to invest more than a stated proportion of the assets in any one stock, thereby guaranteeing a spread of investment. Unit trusts have grown rapidly in recent years and now provide access to differing markets in different sectors and across the world.

Units are open-ended in that units are created or cancelled to meet the needs of buyers or sellers of units. They can therefore be looked on as a totally liquid investment, ie if you need to sell units, you can.

Unit trusts are taxed in a similar way to ordinary shares. Any dividend you receive will receive a tax credit at the rate of 20 per cent. Non-taxpayers can claim back this tax credit. Basic rate taxpayers face no further liability for income tax but higher rate taxpayers will have a further liability.

The underlying funds are exempt from capital gains tax but unit holders will face a potential liability when selling units.

6.5.2   Investment trusts

An investment trust is not really a trust at all, but a limited company in which investors buy shares so as to benefit directly from its asset growth and income. Shares in investment trusts are bought and sold on the stockmarket at market prices determined by supply and demand.

Investment trusts invest in a range of asset-backed investments, principally shares, but also property and may also invest internationally. Investment trusts have therefore, like unit trusts, been set up so as to concentrate in one particular sector, or market or economy, or across ranges of sectors, economies and countries.

The total return from an investment trust can be assessed in terms of capital growth and income. Investment trusts themselves are taxed on their income, but are exempt from capital gains tax. The income paid to investors is taxed in exactly the same way as for ordinary shares. Investors are liable to capital gains tax when they sell their shares.

Being a form of pooled investment, investment trusts are suitable for those investors who want to spread their risk and do not have the expertise or resource to invest directly into stocks and shares. However, they are marketable securities in their own right and their price is not a direct reflection of the value of their underlying assets. Two important factors you must take into account are 'net asset value' and 'gearing'.

Net asset value

Investment trusts have, for many years, often traded at a price which is lower than the value of the underlying assets. These discounts have been an attractive aspect of investment trusts as they clearly contain the potential for higher income and capital growth. However, some trusts are priced at a premium, ie at a price in excess of the current value of the underlying assets. It is important to know what the discount or premium is before investing.

Gearing

Some trusts have raised capital by issuing fixed interest stocks in addition to equity capital. If the trust is wound up, these fixed interest stockholders will have priority over ordinary shareholders. If the trust performs well, the impact on ordinary shareholders could well be magnified (as they will benefit from all the increase). Conversely, if the price falls, the ordinary shareholders will carry most of the loss. The higher the proportion of debt (ie the more highly geared the trust), the greater the potential gain or loss.

If you are unwilling to accept these risks in return for a potentially higher reward, then you are probably better off in a unit trust or single premium bond.

Investment trusts are also free to create different kinds of securities for their investors and this has led to some sophisticated investments such as zero dividend preference shares, capital shares, income shares, annuity shares and stepped preference shares. These are specialised areas of investment where you should get competent advice (further details of them can be found in the *Allied Dunbar Investment and Savings Handbook*) although 'zeros' deserve further details here.

Zero dividend preference shares

These pay no dividends but they aim to generate a capital gain at a fixed date in the future when the trust is wound up. Most zeros are priced at a value below their redemption value so they have the *potential* for capital gain. However, the redemption value is not guaranteed; it will only be paid if the assets of the trust are sufficient (though there is some protection in the fact that, in most cases, zeros have first call on the assets of the trust).

Clearly, a trust that can already cover the future repayment is a better bet but all values are susceptible to stock market movements. Zeros have proved to be a popular investment for the more cautious investor but it is an area where professional advice is called for.

6.5.3 Single premium bonds

These are lump sum investments marketed by life assurance companies. They are also pooled investments in that they cover a wide range of assets including property. However, because they are life assurance products, they are taxed within the umbrella of the taxation of life assurance companies. This has implications for the investor, as it leads to a tax system which, although apparently complicated, has some benefits.

Life assurance funds are income accumulators (ie they do not pay dividends) and so the life company itself will be taxed on the income earned by the assets in the funds and will also have to pay capital gains tax on any gains made when selling assets. These taxes are usually taken into account when fixing the unit prices, which means that the individual bondholder usually faces no further liability to basic rate income tax or capital gains tax. However, this tax may not be reclaimed which tends to make them unsuitable investments for non-taxpayers. Higher rate taxpayers may have some further tax liability.

Surrendering a bond—'top slicing'

When a bond is surrendered, either in whole or in part, the gain is taxed as income. However, as the life fund has already paid some tax on the income earned by the funds, the only tax liability on the bondholder is to higher rate tax.

The total gain is divided by the number of complete policy years that the bond has been held. The resulting figure (known as the 'slice') is then added to the bondholder's other income for that tax year. The rate of tax that the bondholder would pay on this slice is then, *after deduction of the basic rate of tax*, applied to the whole gain.

For example, if you purchased a bond in July 1986 and surrendered it in May 1996 you would have held it for nine years and ten months. If you had made a total gain of £9,000, the slice would be £1,000 (ie £9,000 divided by the number of *complete* policy years). £1,000 would therefore be added to your other income for the 1996-97 tax year for the purposes of calculating the tax rate to be applied to the whole gain.

(1)   If you remained a basic rate taxpayer even after the addition of the £1,000, you would face no further tax liability.

(2)   If you were a higher rate tax payer before the addition of the £1,000, you would have to pay tax at 15 per cent (ie 40 per cent less 25 per cent) on the whole of the £9,000

(3)   If the addition of the £1,000 lifted you into the higher rate band then a composite rate of tax (between 0 and 15 per cent) would be applied to the whole of the £9,000.

This principle of dividing the gain up is called 'top slicing' and can lead to benefits for people who are currently higher rate taxpayers if they defer surrendering their bond until a time when they are receiving a lower income.

'Income' from single premium bonds

Single premium bonds do not pay any automatic dividends. However, there is a facility to cancel units on a regular basis to provide a regular 'income' and there is a specially constructed tax regime to handle these.

(1)   Investors can withdraw up to five per cent of the original investment in any one policy year without incurring any tax liability at the time. A running count is kept of cumulative allowances and amounts withdrawn.

(2)   When the bond is finally surrendered, any previous payments are taken into account in assessing the total overall gain which is then taxed as above.

(3)   If, at any time during your ownership of the bond, the cumulative amounts withdrawn exceed the cumulative allowances, a tax charge arises. The excess is the gain and is treated as above. However, the calculation is done at the end of the policy year which could be in a different tax year from when the money was actually withdrawn.

The structure of the investment

The practical implications of the above are as follows:

(1) It would be very tax inefficient to invest in a single premium bond and then withdraw a substantial percentage in a short time. This would cause the five per cent rule to be breached and could result in a basic rate taxpayer incurring a substantial higher rate tax liability. For example, if you invested £10,000 in a bond and had to withdraw £6,000 a year later, you would have one year's allowance (£500) to set against the withdrawal. The end result would be that, even if the investment was showing an overall loss at the time, £5,500 would be added to your other income to determine the rate of tax to be applied to the £5,500.

This is generally avoided by companies issuing investments in a 'cluster' or series of smaller bonds and encouraging bondholders never to withdraw more than five per cent a year from each element. If larger amounts are needed at any time, then these are raised by surrendering one or more individual bonds completely.

(2) A higher rate taxpayer could withdraw five per cent of the bond each year with no liability to tax at the time and either finally surrender the bond at a time when he was a basic rate taxpayer (eg after retirement).

An attraction for older taxpayers is that the regular five per cent withdrawals do not count as part of 'total income' for the purposes of the higher personal allowances (see 8.4.1). However, there is a sting in the tail for older people in that when the bond is finally surrendered, any gain *is* regarded as part of your total income for the purposes of calculating your entitlement to the age allowance.

6.5.4 Comparisons between pooled investments

All three types of investment provide the opportunity for diversification and professional fund management. It is now possible to choose virtually any type of equity investment anywhere in the world and find at least one investment trust or unit trust company offering the opportunity of investing in it. Investment trusts differ principally on the basis that the share value is not necessarily a reflection of the underlying assets and there is also the potential risk (and opportunity) of 'gearing'.

Both investment trusts and unit trusts are beneficial to non-taxpayers in that any tax deducted from dividends can be reclaimed. This is not the case with single premium bonds, but they offer tax benefits to higher rate taxpayers. As gains on single premium bonds are taxed in the tax year in which they arise, there is the opportunity to defer taking gains until retirement, ie at a time when you might have become a basic rate taxpayer.

Both investment trusts and unit trusts are potentially chargeable to capital gains tax in the hands of the investor which means that changing the area of investment requires the old investment to be sold and a fresh investment made in the new area of interest. Single premium bonds, on the other hand are taxed in a totally different way with a complete absence of any capital gains tax liability on the individual investor. It is therefore possible to switch your investment from one area of investment to another with no tax implications.

6.6   Personal equity plans (PEPs)

Since their introduction in 1988, PEPs have become one of the fastest growing forms of investment media ever known. Their principal benefit is that they have no liability to capital gains tax or income tax. Furthermore, the income earned from a PEP does not count towards 'total income' for the purposes of the higher age-related personal allowance (see 8.4.1).

PEPs can therefore be seen as a very important way of complementing the money being put into a pension plan with the added advantage that they can produce a tax-free income at any time you choose in the future. The only disadvantage is that they are not available to non-residents.

Up to £6,000 a year can be invested into a general plan (and this includes unit trusts and investments trusts which have at least 50 per cent of their funds invested in UK equities and shares quoted on EC stock exchanges). Up to £1,500 a year can be invested in a general plan which does not meet these criteria. You can take out only one plan with one plan manager in any one tax year. In addition, up to £3,000 a year can be invested into a single company PEP.

The important point to remember is that PEPs should not be judged by tax considerations alone. They are principally investments in shares, they carry a degree of risk and there is no guarantee that you will get all your money back. They are therefore long-term investments with the added benefit that they have certain valuable tax benefits. Provided you accept that you wish to invest in asset-backed investments, then the first £6,000 a year of your investment should be via a PEP.

Most PEP managers charge some kind of annual fee though, in the case of unit trust and investment trust PEPs, the charges are likely to be the same as straightforward investment (indeed, the trend is to give preferential fees to PEPs). For single company PEPs, the position is not quite so simple as the fees charged can sometimes be high enough to wipe out any tax savings on the income (although some companies offer special schemes for their shareholders).

6.7 Other tax efficient investments

6.7.1 Enterprise investment schemes

These were introduced in the November 1993 Budget as a replacement for the Business Expansion Scheme. At the time of going to press, the legislation was not in place but the broad principles are as follows:

(1) The scheme is open to all individuals liable to UK income tax (including non-residents).
(2) Up to £100,000 may be invested in any tax year. Up to 5 October, half of the amount invested (subject to an upper limit of £15,000) can be carried back to the previous tax year.
(3) Investment must be in new shares in a qualifying unquoted traded company on or after 1 January 1994.
(4) Tax relief is given at the rate of 20 per cent. Once the shares have been held for five years, there is no liability to capital gains tax.

6.7.2 Enterprise zone trusts

These are specialised investments which are rather beyond the scope of this book. They provide for full tax relief on lump sums invested in a portfolio of properties located in a designated enterprise zone. There is no upper limit on the amount that may be invested but they are very long term (investors should be planning to hold on to their investment for 25 years).

6.7.3 Venture capital trusts

These are merely a proposal at the time of going to press and more detail is expected in the 1995 Finance Act. Broadly, it is proposed to encourage investment in unquoted trading companies through income tax and capital gains tax incentives for a special type of investment trust.

This adds to the tax benefits introduced in the 1994 Finance Act relating to the enhanced form of reinvestment relief (see 8.6.7).

6.8 Offshore investments

An investment is described as 'offshore' if it is incorporated in a low tax financial centre such as the Isle of Man or the Channel Islands. Such funds pay little or no local tax. They offer a wide range of investment opportunity and also offer all the risk advantages of other pooled investments. They may also be denominated in currencies other than sterling.

6.8.1 Offshore funds

Some offshore funds distribute the income they earn on their investments, whilst others accumulate it. A fund that distributes its income will generally have 'distributor' status, but this is not necessarily the case. To be granted distributor status, a fund has to distribute at least 85 per cent of its income.

The distinction is important because the dividends from a fund with distributor status will be taxed as income but will be paid gross. In addition, you will be liable to capital gains tax on any profit made when you sell the investment.

Funds without distributor status are taxed differently. When you dispose of your investment, you will face a liability to income tax, not capital gains tax, on the overall gain. There is therefore no annual exemption and no indexation relief (see 8.6.1). However, as the rolled-up income and gains are only taxed when you dispose of the investment, you have the opportunity to do some tax planning by arranging to cash in your investment at a time when your income from other sources may be lower.

Also, a transfer of such an investment to your spouse does not count as a disposal. Consequently, it would be possible for you to invest in a 'roll-up' fund and, at a time to suit yourself, to transfer the investment to your wife for her to make any profit (and pay any tax) on the sale.

6.8.2 Offshore investment bonds

In the same way as some companies establish offshore funds, some life companies offer a facility for investing in offshore single premium bonds. These offer some advantages within the bond itself as local tax rates will generally be lower than in the United Kingdom.

However, they are usually not a good idea for the UK investor. Although it is possible to take five per cent withdrawals and although 'top slicing' still applies, no allowance is given for basic rate tax. With a UK bond, the rate of tax on any gains can, at current rates of tax, be anywhere between 0 per cent and 15 per cent. With an offshore bond, exactly the same circumstances will produce a tax liability of between 25 per cent and 40 per cent.

6.9 Regular savings

Not everybody has lump sums to invest and others may prefer not to commit large sums of money anyway. In most of the areas of investment covered in this chapter, the opportunity exists to put money away on a regular basis.

6.9.1 Fixed interest savings

TESSAs

A few banks and building societies offer monthly TESSAs. The minimum amount can be as low as £10; the maximum is £150.

National Savings yearly plan

This is effectively an alternative way of investing up to £4,800 in the current issue of National Savings certificates. You may pay between £20 and £400 a month for 12 months after which you will receive your yearly plan certificate.

The certificate should then be held for a further four years to get the maximum tax-free return.

Save As You Earn (SAYE Schemes)

These are offered by a range of building societies and offer tax-free returns on savings of up to £20 per month. At the end of five years, a tax-free bonus equal to 14 months' contributions is added. If savings are left untouched for a further two years, this bonus is doubled.

6.9.2 Asset-backed investment

There are a range of monthly savings plans available to allow regular investment into unit trusts or investment trusts, with or without PEP arrangements. There is generally no limit on the amount that may be invested though if you are contributing to a monthly PEP, your monthly amount is limited to £500.

Monthly investment plans are favoured by some advisers for two reasons. In the first place, nobody can be sure they have got the timing right and paying an amount each month removes any worries about the right time to make the investment. Secondly, there are some benefits in doing things this way due to what is called 'pound cost averaging'.

Each investment you make, whether as a lump sum or a series of monthly payments, will buy you a quantifiable stake in the investment you have chosen either as a number of shares or units. The fans of monthly plans emphasise the fact that regular payments iron out the effect of the fluctuations in prices, buying more shares or units when prices are depressed and less when prices are higher. Over the longer term, this will tend to reduce the likelihood of an investment turning out a disappointment on the grounds that the moment you chose to invest a lump sum just happened to be the wrong moment.

Overall, pound cost averaging is part of the comfort factor. One disadvantage is that it makes the capital gains position rather more complex but the Inland Revenue operates a concession to simplify things (see 8.6.4).

6.10   An overall strategy

There is no single overall strategy; it will be different for every individual. We all look at things differently and our ideal portfolio will be based on our individual wealth and tax position, our own views of the likely movements in interest rates and inflation and our own ideas of what is comfortable.

However, the basic structure is unlikely to differ too widely. The first priority should be to repay all borrowings, as interest is usually payable out of net income at higher rates than can be expected gross from investments (see 6.11.1).

A suggested approach is that for capital up to £5,000 the best home is a building society; for capital up to £10,000 there can be more of a balance between emergency money and the tax efficient forms of short-term saving.

Once past £10,000, more can be directed towards asset-backed investment, preferably of the pooled variety with full use being taken of investment in PEPs. The balance can change to, say, 10:40:50 (emergency:short-term:long-term) as you approach £25,000.

Thereafter, the balance is up to you. Some people will prefer a greater emphasis on asset-backed investment; others will prefer a balance between short-term and asset-backed. One suggestion is that perhaps your retirement investment plans should follow the plans for your retirement itself; long-term, plenty of variety and not too much excitement.

The final point has to be on inflation and interest rates which, at the time of going to press, are the lowest they have been for over 20 years (a fact which has been the cause of more than one portfolio being re-assessed). A higher rate taxpayer looking to match underlying inflation (ie inflation taking into account mortgage repayments) has to get a gross return of 6.7 per cent on his investments and only half that if he is looking to match headline inflation. If you are looking to protect the real value of your capital there is no need to take excessive risk; even if you are hoping that your capital will grow over and above inflation it can be done in a fairly comfortable way.

For the time being, at any rate.

6.11 The home as an investment

No chapter on investment would be complete without a section on houses. For most people, their home represents their biggest single financial commitment and, as we prepare for retirement, it may well represent our biggest single debt. This section of the chapter looks at four topics related to residential property and financial planning:

(1) Paying off the mortgage
(2) Re-arranging the mortgage
(3) Home income plans
(4) Furnished holiday accommodation
(5) Rent-a-room relief.

6.11.1 Paying off the mortgage

The majority of people buy their home with the help of a mortgage and the idea of continuing with a mortgage is almost second nature. However, at or near retirement the idea of such a large debt is not attractive. It may also be that paying off the mortgage makes some sense financially.

The current limit on tax relief on loan interest is on the first £30,000 of the loan. This was fixed in 1983 and has not been adjusted since. If it had, it would need to be nearer £50,000 to keep up with increases in the cost of living. In addition, the rate of tax relief has come down over the years. In 1991, it was changed so that higher rate tax relief was no longer available, a further change in April 1994 limited the tax relief to 20 per cent, with a further reduction to 15 per cent from April 1995. As a result of these factors, many of the arguments for keeping a mortgage need re-examining.

The question, of course, is—if you have the funds available, do you pay the mortgage off, or reinvest the money elsewhere in the hope of doing better with it? For years, the answer has nearly always been that paying off the mortgage was the last thing you should do, but the erosion of tax benefits has made that assertion less valid. The interest you pay on money you have borrowed will always be more than the interest you are likely to get from any guaranteed investment. Add to that the fact that, from April 1995, you will only be getting 15 per cent relief on the first £30,000 you have borrowed compared to paying up to 40 per cent on the interest that you earn and there is probably no way that you will ever be able to match your mortgage interest payments with any certainty.

The only option you have is to invest in asset-backed investments which give you better prospects of matching you mortgage payments but which, in turn, means taking a long-term view (and you still have to pay your mortgage interest in the meantime).

The big hang-up, of course, is having to write out a cheque for such a large amount which then disappears into the building society's coffers, never to be seen again. The decision inevitably comes down to one of comfort. If you are happy to sign the cheque, then pay it off (or at least pay enough of it off to bring you down to the £30,000 level). If you prefer to leave your options open and retain flexibility for the future, then invest the funds elsewhere.

The key point is that it is easy to get stuck into a mortgage and to take it for granted. However, it represents for most people a fairly sizable trans-action and it does no harm to re-examine the overall arrangement from time to time.

6.11.2 Re-arranging the mortgage

At one time, the repayment mortgage was the only option, there were no others. Under the repayment method, repayments of capital are made over the term of the loan, together with an amount representing the inter-est on the outstanding loan. The payments are calculated to be level over the term so the balance between loan repayment and interest paid varies over the period of the loan.

Today, there are two other popular repayment methods, both based on 'interest only' loans. Here, no capital is repaid over the term of the loan. The capital is, instead, repaid out of the proceeds of an endowment policy (see 7.3.2) or out of the tax-free cash lump sum from a pension plan. The use of a pension plan in this way is a popular method because, instead of repaying the capital to the building society (for them to lend to somebody else), you are effectively investing it in your own pension plan with the knock on benefits of tax relief.

A further variant which is accepted by one or two banks and building societies is the PEP mortgage where the value of the relevant PEPs is monitored on a regular basis to make sure there is sufficient potential value in the PEPs to repay the mortgage. Associated term assurance (see 7.2.1) is also generally required as part of these packages.

Another alternative might be for you to look at the structure of your mort-gage and, in particular, the way interest is paid. Many people have the standard, variable rate mortgage but there could be some advantages in taking out a new loan and perhaps moving to one of the fixed rate options that are available. However, there is a caveat. If your current loan was taken out before 6 April 1988 and any element of that loan is for home improvements paid for before that date, you should leave well alone. If you take out a different form of mortgage, you could lose the tax relief on the proportion represented by the home improvement element.

Once again, the message is that it is easy to fall into the trap of doing nothing and assuming that what was good ten years ago is true today. There have been too many changes in the last few years for you simply to sit back and leave things as they are. Once again, *Moneyfacts* contains details of the wide range of mortgages that are on offer from the various sources.

6.11.3   Home income plans

Many elderly people owning their own homes may often find themselves in the position of owning a valuable asset but not having much income; they are 'asset rich but income poor'. Over the years a number of schemes have evolved to allow elderly people the means of convert the equity in their homes into income; such schemes are generally referred to as home income plans.

The original form of home income plan is a special form of purchased life annuity (see 5.1) bought with a loan secured against the value of the house. To qualify, the borrower must be at least age 65 and at least 90 per cent of the amount borrowed must be used to purchase the annuity.

Provided the loan qualifies in this way, the interest on the loan (up to £30,000) will qualify for tax relief. From April 1994, the way interest is treated will be slightly different. Interest relief will be by an income tax reduction whereby the borrower's income tax liability will be reduced (via his notice of coding) by 25 per cent of the interest on the loan (note, not 20 per cent or 15 per cent).

Home income plans can be a useful way for elderly people to turn their home into a source of income particularly if most of their capital is tied up in their home. However, annuity rates are a factor here and the insurance companies offering such schemes often insist on a higher age than 65.

Also, such schemes effectively hand over the rights to the house to a third party with only the balance being returned when the house is eventually sold. There is nothing intrinsically wrong with that but an annuity is generally paid until death however late or early that occurs. Families do not always take too kindly to seeing their inheritance disposed of for what turns out to be a short-term income. It is an area which needs total family involvement.

One of the appeals of home income plans is that the rate of interest on the loan is usually fixed and the annuity purchased will be a guaranteed gross amount as well. This means that future income will be fairly stable and will be affected only by changes to tax rates. There are various types of plan available offering different types of annuity. Some allow the monthly income to be topped up in the future, others are 'capital protected' in that some of the capital will be returned in the event of early death.

Another popular means of obtaining capital from property is through a reversion scheme. All or part of the house is sold to an institutional investor for a proportion of its market value. The seller is then granted a lease so that he can remain there until death or until he decides to sell and move elsewhere. The advantages of this type of scheme are that the cash released is not restricted to £30,000 and that the seller is not obliged to take an annuity. Against that is the absence of a stable income.

A variant which is not recommended is the 'roll-up' scheme where a mortgage is arranged but with the interest being added to the loan. As interest is then due on the unpaid interest as well as the original capital, the debt can build up quite rapidly and even overtake the value of the house. A loan of £30,000 for example would, at an interest rate of only five per cent, roll-up to nearly £50,000 in ten years.

6.11.4   Furnished holiday accommodation

In concluding the section on property, it is worth covering two areas where property can be used as an investment, providing you with an income with some useful tax benefits. The first is the area of holiday letting and it extends to property in the United Kingdom which is used for the specific purpose of furnished holiday accommodation (ie the benefits do not apply to overseas property).

There are certain requirements that must be fulfilled:

(1)   The property must be let on a commercial basis (ie it must be let at a realistic rent).
(2)   It must be furnished.
(3)   During any 12 month period:
    (a)   The property must be available for letting as holiday accommodation for at least 140 days.
    (b)   It must be let for 70 such days.
    (c)   It must not normally be occupied by the same person for more than 31 days during a period of seven months in the 12 month period.

Tax benefits

Provided these conditions are fulfilled, the following consequences follow:

(1)   Interest on loans used to buy the property should qualify as an expense.
(2)   You may get capital allowances for equipment, furniture and furnishings.
(3)   Expenditure incurred before you actually start letting your property may be allowed as a loss.

(4)   Any overall loss (after taking into account items (1), (2) and (3)) may be off-set against your other income.

(5)   Your profits could be regarded as 'relevant earnings' (see 4.7.1) for the purposes of personal pension plan and retirement annuity contributions.

The term 'holiday accommodation' should not be taken to imply that it must be a cottage in the country or by the sea. Provided it is used for the purposes of holidays, it could be in the centre of a town and it could just as easily be a mobile home.

Overall, there are some attractive features to the purchase of property for use as holiday accommodation, though it is clearly an area where an accountant's advice is needed. It is also, of course, an investment for the long-term and one where you will be expected to contribute some of your time as well as your money.

6.11.5   Rent-a-room relief

Under this relief, you can get total exemption from tax for income of up to £3,250 *per annum* for letting part of your only or main residence for use as a separate residence. Not only can this be a useful source of income, it is also one of the forms of income which does not form part of your 'total income' for the purposes of your eligibility to the higher age-related personal allowances (see 8.4.1).

7 Financial protection

In any plans for the future, particularly plans as long-term as those for retirement, it is a little unrealistic to believe that nothing will ever intrude to spoil our arrangements; as John Lennon once said 'life is what happens to you when you are busy making other plans.' Consequently, any prudent arrangements for a smooth transition from earning a salary to living on a retirement income must take account of the fact that there may be trouble ahead. There is nothing new in this; the practice of insuring life can be traced back to Roman times.

This chapter looks at the most common forms of financial protection and covers the following topics:

(1)   Introduction
(2)   Life assurance
(3)   Personal life assurance
(4)   Business assurance
(5)   Illness protection
(6)   Medical insurance
(7)   Redundancy and unemployment.

7.1   Introduction

This chapter is going to look at a number of ways in which we can insure ourselves. However, there has to be a balance. If we paid all the necessary premiums on every form of insurance, to protect ourselves up to the hilt from every one of life's potential problems, then we would certainly be well protected. We might also be destitute.

The other side of the coin is to believe that we are totally immune from the problems that life can throw up. Life is for living, we say, and we should enjoy the things we can do while we are young enough and fit enough to do them.

This may be a perfectly understandable approach but, nevertheless, you have to face up to the risks and make a conscious decision not to protect yourself. You may well sail through life without a serious illness or accident but taking it for granted that you will have such a easy ride is to take a risk. And, like all risk takers, you have to accept the consequences if things go against you.

It may not even be you who is the one to suffer. Your business could be affected by the absence of a key individual, somebody who may also have believed himself to be immune. His belief in his own immortality is no reason for your business and your financial plans to suffer.

There are no magic formulae. The only thing you can do is to ask yourself the question of what the financial implications would be, for you or your family, following the death, ill health or accident either of yourself or somebody close to you. Then you have to find out the cost of covering yourself or your family against these implications. The decision you face is whether you are prepared to accept a modest fall in your current living standards today in order to maximise the chances of maintaining that slightly lower standard of living in the future if the worst happens.

One of the all-time favourite stories of people selling life assurance is to invite the potential customer to imagine that he has just inherited a magical machine that pays out £2,000 a month, month in, month out. The only drawback is that the machine could explode, literally at any moment. The good news is that the machine will never explode if the customer, on receiving the £2,000, immediately puts £200 back, ie if he is prepared to accept £1,800 a month, he can have it forever. But the decision is his. The machine won't pay him a net £1,800; he has to make the conscious decision to put the £200 back.

On the assumption that the customer says that of course he would do that, he is then invited to believe that he is that magical machine.

A simple approach but often effective. Most insurance means giving up something today to ensure that we don't have to give up everything tomorrow and, as such, has a vital part to play in our retirement planning.

7.2 Life assurance

Life assurance is probably one of the most frequently encountered forms of personal protection. It certainly has a long history but, although a simple form of life assurance was available in England in the 16th century, the birth of the modern life assurance industry is generally regarded as having taken place in 1762. It was then that policies where the premiums were related to age and type of policy were first issued.

It is not hard to see why it is such a vital part of most people's protection. It is one of only two forms of investment that will provide a predictable sum of money at a totally unpredictable time in the future—and usually when it is desperately needed. The other form of protection that provides this type of cover is critical illness cover which is covered in 7.5.1.

Life assurance is also one of the few permanent forms of insurance. Once you have been accepted, and provided you continue to pay the premiums, you are covered regardless of what happens to you in the future.

7.2.1 The types of life assurance

There are three broad categories of life assurance:

(1)   Term assurance
(2)   Endowment assurance
(3)   Whole of life assurance.

Term assurance

This is the simplest form of life cover and will provide a guaranteed amount if death occurs within a certain fixed period (the term). The term can be set for any number of years to suit the purpose. At the end of the term, the cover lapses and there is no residual cash value.

Endowment assurance

Endowment assurance also has a term but it also has a growing investment value as well. Throughout the term, the policy provides life cover; at the end of the term (the maturity date) the plan provides a sum of money.

Whole of life assurance

These policies provide a guaranteed level of cover for as long as premiums continue to be paid. They may also build up a cash value.

7.2.2 The forms of life assurance

The principal aim of a life policy is to provide the funds to cover any financial difficulties likely to arise on the death of a named individual (the life assured). The amount of cover will be agreed at the start of the plan and, provided premiums are maintained at the agreed level, this life cover can never be taken away.

With modern life policies, the initial premiums are set at the best rates the life company can offer, based on assumptions of future mortality and investment conditions. At the end of a period of time (usually ten years), the position is reviewed. If the overall environment has been better than the assumptions, the level of cover will be increased; if worse, then premiums are increased to maintain the same level of cover. This then remains the position until the next 'policy review'.

There are two main types of policy: with-profits and unit-linked.

With-profits policies

The underlying value of the policy is related to the value of assets in which the life company invests the premiums. Any growth which can be passed on to the policyholder is passed on by periodic bonuses through-out the term of the policy (called 'reversionary bonuses') with a final bonus (the 'terminal bonus') payable at maturity. Once declared, a bonus is guaranteed but, in the case of endowment policies, companies reserve the right to re-calculate the figures if the policy is surrendered before its maturity date.

Unit-linked policies

The underlying value of the policy is expressed in the number and value of units that the policy holds in the relevant funds. The funds themselves reflect the value of the underlying assets and so, as the value of the assets fluctuates, so does the value of the policy.

The value of the policy can therefore be continuously assessed; there are no periodic or final bonuses as for with-profit policies.

7.2.3 The variations in life policies

The simplest form of policy is an 'own-life, own-benefit' arrangement. The policy is arranged by the policyholder on his own life and, when he dies, the proceeds of the policy will form part of his estate for inheritance tax purposes (see 9.2).

Other forms are joint-life policies, written jointly on married couples. Here, the life cover can be paid out either when the first person dies (joint-life, first-death) or when the second person dies (joint-life, second death).

It is also quite common to take out life assurance on somebody else's life if you would suffer financially if that person died (referred to as having an 'insurable interest'). Such policies are called 'life of another' policies. The insurable interest (and hence the maximum amount of life cover) is the potential financial loss to you if the life assured died.

Husbands and wives have unlimited insurable interest in each other. A policy taken out by one spouse on the life of the other can come under the provisions of the Married Women's Property Act 1882, which gives the policy a certain element of protection (eg a policy taken out by a wife on her husband would be protected in the event of the husband's bankruptcy).

Policies may also be taken out under the terms of a simple trust. This is usually done to ensure that the proceeds of the policy do not fall into the life assured's estate on death but, instead, become payable to nominated beneficiaries. This is frequently used in conjunction with joint-life, second death plans for the mitigation of inheritance tax (see 9.5) and also in certain types of business assurance (see 7.4).

There is also the straightforward practical point that policies written in trust means that cash is available without having to wait for grant of probate. Consequently, there is a case for saying that every life policy taken out for family protection should be written in trust.

7.3   Personal life assurance

7.3.1   The need for personal life cover

It would be rare for anybody with any level of family or financial responsibility to have no life assurance. Anybody taking out a loan or a mortgage, for example, will usually have life cover equal to the loan whether they want it or not because the lender will usually wish to ensure that the loan is protected in the event of the borrower's death.

If you have family responsibilities, where others are dependent on your income, then you have to consider what they would do without that income. The life cover you need is the sum of money which, when invested (and taking into account the level of interest rates generally available), will produce the income they need and which would also cover any outstanding debts or future financial commitments.

Tax relief

There is no general relief for life assurance premiums but certain policies taken out before 13 March 1984 continue to benefit from life assurance premium relief (LAPR). This relief is currently equal to 12½ per cent of premiums paid and represents a good reason for continuing to pay the premiums on such policies for as long as the policy remains eligible.

7.3.2   The uses of personal life cover

The type of life cover will generally follow the requirement it is needed to fulfil.

(1)   A short-term debt (eg a bank loan) could be covered by term assurance with the life cover equal to the amount borrowed.

(2)   A mortgage on a house is frequently covered by endowment assurance. The basic intention is for the maturity value to pay off the loan at the end of the term but the life cover ensures that the mortgage is protected during the term of the loan.

(3)   Where the need for cover is effectively limitless (eg family protec-

tion), whole of life plans are used to provide the required level of cover. Such plans are also written in trust where family protection or inheritance tax mitigation is the objective (see 9.5).

7.3.3 Pensions related life cover

Occupational pension schemes

Company schemes often provide a level of life cover while you remain employed and a member of your company scheme. Inland Revenue rules allow life cover of up to four times your final remuneration to be incorporated in your pension plan and, in this context, final remuneration means your remuneration at death. This definition means that your life cover keeps pace with your earnings, a form of in-built indexation.

For post-1989 members (see 3.3.1), the earnings cap affects this which means that for 1994–95, the maximum level of life cover is £307,200 (ie 4 × £76,800).

The recipients of the lump sum payment are at the discretion of the trustees and the payment will normally be free of inheritance tax. However, the rules of the scheme would usually allow you to nominate your preferred beneficiaries although, strictly speaking, the trustees are not bound by your nomination.

Additional voluntary contributions

Generally, any additional voluntary contributions (see 3.9) paid to a company scheme will be returned in full, although the rules of the scheme will determine whether or not they are returned with interest. Usually, the full investment value is repayable.

With free standing additional voluntary contributions (see 3.10), the full investment value is payable to the beneficiaries.

Funded unapproved Retirement Benefit Schemes (FURBS)

With funded unapproved retirement benefit schemes (see 3.12), any employer looking to increase the life cover of an employee caught by the earnings cap would have to set up an ordinary life assurance policy written in trust (and the premiums paid would be regarded as a benefit in kind and so taxable).

On death, the benefits would be distributed by the trustees and it is unlikely that any inheritance tax would be due.

Personal pension schemes

In the event of death before retirement, it would generally be the case that the retirement fund would be payable as a death benefit. The total death benefit under personal pension schemes can be written in trust and with generally favourable inheritance tax consequences. The form of trust can either be interest in possession or discretionary (see 11.3). Putting existing schemes into trust may have some inheritance tax implications, as might death occurring before taking benefits if it has been decided to defer benefits beyond the expected retirement date (although, if you defer taking benefits, you are potentially increasing the capital sum which can be returned to your beneficiaries in the event of your death).

However, it is possible to arrange a totally separate life policy within a personal pension scheme, with a big benefit being that the contributions are fully allowable against tax. The maximum amount that may be paid into a life policy set up separately from the personal pension scheme is five per cent of net relevant earnings (see 4.7.2). This is a drawback as the percentage does not vary with age, unlike the proportion that may be invested to provide retirement benefits. The five per cent also counts towards the overall maximum percentage that may be contributed to a personal pension scheme (see 4.8).

Life assurance policies set up together with a personal pension scheme may be assigned which can make them useful as collateral security in certain business assurance situations (see 7.4.3).

7.4   Business assurance

Just as there is a need to protect the family against sudden death, there is an equal need within the business. Covering the financial consequences of the loss of a key person (including such things as the repayment of guaranteed loans, arrangements to prevent the breakup of shareholdings and partnerships and so on) are all areas where the smaller business can turn to a suitably arranged life policy. This is a complex area and one where competent advice should be sought. The following sections provide only an outline of the types of areas where life assurance can play a part in business protection.

This section covers the following topics:

(1)   Key person assurance
(2)   Share purchase assurance
(3)   Partnership assurance.

7.4.1   Key person assurance

Area of risk

A key person is an employee or working director whose existence is crucial to the continued activities of the company. His or her loss could lead to a drop in sales, a drop in profits or a drop in confidence. In an extreme case, it could mean the winding up of the company. The individual could have given personal guarantees for loans and may even have made personal loans to the company.

Regardless of the specific circumstances, cash could be required to repay loans, hire and train replacements, spend time on reassuring nervous customers and so on.

Amount of risk

The potential loss in each case will vary. Where a loan is guaranteed, the position is clear. Where a sales director is being considered, the potential loss is less easy to ascertain. It could be a multiple of salary (ie a replacement cost), the loss in net profits or the potential fall in share value.

Type of policy

The most appropriate form is often a term policy but whole of life plans may give further options. It will generally be taken out on a 'life of another' basis as the proceeds will belong to the company.

From the tax point of view, the general view is that if the proceeds are likely to be treated as a trading receipt (and therefore taxable), the premiums will be allowable as an expense for corporation tax purposes. This would tend to be the case when life cover was arranged on a short-term basis to meet the expense of replacing a key person. Where, however, the proceeds are unlikely to be seen as a trading receipt (eg if the policy was taken out to protect a loan), then the premiums will not be allowable as an expense against corporation tax.

In all cases, you should get confirmation of the tax position from your local Inspector of Taxes.

7.4.2 Share purchase assurance

Area of risk

There are many thousands of companies with just two or three shareholders. The death of any one of them could have problems for the future direction of the company as the remaining shareholders may not welcome the involvement of the deceased shareholder's family. When a shareholder dies, his shares fall into his estate and will pass to his beneficiaries under the terms of his will. If there is no will, the rules of intestacy will apply (see 10.2), leading to a potentially even more unwelcome situation.

The most likely position is that the existing shareholders will wish to regain the shares so that they can regain full control of the overall shareholding. However, that may not always be easy; the new shareholders may be unwilling to sell or may put too high a price on the shares.

Amount of risk

The most popular solution is an arrangement with options to buy and sell the shares. This is usually referred to as a 'cross-option' agreement.

The agreement gives the holders of the shares (ie the deceased's executors) the option to sell the shares at the market price and gives the other shareholders the option to buy them.

The agreements provide for adequate life cover to be taken out to cover the costs of purchase of the shares. Determining the precise level of life cover is not easy because it is related to the market value of shares. This points to the need for a flexible type of policy which will allow for future increases in the level of life cover to be arranged.

Type of policy

The most usual arrangement is for each shareholder to take out a policy on his own life, written in trust for the other shareholders. On death, the proceeds are paid to the other shareholders who now have the money to buy the shares from the executors. Either a term policy or a whole of life policy may be used; a whole of life plan will often provide greater flexibility in what often proves to be an open-ended situation.

7.4.3   Partnership protection

Area of risk

As for shareholders, so too with partners. The death of a partner is legally the end of the old partnership and the start of a new one. The partner's widow will be in a difficult position; the main source of her income may have disappeared and, while she may have inherited her husband's share in the partnership, she may well have little interest in it. Her need is for cash but a share in a partnership is a difficult thing to sell except to the remaining partners and they may not have the money. She may be able to have the partnership dissolved in order to realise her interest in it, but this could be a lengthy and unsatisfactory process which could be a major problem for the remaining partners as well.

Amount of risk

Once again, a suitably arranged life policy can provide the answer. The most usual arrangement is for each partner to take out a policy written in trust for the benefit of the other partners for a sum assured appropriate to his share in the partnership. Once again, a suitable form of option agreement will be set up including the necessary cross-option arrangements to make sure that a willing seller is bound to find some willing buyers.

Type of policy

From the point of view of a traditional life policy, a whole of life arrangement may provide greater flexibility. However, this is one area where a life policy taken out as a separate plan alongside a personal pension scheme may also be appropriate with the added advantage of full tax relief on the premiums.

7.4.4 Tax implications

The tax implications of share purchase and partnership arrangements can be quite complex. The major impact is on inheritance tax and has specific implications for business property relief (see 9.8).

Clearly, no inheritance tax applies if property is left to the spouse, but, in all other cases, inheritance tax may be payable. This is a case where business property relief comes into its own as up to 100 per cent relief can be given on the transfer of shares and interests in partnerships. However, this relief could be lost if, at the time of death, there is a binding contract for sale. This could be a problem where there is a long-standing 'buy and sell' agreement because that may well constitute a binding contract for sale.

However, the Inland Revenue view is that a cross-option agreement is not regarded as a contract for sale for these purposes and so the relief will not be lost. That merely emphasises that a correctly drawn up cross-option agreement is an essential part of all shareholder and partnership protection. Most life companies will be able to advise you on a suitable form of agreement.

In general, there will be no inheritance tax implications on the payment of premiums or payment of proceeds, particularly where there is an arrangement within a group of people to 'cross insure' each other for commercial purposes; under these arrangements the premiums are not regarded as gifts.

There could well be tax implications if a new shareholder or partner joins an existing arrangement.

7.5 Illness protection

Most people will, if pushed, reluctantly concede that they are not immortal and that their life will at some point come to an end ('but not for some years yet'). Serious illness, however, which does not require immortality for its survival, is often regarded as an even more unlikely occurrence, a view which flies in the face of all the evidence.

The chances are that one in four men reading this book have either had, or will have, a critical illness before they reach State retirement age. Each year, hundreds of thousands of people are diagnosed as having cancer, or suffer from a heart attack or stroke.

Over and above these critical illness figures, many hundreds of thousands of people are unable to work as a result of sickness, accident or disability. For all manner of reasons, over half a million people are unable to work at any moment in time for medical reasons and have been unable to work for at least three years.

This section looks at three areas of financial protection against illness and covers the following:

(1)   Critical illness cover
(2)   Income protection
(3)   Waiver of contribution.

7.5.1   Critical illness cover

Not so very long ago, a critical illness, such as a heart attack, was frequently fatal; very few people would expect to survive. Today, medical science has made dramatic improvements in the treatment of a whole range of such illnesses and an increasing number of people survive them. Each year, half a million people suffer heart attacks, or strokes or are diagnosed as having cancer but, 12 months later, well over half of them are getting on with their lives.

However, while they may survive, their finances often do not. A heart attack may not lead to a permanent disability but it may well lead to a permanent change of lifestyle. It could mean a less stressful (and less well-rewarded) job; it could mean no job at all.

Critical illness cover is a relatively new type of insurance which is designed to meet the financial problems of survival. It provides a cash lump sum on the survival of a range of critical conditions or certain types of major surgery. The cash can be used for any purpose such as necessary home alterations or paying off the mortgage.

The range of plans available is growing all the time. They are also growing in terms of the options they can provide; some plans now provide additional life cover and some can be written on a 'joint-life, first claim' basis.

They may also be incorporated into cross option agreements for shareholder and partnership protection (see 7.4.2 and 7.4.3) to cover the purchase of business interests in the event of serious illness, as well as death.

7.5.2 Income protection

An illness does not have to be a critical illness in order to prevent you from working. Some of the less severe illnesses can lead to long periods of absence, as could an accident or other forms of disability.

A regular income at times like this can arise from three sources: the State, a company scheme or a personally arranged income protection plan.

State benefits

The two key benefits are sickness benefit and invalidity benefit. These are described in more detail in Chapter 13 but the essential aspects are as follows:

(1) Sickness benefit is a short-term benefit payable for up to 28 weeks. It is payable if you are unable to claim statutory sick pay from an employer.

(2) If the illness persists beyond 28 weeks, invalidity benefit would then be paid for as long as you remained incapable of work, and until you start to draw State retirement benefits.

Both benefits are available to the self-employed.

Sickness benefit and invalidity benefit are to be replaced from April 1995 with a new incapacity benefit (see 13.6.3). The overall effect will be a reduction in the amount of State help after an initial 28 week period.

Company benefits

The principal benefit is statutory sick pay which employers pay for up to the first 28 weeks of illness. There are a number of requirements to be fulfilled by the employee. Once statutory sick pay ends, then you may well have to rely on State benefits.

Some occupational pension schemes also provide a disability pension but this will only usually be paid if you are so disabled that you are in no position to continue with your job and have to leave the company.

For many people, therefore, the possibility of a long illness could leave them protected by a sick pay scheme of some sort or other for just over six months with the prospect of having to live on State benefits after that.

Income protection plans

These are contributory insurance plans which will usually provide you with up to 75 per cent of your gross annual salary (or net relevant earnings), less any entitlement to sickness benefit or invalidity benefit. These plans are designed to replace your earned income and so will usually commence paying benefit when your regular source of income stops as a result of your illness or disability. The income will then continue until you are fit to resume work or until the cover ceases (which will usually be your date of intended retirement).

The income is tax-free for the first twelve months of payment.

There is usually a range of options. One is to choose that the income does not start for a defined period of time after you have to give up work. This allows the plans to mesh in with other sick pay arrangements. These 'deferred periods' are typically one, three, six or 12 months and the longer the deferred period, the lower the premiums.

Other options include the facility to index-link your benefits in line with your rising income.

7.5.3 Waiver of contribution

Many forms of financial protection (life assurance policies, critical illness plans and pension schemes) require that you pay regular contributions, often monthly. Although many of them have the facility to catch up on any missed payments, there are usually limits to the extent you can do this, some imposed by the Inland Revenue.

A number of these plans therefore incorporate a 'waiver of contribution' where, in return for a small increase in your regular contributions, you have the reassurance that your contributions will continue to be accounted for if you are off work due to illness or disability. There is usually a built-in 'deferred period' of three months before this starts.

With personal pension schemes, it may seem odd that contributions can continue to be paid during a period of incapacity, ie at a time when, by implication, net relevant earnings are not arising. However, the answer lies in the name of the benefit; contributions are not paid on behalf of the planholder, the life company waives them.

Overall, this benefit can be very important in maintaining plans that are being used for inheritance tax mitigation or as the repayment vehicle for a mortgage and extremely important if it maintains your personal pension scheme during a period of incapacity.

7.6   Medical insurance

Whilst more and more people are prepared to insure themselves against the financial impact of illness, the same cannot be said when it comes to treating the illness. The State is still expected to fund the greater part of medical treatment with an apparently endless conflict between, on the one hand, providing that treatment in an efficient and cost-effective way and, on the other, providing treatment for more and more people as medical science develops increasingly sophisticated ways of successfully treating more and more illnesses. Added to that, there appears to be some reluctance on the part of the taxpayer to foot the bill.

Regardless of political persuasion, most people might accept the view that the NHS offers an unbeatable level of care in emergencies but that for more routine, non-life threatening conditions, we either join the queue at the NHS hospital or pay extra and go to a private hospital.

The growth of private medical insurance has mushroomed in recent years, particularly in corporate schemes, usually presented as a 'staff benefit' but probably more for the purpose of getting expensive staff back to work as fast as possible. Nevertheless, prompt medical treatment can remove a source of stress and, for the self-employed and people in their own business, being repaired and made well could be a key ingredient in preserving their income and their business.

However, the increasing number of people taking out medical insurance has led to pressure in the private sector with a resultant increase in costs. Medical insurance companies are now very much more rigorous when it comes to paying for treatment and a range of options has emerged which will allow you to select the type of treatment that you want (for example, only resorting to private treatment if NHS treatment is unavailable to you within a certain time-scale). This is an area where it is wise to shop around and to pay very close attention to the rules of the scheme. It is also important to look at the premium structure because you will find that premiums tend to increase quite rapidly at older ages.

When treatment seems likely, you should always check with your insurers first to ensure that your bills will be within their limits. If you take on treatment which is outside their limits, you will have to pay the difference yourself.

One point to be aware of is that medical insurance does not cover residential or nursing home care. This can be provided for to some extent by long-term care insurance (see 15.6).

Tax relief

There is no general relief for medical insurance premiums except for people aged 60 or older. However, this relief was reduced from 5 April 1994 (see 8.4.2). In the case of a joint policy, tax relief is given if either the husband or wife is over 60.

7.7   Redundancy and unemployment

If illness and disability are not enough, there is always a possibility of losing your income through other factors beyond your control. It is an unpalatable fact that older people are often first in the queue when it comes to 'rationalisation/slimming down' and the built-in ability and experience often carry little weight with companies looking for youth and vitality which, fortunately for them, often comes with a lower salary.

If you do face the 'five o'clock walk', it is vital to know your rights and to do everything possible to protect your position. This section covers the following:

(1)   Your statutory rights
(2)   Redundancy insurance
(3)   Unemployment benefit.

7.7.1   Your statutory rights

You will be entitled to a statutory redundancy payment if you have worked continuously for your employer for at least two years (five years is you are in part-time work) and you had to leave your job because it ceased to exist and there was no suitable alternative. The amount of payment is a multiple of your normal weekly gross earnings at the time you were made redundant (up to a maximum of £205 per week) for every year you have worked for your employer, up to a maximum of 20 years' continuous employment. The multiple depends on your age:

(1)   For each complete year of work following your 21st birthday, you will receive an amount equal to your weekly gross earnings up to £205.

(2)   For each complete year of working following your 40th birthday, you will receive 1½ times your weekly gross earnings.

The overall maximum level of statutory redundancy pay for an older person being made redundant after 20 years of work is therefore £205 × 20 × 1½ = £6,150. The calculation is different (ie less attractive) if, at the time of your redundancy, you are less than 12 months from State retirement age.

These are your statutory rights; there is nothing to stop your employer making a more generous payment. The taxation of these payments is covered in 8.2.1.

What is, of course, important is that you take all the steps you can to protect your pension. You should make quite sure that your pension arrangements are an integral part of your negotiations with your employer, particularly if you are taking voluntary redundancy. There are full details on your options when leaving your employment in 3.14.

7.7.2 Redundancy insurance

Redundancy insurance is less useful than it might at first appear. It tends mainly to apply to loans and mortgages and, specifically, to new loans and mortgages. There are also a number of conditions on most forms of redundancy insurance which tend to limit eligibility.

The premiums can be quite high. The borrower decides the level of cover he needs and the insurance cost could be in the region of £7 per £100 (eg to protect a monthly payment of £500, the additional monthly payment would be £35).

The definition of redundancy will usually be fairly strict:

(1)   For employed people, the redundancy must be through no fault of their own and must not be voluntary.
(2)   Self-employed people may only be able to claim on being made bankrupt.
(3)   Company directors may only be able to claim if their company is in compulsory liquidation.

One frequent problem with many types of redundancy insurance is that the test for eligibility is done at the time of claim, not at the time of taking out the insurance. It is often the case that a policyholder, having paid the premiums for some time, only finds when he comes to claim that, for example, a subsequent change of job has rendered him ineligible.

7.7.3 Unemployment

If you lose your job, then you will be eligible for unemployment benefit. This is described in more detail in Chapter 13.

Unemployment benefit can, of course, only be claimed by people who have been employed, ie the self-employed are not covered. More specifically, it is only paid to those people who have actually paid (rather than been credited with) Class 1 national insurance contributions (see 2.2) in one of the last two complete tax years before the year benefit is claimed.

Once you become eligible for benefit, and for as long as you qualify for benefit, you will be credited with national insurance contributions in order to preserve the full value of your State pension and other benefits.

8 Income tax and capital gains tax

This book is being prepared at a point more or less mid way between the tax increases imposed by Norman Lamont's last Budget and those introduced by Kenneth Clarke's first Budget. The overall effect of these is the biggest increase in taxation ever imposed on the British public since the end of the Second World War.

Against this background, it is essential that in planning for your future retirement, you take every step you can to reduce your tax burden to the absolute minimum. As Lord Clyde remarked in a famous judgment, nobody is obliged to arrange his affairs 'to enable the Inland Revenue to put the largest possible shovel into his stores'. The Inland Revenue will take every opportunity it can to reduce our income and our wealth and we have the right to take every legal step we can to protect our income and our wealth.

This chapter looks at taxation specifically from the point of view of people approaching or in retirement and covers the following topics:

(1) Introduction
(2) Employees about to retire
(3) Self-employed people about to retire
(4) Taxation in retirement
(5) Independent taxation
(6) Capital gains tax
(7) Tax saving areas.

8.1 Introduction

The basis of the tax system is that all our income and capital gains for a tax year, after deducting certain reliefs and allowances, and allowing for certain exemptions, are effectively aggregated together and taxed at varying rates according to the total amount. Within this system, you have some control over the total amount of tax you pay by following three simple guidelines:

(1) Claiming your entitlements
(2) Checking Inland Revenue documents
(3) Keeping your tax affairs in order.

You should also be aware that there are to be changes in the way we settle all or some of our tax bills.

8.1.1 Claiming your entitlements

Although the range of reliefs, allowances and exemptions has diminished over recent years, there are still a valuable number to be claimed. It is up to you to see if you are entitled to a particular allowance or not because it will rarely be the case that the Inland Revenue will alert you to the relief and allowances you are not using. This chapter does not detail all the allowances and reliefs that are available because that would be beyond the scope of the book. The most important ones from the point of view of retirement planning are covered; details of others can be found in the *Allied Dunbar Tax Handbook.*

8.1.2 Checking Inland Revenue figures

Given the money that they have invested in computer technology, it might seem odd for the Inland Revenue to make mistakes in its calculations. Unfortunately, it does and the author has personal experience of incorrect notices of coding, incorrect assessments and incorrect payment claims.

Once again, it is up to you to make sure that you are not being over-taxed (or under-taxed), and to notify the Inland Revenue accordingly. Any errors should immediately be brought to the attention of your Inspector of Taxes, including any that are in your favour (if you 'benefit' from a mistake by the Inland Revenue and fail to declare it, you could face stiff penalties).

8.1.3 Keeping your tax affairs in order

Legislation introduced over recent years has given the Inland Revenue much greater powers in dealing with tax offenders. Failing to declare sources of income, making late returns and even making mistakes in returns all carry quite serious penalties in contrast to the redress you have against the Inland Revenue for mistakes made against you.

Once again, the onus is on you. If you have been sent a tax return covering your personal tax affairs, you must have that return, fully completed, in the hands of your Inspector, by 4 pm on the last business day of October following the end of the year of assessment (eg for the 1994–95 tax year, the final day is Tuesday 31 October 1995).

If no tax return has been issued, you are obliged to tell your Inspector about any income or gains (that have not already been taxed) within 12 months of the end of the year of assessment eg by 5 April 1996 for any untaxed income and gains arising in the 1994–95 tax year.

Once you receive an assessment for tax due, you should immediately check it and, if correct, make arrangements for the tax to be paid on the due date. This will generally be 1 January in the year of assessment for bank interest and income from property and 1 December following the year of assessment for taxed investment income and capital gains. If you disagree with your assessment you should immediately appeal (if you disagree with the fact that you should be taxed at all) or apply for a postponement of part of the tax (if you feel your assessment is too high). In either case, if it turns out that your assessment was correct, you will be charged interest on any payments that are made late.

The overall message in this section is that tax and taxation are not particularly straightforward and it will pay you to keep everything in order and to double check all the information you send to the Revenue and all the information you get back from them.

8.1.4   Changes on the way

In future, the responsibilities for taxpayers to make returns are likely to become even more onerous. The Government is planning to introduce a form of self-assessment which will come into force from 1996-97. From that time, you will have to decide whether or not to calculate your own tax liability. If you do, you will have until 31 January following the end of the tax year to get your return (together with all the relevant calculations) to your Inspector of Taxes. If you decide to leave things to the Revenue, your fully completed return will have to be submitted by 30 September following the end of the tax year.

However, neither method will mean deferred tax bills. The Revenue will require interim payments of tax on 31 January during the tax year and 31 July following the tax year; these will both be 50 per cent of the previous year's tax bill. Any under or overpayment will then be picked up when the tax return is finally submitted to the Inland Revenue.

The new system will apply mainly to the self-employed and those with investment income. Employees will continue to be taxed under PAYE, as will pension income.

8.2 Employees about to retire

The most valuable exercise you can undertake is a general 'clean-up' of your tax affairs in the year immediately before the year in which you intend to retire. The last thing you want to be doing is carrying forward unpaid tax bills into your retirement.

You should check your notice of coding carefully. This will usually come out in advance of your final tax year of employment. You should make sure that it accurately reflects the deductions that should be made on account of your allowances and any additions made on account of any benefits in kind to which you are entitled.

Benefits in kind

The impact of the taxation of benefits in kind (eg a company car) will be spread over the 12 months of the tax year. Consequently, if you retire part way through a tax year, you should apply, shortly before you retire, to your Inspector of Taxes for your notice of coding to be amended with effect from your date of retirement. This will then ensure that the correct amount of tax is deducted from your pension payments (if you start these straight away) and that your net pension payment will be more or less correct. Clearly, you cannot avoid some tidying up to be done after the end of the tax year (your form P11D, for example, will not generally be sent out by your employer until a couple of months after the end of the tax year) but keeping the Revenue informed will help to ensure that the position is as stable as possible.

Car fuel benefit

If you are in the position where all your petrol, including your petrol for private use, is paid for by your employer, you will be taxed on the full benefit regardless of the amount of fuel provided. If you only fill the tank once during the tax year, you will have to pay tax on the full amount of car fuel benefit (though if you give up your company car part way through the tax year, you will only have to pay tax on a proportion of the car fuel benefit).

Depending on your anticipated private mileage in the tax year during which you intend to retire, it could pay you to forgo this benefit and to reimburse your employer for the full cost of fuel used for private purposes. If you intend to take this decision, you should make quite sure that the decision is clearly recorded in writing between you and your employer before the end of the preceding tax year.

8.2.1 Termination payments

It could be that you are retiring early from your job because your employment has been terminated. Under these circumstances, it can make some difference whether your employment is terminated at the beginning or end of the tax year. Part of any payment that you receive may be treated as taxable income in the year in which your employment is terminated; if this takes place at the beginning of the tax year, it could mean a lower rate of tax being applied to it if your other income for the remainder of the year is low (eg it might be tax efficient to defer taking your pension for a few months).

Redundancy payments

If you are taking early retirement as a result of redundancy, any statutory redundancy payment (see 7.7.1) is exempt from tax although it may need to be taken into account in computing the tax payable on a termination payment (see below). Payment from a non-statutory redundancy scheme will be exempt if it meets certain Inland Revenue requirements.

Golden handshakes

If your contract of service is terminated, it may be possible for a compensation or *ex gratia* payment to be made either wholly or partially tax-free provided you are not entitled to it under the terms of your contract, and it is not regarded as benefit under a retirement benefit scheme.

The various types of termination payments that are wholly exempt from tax are as follows:

(1)   Any made where you have to give up your job because of illness or disability.

(2)   Any special contributions made by your employer into an approved retirement benefit scheme.

(3)   Any payment made where you have worked abroad for your employer (subject to certain, fairly lengthy, minimum periods of service abroad).

The £30,000 exemption.

Where a termination payment is not wholly exempt, the first £30,000 is normally free of tax. If you receive both a statutory redundancy payment and a termination payment, the statutory redundancy payment will be taken to use up part of the £30,000 exemption.

There is always the possibility that an *ex gratia* payment may be viewed as an unapproved retirement benefit and so taxable in full with no benefit from the £30,000 exemption. There are no clear cut rules on this, although the general practice of the Inland Revenue is that if the payment is made in connection with your retirement, then it will be taxable in full.

Restrictive covenants

When you leave your company, you might be asked to give an under-taking that would restrict your future activities (for example, you may decide to become a consultant in your specialised field but agree with your current employers not to offer your services to certain competitors). Any payment you receive in respect of that agreement is treated as salary in the year it is received. This applies even if the covenant is not strictly legally enforceable.

8.3   Self-employed people about to retire

The payment of tax by self-employed people is undergoing a major upheaval in that the whole basis of assessment is changing. This will have an impact on all self-employed people whether they continue to trade or whether they are planning to retire. The following sections provide only an outline and you should get professional advice in specific cases.

8.3.1   Your existing business

The profits on which you are taxed will usually be determined on the 'pre-ceding year' basis, ie your assessment for profits in 1994-95 is deter-mined by your profits for the accounting year which ends some time between 6 April 1993 and 5 April 1994.

When you started up in business, the preceding year basis was not rele-vant. You would normally have moved to a preceding year basis in the fourth year but, in the first three years, you had the option to have both years two and three assessed on an actual profits basis.

The preceding year basis is to be abolished altogether from April 1996, according to the following schedule:

(1)   The 1995-96 assessment will be on the preceding year basis.
(2)   The 1996-97 assessment will generally be based on the average profits for the two years' accounts which end in the 1996-97 tax year.
(3)   The 1997-98 assessment will be on the 'current year' basis.

The current year basis means that the assessment will be based on the accounting year which ends in the year of assessment.

Also, your accounts will normally be prepared to reflect your earnings rather than cash received. This will certainly be the case during the first three years, but thereafter you may switch to the cash basis provided that you undertake to issue bills for completed work at regular and frequent intervals. Where accounts are treated on the cash basis, this treatment applies to expenses as well as to income.

8.3.2 Closing down your business

If you are a sole trader then, when you leave the business, the business—for tax purposes—ends, regardless of whether you sell it, give it away or close it down.

Final year profits

The profit charged to tax in the year in which the business ends is not worked out on the preceding year basis but on the profit (or loss) made in the tax year in which the business ends (ie the year from 6 April to the date on which you leave the business).

This could involve you in making an overall tax gain and, to overcome this, the Inland Revenue has the power to change the basis of taxing the last two full years of business from the preceding year basis to an actual profits basis. They will do this if it increases the amount of tax you are liable to pay although they must reassess both of the last two tax years; they cannot change one year only.

Because of this power of changing the basis of taxation, it may be worth deferring your retirement until just after 5 April. However, you should note that the current method will end with effect from 5 April 1997.

If you have been assessed on the cash basis, any income received after cessation will normally be taxed in the year you receive it, although you may elect for this income to be treated as though it had been received in the year you ceased trading.

Terminal losses

If your business ends up making a loss in its final year, this loss may be carried back against your profits for the previous three tax years. The relief will be given against the latest year's profits first.

Other tax considerations

Any item of plant or machinery or other assets on which capital allowances have been granted may have to be re-assessed and made subject to a balancing charge or balancing allowance.

(1) If sold, there may be extra tax to pay in the form of a balancing charge if the proceeds exceed the cost less previous allowances (if the asset is taken over for private use or given away, it will be regarded as having been sold at market value).

(2)   If the item is scrapped, there may be a balancing allowance.

Your accounts will include your stock-in-hand at your year end (unless your accounts are on the cash basis). This stock will normally be valued at the lower of cost and realisable value but, when you close your business, any stock must be valued at open market value. This may be higher and this hidden profit will be liable to tax.

VAT

If you are registered for VAT, you are regarded as running your business for the purposes of VAT even though you are closing it down. Any disposals of assets, and even the sale or gift of the business itself as a going concern, may be subject to VAT.

Once you have sold or disposed of the business, you must de-register for VAT purposes within 30 days.

8.3.3 Capital gains tax and inheritance tax

If you dispose of your business, you could be liable for capital gains tax on the proceeds and this is covered in section 8.6.5.

If you give all or part of the business away, or sell any part of it at less than market value, there will be inheritance tax implications (see 9.8).

8.3.4 Partnerships

The profits of a partnership are computed in the same way as a sole trader's profit.

If you retire from a partnership, the strict position is that the old business stops and the new business starts. However, provided all partners (including those before and after your departure) agree, the partners may elect for the change of partners to be ignored. This is called a 'continuation election' and must be made within two years of your retirement. It will generally be favourable to do this from the tax position because if it is not done, the Inland Revenue reserves the right to change the basis of taxation of the new partnership to an actual basis for the first four years.

The need for a continuation election will cease with effect from 6 April 1997.

8.3.5 Personal pension schemes

Although you may have retired having sold your business, there may still be scope for continuing to pay contributions to a retirement annuity or personal pension plan by making use of the 'carry back' provisions (see 4.9.2). You may be able to carry back contributions for up to two years to a period when you were in business in order to obtain a tax refund.

8.4   Taxation in retirement

When you retire, you will be expected to make returns in the usual way, or at least notify the Inland Revenue of any untaxed income or gains you have received but not accounted for. The Revenue will give you a notice of coding—this will go to your principal pension provider so that they deduct the right amount of tax from your pension payments. This notice of coding will also take into account any State retirement pension you are receiving (which is always paid gross).

8.4.1   Personal allowances

Personal allowances may be claimed by anyone resident in the United Kingdom and also by any British subject. This means that you are able to claim personal allowances on any income you receive in the United Kingdom even if you have gone to live abroad (see chapter 12).

A claim to any personal allowance must be made within six years of the end of the relevant year of assessment (ie a claim for the 1988-89 tax year may be made up to 5 April 1995). A claim is made on the day it is received by your Inspector of Taxes, not the day it is posted.

The basic personal allowance for 1994-95 is £3,445. A higher allowance is given to those people who have reached the age of 65 and who are of limited means. Up to age 74, the allowance is £4,200 and rises to £4,370 for those people aged 75 or over. You get the higher allowance for the whole of the tax year in which you attain age 65 or age 75.

However, the higher allowances are reduced by £1 for every £2 by which your 'total income' exceeds £14,200 as follows:

(1)   If you are aged between 65 and 74, the £1 for £2 operates on 'total income' between £14,202 and £15,710.

(2)   For those aged 75 or over, the deduction operates on 'total incomes' between £14,202 and £16,050.

Your personal allowance can never fall below the basic single person's allowance.

This reduction in age-related personal allowances is quite an imposition and so, if you are a marginal case, it is important to rearrange your investments as far as possible to reduce your 'total income' (see below).

Personal allowances are just that, ie entirely personal to both husband and wife and any reduction in their age-related increases will be determined by their individual 'total incomes'.

8.4.2 Total income

Your 'total income' differs from your real income, firstly because not all your real income counts toward total income, and, secondly, because certain deductions can be made from your real income in calculating your total income.

(1) Income which does not count towards total income includes:
  (a) Exempt letting income under the 'rent-a-room' scheme (see 6.11.5).
  (b) Interest credited to a TESSA (see 6.3.2).
  (c) Dividends earned by a Personal Equity Plan (see 6.6).
  (d) Growth in National Savings certificates (see 6.3.1)
  (e) Withdrawals from single premium bonds up to the five per cent limit (see 6.5.3).
(2) The principal deduction that can be made from any other income in arriving at total income is any interest paid on certain types of qualifying loan (though not normally on your mortgage as relief on this will probably have been given through the MIRAS system). However, you may also deduct certain other outgoings such as:
  (a) Contributions paid to an occupational or personal pension plan.
  (b) One-half of any Class 4 national insurance contributions (see 2.2).

Up until 5 April 1994, it was also possible to deduct premiums for private medical insurance. However, the tax relief for these was restricted to 20 per cent with effect from 6 April 1994 and it was also eliminated as a deductible item in assessing total income, a 'double whammy' which became a 'triple whammy' with the imposition of the new insurance premium tax with effect from October 1994.

8.4.3 Married couple's allowance

The basic rule is that a married man, whose wife is living with him, may claim the married couple's allowance of £1,720. This is increased to £2,665 if either husband or wife is aged between 65 and 74 and to £2,705 if either is aged 75 or over. These higher allowances are for 1994-95 and are due to rise by a further £330 in 1995-96. The additional age-related allowances are also dependent on total income but it is only the *husband's* total income that is taken into account.

The Inland Revenue position on 'living with' can be quite strict. It would rule out circumstances where a separation is likely to be permanent and that has been known to rule out a claim for a married couple's allowance where one of the couple was terminally ill and unlikely to return home.

While the married couple's allowance would normally be claimed by the husband, a wife may claim half for herself. Also, a couple may jointly elect for the whole of it to be given to the wife (although the husband could subsequently claim his half back without his wife's consent). Neither of these elections will have any impact on the rule that any reduction in the age-related allowance is determined by the husband's total income.

An election must be made before 6 April if it is to apply for the following tax year (although if you have notified your *intention* by the 5 April deadline, you have until 5 May to submit the official forms). Once made, the election stays in force until revoked.

This election to transfer the married couple's allowance applies only to the basic allowance of £1,720; it does not apply to any age-related additional allowance. Also, it is a general right which has been in place for some time and is not a result of the introduction of independent taxation. However, independent taxation also provides a mechanism for transferring the married couple's allowance and this is covered in 8.5.2.

8.4.4   Widow's bereavement allowance

If you are living with your husband at the time of his death, you may claim, in addition to your basic personal allowance, a widow's bereavement allowance of £1,720. This will usually be given for the tax year in which your husband died and also for the following year.

The allowance does not qualify for any age-related increase and is strictly for widows, not widowers.

8.4.5   Reduced taxation levels

From April 1994, relief for the married couple's allowance (including the age-related increase) and the widow's bereavement allowance will be given at the 20 per cent rate of tax only, reducing to 15 per cent from April 1995. The same reduction in relief will apply to mortgage interest on the first £30,000 of a qualifying loan.

The general view is that this move to 15 per cent signals the intention of the government to phase out the married couple's allowance and tax relief on mortgage interest.

8.4.6   Taxation of pensions

All state retirement pensions are paid gross without deduction of tax. All occupational pensions are taxed under Schedule E and PAYE. Until 6 April 1995, personal pensions will be taxed under Schedule D; from

6 April 1995 they will fall into line with occupational pensions and be taxed under Schedule E and PAYE.

8.5 Independent taxation

8.5.1 Introduction

Independent taxation was introduced on 6 April 1990, since when all tax-payers, married and single, male and female, have been taxed separately on their own income. This means they are required to make their own tax returns, declare their own income and claim their own tax allowances and reliefs. For many married people, it also means that a well thought out rearrangement of assets can result in tax savings.

8.5.2 Married couple's allowance

Both husband and wife will have their individual personal allowances and a married couple will also have the married couple's allowance which will *usually* be claimed by the husband. Over and above the general right for half or all the basic amount of the married couple's allowance to be transferred to the wife (see 8.4.3), if the husband has insufficient income to use the married couple's allowance in full, he may ask for all or part of this allowance (including any age-related incre-ments) to be transferred to his wife.

In assessing your total income for this purpose, you calculate it in the same way as described in 8.4.2 except that you may not deduct the items described in paragraph (2) of that section.

Transferring the married couple's allowance under these rules also has different time limits from those described in 8.4.3; you may request a transfer at any time up to the sixth anniversary of the year of assessment.

8.5.3 Income

Under independent taxation, a husband's and wife's incomes are calcu-lated separately. In the case of a wife, this will include any State retire-ment pension to which she is entitled, even if on the basis of her husband's national insurance contributions. It is her income and she can set her allowances against it.

Income from jointly-held assets will normally be split equally between husband and wife for tax purposes (the 50:50 rule). However, if the hus-band's actual entitlement to a jointly-held asset and the income from it is different from that of his wife, they may make a joint declaration of their actual beneficial interest in the asset. If no declaration is made, the 50:50 rule will apply.

A couple may choose to make a declaration for some of their assets, but not for others. The declaration applies only to the assets listed in the declaration; further declarations can be made at any time in the future.

Income will be taxed as required, from the date of declaration, provided the declaration is received by your tax office within 60 days of the date of the declaration. Declarations cannot be backdated and, once made, cannot be withdrawn except in the cases of death, marital breakdown or a change in beneficial interest of the assets concerned.

8.5.4 Capital

Just as husband and wife have individual incomes, they can each own individual assets and each may qualify for the annual capital gains tax exemption (see 8.6).

8.5.5 Rearrangement of assets

With the introduction of independent taxation, it immediately became apparent that transferring assets between husband and wife could result in some significant tax savings. Over and above the advisability of dividing up assets for inheritance tax purposes (see 9.4.2), there are, for example, obvious attractions for a husband who is paying higher rate tax on his investment income in transferring some of the income-producing assets to his non-tax paying wife.

However, be warned. The view of the Inland Revenue is that a transfer of assets is a perfectly legitimate result of the introduction of independent taxation. Nevertheless, it must be an outright gift with no strings attached. Whilst there is nothing whatever to prevent your wife using the capital or income in a way that benefits you, any conditions attached to the gift which *require* her to use the capital or income for your benefit, will result in the benefit being regarded not as a gift but as a settlement and therefore taxable (see 11.9).

You need to be careful with any subsequent re-transfers. It could well be that you transferred assets while you were a higher rate taxpayer because it seemed to be the correct thing to do at the time. When you are retired, and perhaps a basic rate taxpayer, those arrangements might not look quite so attractive. But, if you attempt to 'unravel' the situation, the Revenue may claim that the first transfer was artificial and treat it as though it never happened, ie you may receive a bill for unpaid tax and probably with interest.

8.6 Capital gains tax

Capital gains tax is quite a complex tax, so this chapter will only give a basic outline. More detailed information can be found in the *Allied*

Dunbar Tax Handbook.

In general terms, capital gains tax is levied if a chargeable person disposes of a chargeable asset in a way which constitutes a chargeable disposal. You should note that it is not simply the *sale* of an asset, it is the *disposal* of an asset.

You are chargeable to capital gains tax if you dispose of assets whilst you are resident and ordinarily resident in the United Kingdom (see 12.3.1). For most practical purposes, this will include you unless you are planning to go and live abroad.

Gains on virtually all types of assets are potentially liable to capital gains tax. However, certain assets are not regarded as chargeable assets, the main exemptions being chattels sold for less than £6,000, motor cars, gilt-edged securities, shares held in a Personal Equity Plan and your principal private residence.

The most obvious form of chargeable disposal is the outright sale of the asset but, in certain cases, the gift of the assets may also be a chargeable disposal (though not gifts made between husband and wife). There are also other forms of disposal on specific types of asset that would constitute a chargeable disposal.

You cannot be liable for capital gains tax unless your total net gains (for 1994–95) exceed £5,800. Any gains in excess of that amount are added to your other income and taxed at income tax rates. If your other income is particularly low, you are not allowed to deduct any unused personal allowances from your capital gains in order to reduce your capital gains tax bill.

8.6.1 Calculation and indexation

The basic calculation for capital gains tax is that your gain equals the sale proceeds, minus the initial costs.

In calculating your liability to capital gains tax, you are allowed to take into account the costs of buying the asset and the costs of selling the asset. If, for example, you have bought and sold some shares, any commission and stamp duty would be taken into account in computing the overall gain (or loss).

You are also allowed to offset the effects of inflation (ie you are taxable on real gains not paper gains). Indexation works by inflating the initial cost of the asset by reference to the change in the retail prices index between the date of purchase and the date of sale.

This is the general rule and it applies to all assets acquired since 31 March 1982. All assets owned at 31 March 1982 were, in most instances, revalued as though they had been acquired at 31 March 1982. Assets owned for longer periods of time may be subject to more complex rules.

8.6.2 Losses

In any one tax year, you will be assessable to your total gains made in that year, adjusted by indexation where relevant. You are also able to reduce your overall gains if you have made any capital losses in the same tax year, ie if you have sold assets at a lower price than you paid for them. The overall impact is that you are only liable to capital gains tax on your overall net gains made during the tax year.

Up until 30 November 1993 (Budget day) it was possible to index the original cost in the same way as for gains so as to calculate the loss in real terms. For example, if you had bought an asset for £10,000 ten years ago and sold it for the same amount today, you would regard that as a loss because £10,000 was worth more ten years ago than it is worth today.

Unfortunately, the Treasury no longer agrees with this view of the real world and only nominal losses may be deducted from your real gains. This means that, in general terms, for all transactions after 30 November 1993, indexation relief may only be used to reduce or extinguish a capital gain; it may not be used to create or increase a capital loss. However, the rule was relaxed slightly as the 1994 Finance Bill made its way through the committee stages. Losses will be allowed but only for the 1993–94 and 1994–95 tax years and only up to an overall limit of £10,000.

8.6.3 'Bed and breakfasting'

Any unused capital gains exemption cannot be carried forward to a future tax year so, if you don't use up your exemption (£5,800 in the 1994–95 tax year) by 5 April, you will lose it altogether. If you have assets that are showing substantial gains, but which you wish to hold on to, you may be able to make use of your exemption by 'bed and breakfasting'.

By selling your assets on one day and buying them back the next day, you will realise the gain (tax-free if it is less than £5,800) and will usually be able to repurchase them at roughly the same price. You will therefore have acquired the assets at a higher price, so reducing your potential liability to capital gains tax on those assets in the future.

However, you will still have to pay the dealing costs (which could be around five per cent of your total holding) and there is no guarantee that you will be able to repurchase at the same price; you might have to pay more though you could, of course, conceivably pay less.

'Bed and breakfasting' is a fairly popular activity shortly before the end of the tax year but it should only be undertaken as part of a general review of your finances and not as an automatic attempt to claim a tax benefit.

8.6.4 Pooling

Pooling is a device used to calculate your capital gains tax liability if you buy more shares of the same class in the future. This may happen, for example, if you have shares in a company that offers you shares instead of dividends or if you decide to top up a unit trust holding with a further investment.

Pooling works by recalculating the cost of the original number of shares as at the date of purchase of the new shares (using indexation if the shares are showing a profit). This recalculated cost is then added to the cost of the new shares which then gives you a new base cost for your total shareholding.

Monthly savings plans

Pooling and indexation could be a nightmare if they were strictly applied to the regular purchase of units in a unit trust or investment trust monthly savings plan. Fortunately, the Revenue may accept a simplified calculation which assumes that you made a single purchase in the seventh month of the trust's accounting year (note, not the tax year) equal to your regular savings in that year plus any re-invested income. You will have to elect to use this alternative method and it may only be applied if, in the tax year when you sell units purchased via a monthly savings plan, your total gains exceed the annual exemption or your total *disposals* either exceed twice the annual exemption or result in capital losses.

8.6.5 Business considerations

If you are in business, and decide to dispose of your business or your business-related assets when you retire, then you will face a liability to capital gains tax. The two aspects of capital gains tax legislation that will affect you are retirement relief and roll-over relief.

8.6.6 Retirement relief

Retirement relief is available, if you are aged at least 55 or are having to retire early because of ill health. The effect is that the first £250,000 of gains plus half the gains between £250,000 and £1,000,000 are exempt from capital gains tax. The maximum exemption is therefore on £625,000 of gains.

The exemption may be reduced if you have been running the business for less than ten years or if the business holds investments.

If the business is run jointly by you and your wife, both of you qualify for the exemption, ie the relief is doubled.

Within that apparently simple rule, there is plenty of room for debate with the Inland Revenue on whether you are selling the business itself (in which case retirement relief will be available) or selling assets used in the business (in which case retirement relief will not be available). There have, for example, been cases with farmers where the farmer has disposed of part of his land; the Revenue has held that the land is not the business itself but an asset used in the business and retirement relief has been disallowed.

8.6.7   Roll-over relief

In general terms, roll-over relief is available where a person sells an asset which is used by him in a trade and re-invests the proceeds in replacement assets for the same trade. Any gain made is not taxed, but is deducted from the acquisition cost of the replacement asset (ie the future capital gain on the replacement asset now incorporates the gain made on the old asset). This aggregation of capital gains tax to some time in the future is called 'roll-over relief'.

If, as a sole trader or partner, you are selling your business, you may invest the proceeds in a new or existing business and defer any liability to capital gains tax on the original sale. A potentially quite attractive way in which this might be done would be to invest in property bought for the purpose of furnished holiday lettings (see 6.11.4). Under these circumstances, you would be regarded as having acquired an asset for the purposes of a trade and roll-over relief may be available.

Re-investment relief

The principle of relief for capital gains tax was further extended in the November 1993 Budget to apply to all individuals who would like to defer a capital gains tax bill. Provided the gain is re-invested into an unquoted trading company that fulfils certain conditions, and provided that you don't emigrate within three years of buying the shares, you can defer the original capital gains tax bill almost indefinitely. You have up to three years after the sale of the asset in which to make the re-investment; you may also claim for an investment that was made up to 12 months before the sale.

However, the fact that the re-investment has to be in an unquoted company makes it a more risky use of funds.

8.7   Tax saving areas

One of the most frequently quoted rules of investment is never to do something just because it saves tax. Your actions should be based primarily on the merits of the investment in question; tax considerations should be secondary. Nevertheless, within some of the principal areas of investment, the opportunity exists for tax benefits as well and you should take full advantage of these.

The principal guidelines on tax saving are:

(1) Make sure you claim all the tax allowances and reliefs you are eligible for and make sure that the calculations of your tax liability from the Inland Revenue are correct.

(2) Make sure you use the exemptions to which you are entitled.

(3) If you are a married couple, make full use of independent taxation in order to minimise your tax bills, but do bear in mind the following:

    (a) Any transfers must be seen as once-and-for-all gifts with no strings attached. It may even be beneficial to set up separate bank accounts.

    (b) If you are approaching retirement, do bear in mind that your tax position may change, so try not to do anything now that might work against you in the future.

    (c) If you are in your 60s, don't do anything that might jeopardise a claim for age-related higher personal allowances if your income is marginal.

    (d) If a jointly-owned income-producing asset is not owned in equal shares, consider applying for the interest to be paid (and therefore taxed) in the correct proportions.

(4) If you hold asset-backed investments, consider investing as much as you can in personal equity plans (see 6.6).

(5) If you hold other asset-backed investments, consider transferring some or part of your holding to single premium bonds (see 6.5.3) so as to get the benefit of tax efficient 'income'

(6) Do some projections of future income and tax bills when you come to take your pension. If you don't need all the income from your pension now, and if you have the option of deferring all or some of the benefits, you will not be paying tax on 'unwanted' income and your deferred benefits will continue to get the benefit of potential growth in a tax-free fund.

9 Inheritance tax

One of the most popular booklets Allied Dunbar ever produced was on inheritance tax (IHT); literally thousands were distributed. Its success stemmed from the interest in inheritance tax, a tax which still seems to rattle a good number of people. A colleague in the world of financial journalism once remarked that if he ever felt his postbag was starting to get a bit light, all he had to do was to publish an article on inheritance tax and the letters would start flowing in.

This chapter is based on the booklet and explains what inheritance tax is, what you can do to limit its impact and how you can best prepare for the often inevitable bill. It explains a tax which was described by Roy Jenkins as 'a voluntary levy paid by those who distrust their heirs more than they dislike the Inland Revenue' and covers the following topics:

(1) Introduction
(2) A tax on property
(3) The scope of inheritance tax
(4) Tax planning
(5) Life assurance in the mitigation of IHT
(6) Making gifts
(7) The main exemptions
(8) Inheritance tax and businesses
(9) Pension plans and IHT.

9.1 Introduction

Inheritance tax was introduced in the Finance Act of 1986. It replaced capital transfer tax, which had itself replaced estate duty in 1975. One of the dangers with inheritance tax lies in its very name. The majority of people probably don't regard themselves as wealthy and tend to ignore the things which are associated with 'inheritances' and 'estates'. However, even fairly modest estates can attract the attention of the Inland Revenue because inheritance tax starts to bite at a relatively low level. As a result, for example, of increasing house prices over the past decade, a significant number of older people have built up a potential liability to inheritance tax without fully realising it and their children may have to pay the bill.

One of the most potent ways of redistributing wealth is through capital taxation—and that is what inheritance tax is. Capital taxation is here to stay because although the various political parties may disagree on the extent to which capital should be taxed, they are all in agreement in the fact that it must be taxed. The overall objective of death duties is to tax the passing on of large estates by inheritance. As a consequence, inheritance tax tends to come into its own on death but, like all other taxes, there is no need for anybody to pay more than necessary. Within limits, everyone is entitled to organise his affairs in such a way that his liability to tax is reduced—there is no obligation on anybody to pay more than his fair share.

This is particularly true of inheritance tax because it can be reduced by prudent and sensible planning. Indeed, as far as this is concerned, the Inland Revenue relies on our failure to make sound plans. Without some straightforward sensible planning, it's quite possible that a good proportion of your lifetime efforts may go to the State rather than to your heirs. Of inheritance tax, above all other taxes, it can be truly said that the Revenue is the beneficiary of our inertia.

9.2 A tax on property

Inheritance tax is a tax on property. The tax liability does not arise merely as a result of the ownership of property (because that would be a wealth tax); the tax liability arises when the property passes from one person to another, ie when you give ownership of the property to somebody else when you are alive or when you die.

For the purposes of inheritance tax, property can either pass during your lifetime or on your death. During your lifetime, it may pass by gift; on death, it is considered to pass automatically because, being dead, you cannot retain ownership of that property. The ownership must, therefore, pass to someone else. In both cases, inheritance tax is potentially chargeable on this movement of property from you to someone else.

The taxation of lifetime gifts comes as a surprise to many people. They find it hard to believe that, having worked hard and saved money, they do not have total discretion of how they dispose of it while they are alive. The reality is that if you spend it on yourself in a never-to-be-repeated spree in a gambling casino, the Inland Revenue will not bat an eyelid. If you give it to your children and set them loose in a casino, the Revenue may demand its share too.

'Property' means all your personal possessions of all types. As far as the majority of people who have their permanent homes in the United Kingdom are concerned, it also includes any property situated outside the United Kingdom such as overseas property and overseas bank accounts.

Overseas assets

If you are domiciled in the United Kingdom, inheritance tax is charged on all your property no matter where in the world it is situated. That doesn't, of course, mean that you won't also have an inheritance tax liability (or similar liability) in the country where you have assets situated. In some cases, there exist 'double taxation treaties' between the United Kingdom and other countries so this problem is avoided. However, it pays to check and, if necessary, to make arrangements in the country where you have assets. That could mean having a foreign will as well as a UK will. All these matters are covered in more detail in chapter 12.

9.3 The scope of inheritance tax

'Estate' is simply the legal label that is given to the sum total of everything that you own when you die. It includes your house, your car, your possessions, your bank account, your cash, your stocks and shares, investments and so on. If you have a life assurance policy on your own life then, when you die, the proceeds also fall into your estate.

If you have any outstanding debts (eg a mortgage) then the total of these is deducted from your gross estate to give your net estate. The more common deductions are as follows:

(1)   Funeral expenses
(2)   Most debts
(3)   Legal and professional fees owing at the date of death
(4)   Liabilities for income tax and capital gains tax up to the time of death.

It is your net estate which is potentially liable to inheritance tax. Everything that you leave to your heirs over and above the first £150,000 is likely to be taxed. The following example shows how inheritance tax works and will be referred to throughout the chapter.

9.3.1 Example—Total net estate

A man's total list of assets is as follows:

House	£170,000
House contents	£32,000
Car	£8,000
Term assurance policy	£18,000
2 weeks' timeshare	£12,000
Savings and investments	£5,000
Mortgage protection policy	£20,000
Bank account/building society	£5,000
Total gross estate	£270,000
Less Mortgage	£20,000
Total net estate	£250,000

If he dies he will leave a gross estate of £270,000. The mortgage protection policy would be used to pay off his mortgage, leaving a net estate of £250,000. He therefore, 'owns' £250,000 net—but probably regards himself as 'worth' only £10,000 (his bank accounts and savings). After all he can't spend the house and contents, and the life policy is only there when he isn't.

9.3.2 How inheritance tax is calculated

Inheritance tax is currently charged in two bands. The first band (currently of £150,000) is charged at the 'nil rate' and no inheritance tax is payable. Everything in excess of that band is chargeable to inheritance tax at a rate of 40 per cent. What that means is that if your net estate totals £250,000 (ie £150,000 plus £100,000) there is a potential liability of 40 per cent of £100,000, ie £40,000. That normally has to be paid, in cash, to the Inland Revenue within six months of death, with an added complication being that (assuming for the moment that the man has no surviving wife) the beneficiaries will not be able to get access to any of the assets until the tax has been paid.

In the above example, on the assumption that money has been borrowed to pay the inheritance tax bill, the beneficiaries will eventually be able to get access to the savings (of £10,000) and the proceeds of the term policy (£18,000). The beneficiaries are £12,000 short and this will either have to come out of their own resources or through selling some of the assets they have been left.

For inheritance tax purposes, your assets are normally valued at their open market value at the date of death. By and large, the Inland Revenue is sympathetic to fluctuating values, particularly where quoted securities are sold for less than their 'date of death' value within 12 months of death. In such cases the people liable to pay the inheritance tax may be able to claim that the sale price should be substituted for the 'date of death' value. If, however, these same people have sold the investments and then reinvested the proceeds, this relief may be lost.

The position on land is rather more complex but, basically, if the person paying the tax on certain land sells it within four years of death for less than its value at the date of death, the sale proceeds can often be substituted in place of the higher value.

9.3.3 Reducing the burden

There are a number of ways in which you can reduce the burden of inheritance tax but they do need to be carefully planned for. However, before looking at some of these methods in more detail, there are two important points to make:

(1) The tax on your estate will be determined by the law at the time of your death—not the law now. The first important consideration, therefore, in all planning for inheritance tax is to keep your plans flexible. The rules will almost certainly change from time to time so you must avoid taking irrevocable actions that aren't strictly necessary.

(2) You should be realistic with your plans, and not put tax saving as a prime requirement. For example, one possible way to avoid inheritance tax would be to dispose of all your capital but that would hardly be a wise thing to do. The prime requirement is to have sufficient resources to live on right up to the date of your death. Inheritance tax planning means doing that—and at the same time trying to ensure that the balance of the proceeds of your life's work pass largely to your family and not to the Inland Revenue.

The next three sections (tax planning, life assurance and making gifts) look in rather more detail at three basic ways either to reduce the amount of inheritance tax that has to be paid on your estate or to provide for the unavoidable inheritance tax bill when you've done everything possible to reduce the amount. There is nothing particularly difficult about any of them and they might have quite a dramatic impact on the way your beneficiaries might remember you.

Once again, it is important to emphasise the need to keep all plans as simple and as flexible as possible. In this way, it may be easier to change them. Although the detailed rules on taxing estates on death do change from time to time, the broad basis of death duty planning has remained unchanged for a number of years now and that provides the framework for the three strategies.

9.4   Tax planning

This section covers three of the most straightforward ways of ensuring that the potential inheritance tax bill is kept as low as possible. It also covers a specific form of planning called the will trust plan and also looks at situations where planning might not always be to the beneficiaries' advantage.

(1)   Writing a will
(2)   Dividing up assets
(3)   Writing life assurance policies in trust.
(4)   The will trust plan
(5)   Refusing a legacy.

9.4.1   Writing a will

One of the most important exemptions in the inheritance tax rules is that nothing left to your spouse attracts any liability to inheritance tax at all. If the husband were to die first, and left his entire estate to his wife, then no inheritance tax would be payable. (When, subsequently, the wife dies and leaves the estate to the children, that is when the inheritance tax burden would arise.)

This point is often misunderstood. It is often believed that, because there is no inheritance tax to pay, this therefore means that the entire estate automatically passes to the wife or husband. In reality, it is the other way round. Provided you *guarantee* that everything is left to your wife, then there will be no inheritance tax to pay on your death. The only way that a husband can guarantee that everything passes to his wife, and *vice versa*, is to make a will.

The background

Wills are covered in much more detail in Chapter 10. What follows is a limited description to put wills into context as part of inheritance tax planning.

A will is essentially a very simple and straightforward statement of exactly what you wish to happen to your property when you die. If you die without leaving a will (known as dying 'intestate') it may be that certain of your intended beneficiaries will be unable to make a legal claim for any part of your estate, no matter how deserving they may be and no matter what promises you may have made them.

The intestacy rules

Your principal beneficiaries (ie usually your wife and other immediate family) may be protected to some extent because the law provides for your estate to be broken up amongst your family according to the 'intestacy rules'. These rules do not cater for individual needs and requirements and they are not concerned with how you may feel about your family, or how your wife may feel about her in-laws.

The intestacy rules have certain minimum levels so that a small estate (ie up to £125,000 plus personal belongings) would pass directly to the spouse. In all other cases, the first to die will only inherit everything in certain circumstances. If, for example, a man has not made a will, his wife is guaranteed to inherit everything only if *all* the following conditions are fulfilled:

(1)   The couple have no children
(2)   The husband's parents are both dead
(3)   He has no surviving brothers or sisters or nephews or nieces.

The rules in Scotland are different—and they are likely to work rather more in favour of your close family if you don't make a will. Nevertheless, the basic principle is the same—it is always better if you leave clear, legally enforceable instructions about what you want to happen, ie a will.

Tax planning through wills

As well as ensuring that your property is distributed in the way that you wish, writing a will can often be very effective in inheritance tax planning. Everything you leave to your spouse is free of inheritance tax but you also have the 'nil-rate' band (currently £150,000) which allows property up to that value to be distributed to anybody else without attracting any liability to inheritance tax.

Suppose in the example in 9.3.1 that the man is in fact married. By leaving everything to his wife, her potential estate is increased (which could mean a higher inheritance tax bill when she dies) and a valuable opportunity to reduce her potential estate has been lost. However, the man and his wife might, for example, decide that she will not have any real use for the timeshare if he dies first. By making this a specific gift to their children in his will, there is an immediate potential inheritance tax saving of £4,800 if he is the first to die. The reason is that the estate passing on to the wife is reduced by £12,000 so that, on current figures, the eventual inheritance tax saving when she leaves her estate to her children will be £4,800 (ie, £12,000 × 40 per cent) lower than would otherwise have been the case.

Drawing up a will is a vital part of everybody's financial planning. It ensures that your property is distributed in the way you would wish and can incorporate real inheritance tax efficiency. Not writing a will could result in your property being divided up in a way which you would not wish and at the same time create a tax liability for your beneficiaries which they certainly won't want.

9.4.2 Dividing up assets

Although throughout this book we have concentrated on 'he' and 'him' for simplicity, the statistics confirm quite starkly that there are considerably more widows than widowers. Consequently, most inheritance planning tends to assume that the husband will be the first to die. However, it is quite incorrect to do this. The wife may die first, but be unable to take advantage of the inheritance tax 'nil-rate' rules if she doesn't own any property. She would be unable to leave anything to her children, who would face a potentially larger inheritance tax bill when the husband died.

It can therefore make inheritance tax planning sense for husband and wife to divide their assets between them so as to 'equalise', at least in part, their estates. They are both then able to write their wills in a similar way and to make separate bequests with a view to the potential inheritance tax savings. This, of course, is in addition to any tax savings they might make under independent taxation (see 8.5).

9.4.3 Writing life assurance policies in trust

Another way of reducing the inheritance tax burden is through a declaration of trust—and this is particularly relevant to life assurance policies. Many policies are arranged on an 'own life, own benefit' basis which means that the proceeds will become part of the policyholder's estate when he dies. His beneficiaries may need this cash to pay the inheritance tax liability but the position is complicated by the fact that the cash itself adds to the inheritance tax problem. If the policyholder's estate, including the policy proceeds, is over £150,000, 40 per cent of the proceeds of the policy will end up with the Inland Revenue.

It is possible, however, to have the policy written under a declaration of trust so as to nominate the beneficiaries in advance. If you were to make a stipulation that the proceeds of your life policy were to be paid to beneficiaries (ie it now becomes their property and not yours), the proceeds fall outside your estate and therefore don't attract inheritance tax.

Suppose in the example in 9.3.1, the man and his wife decide that she will have enough to live on after his death without depending on the proceeds of the term assurance policy. He therefore decides to complete a simple declaration of trust—and he makes the children the beneficiaries. When he dies, the proceeds of the policy (£18,000) will not become her property, meaning that the eventual inheritance tax liability on her death is reduced by £7,200.

Writing policies in trust is a very common way of avoiding inheritance tax on the proceeds and many life assurance companies will have standard forms drawn up for you to use, often at no charge. Although it is normal to place the policy in trust when it is first taken out, there is nothing to prevent you placing an existing policy in trust (but see 9.7.3).

In the original example in 9.3.1, the beneficiaries were short of £12,000 on an inheritance tax bill of £40,000. By the simple expedient of making a specific bequest in a will (of the timeshare) and asking for an existing life assurance policy to be placed in trust (something that most life companies will arrange at no charge), that £12,000 liability has been completely removed.

Many of these aspects of planning are merely devices to rearrange your affairs in the most tax efficient way. In the main, they merely require letters and forms to be filled in. You then make a clear expression of what you wish to happen—and that's what will happen.

9.4.4   The will trust plan

Single premium bonds (see 6.5.3) also offer the opportunity for a specific type of inheritance tax planning. Most married couples leave their total assets to each other on their death. There is no inheritance tax liability at this time but the nil rate band exemption is lost. However, many people may be unwilling to make use of the exemption, either in whole or in part, because of the loss of the assets, and the income from them, to the survivor.

A particular arrangement of single premium bonds can overcome this problem in a particularly simple way, as follows:

(1)   You and your wife each take out a single premium bond of up to the 'nil rate' band limit (currently £150,000). You will both be the joint lives assured on each bond but, individually, you will be the sole owners of your respective bonds.

(2)   You each amend your wills so that the first to die leaves their bond to their heirs under the terms of a simple will trust (see 11.1.3).

(3)   On the first death, the relevant bond will pass into the will trust. As it is within the nil rate band, no inheritance tax will be payable.

(4)   If the survivor needs to supplement his or her income, they make requests to the trustees (of whom they will be one) for loans from the trust. Such loans, if granted, will be a debt against their estate so reducing the eventual inheritance tax liability when they die.

Under this arrangement, your bonds remain your property to do with exactly as you wish while you are alive; the relevant bonds only become subject to the terms of the trust on the first death.

Single premium bonds are particularly suitable for this kind of arrangement because the fact that they do not distribute income in the form of dividends makes them extremely simple to administer. Also, because they are essentially life assurance products, the trust may be protected. It will often be the case that, on the death of the survivor, the value of the residual bonds (less, of course, any units that have been withdrawn to make loans) will never be less than the original investment, regardless of prevailing investment conditions.

9.4.5 Refusing a legacy

Just as there are good tax reasons for writing a will, it always pre-supposes, to some extent, that you fully understand the financial position of your beneficiaries. However, it would not be unusual for them to prefer that you had left your property in a rather different way or that you had even drafted your will in a different way. There are two ways in which the position can be remedied by beneficiaries. They can either disclaim the legacy or arrange for a 'deed of variation' to be drawn up. Both are equally effective in tax planning after the event, ie they will not have an adverse effect on the inheritance tax position and are often undertaken to improve it.

Disclaimer

If you have become entitled to property under the terms of a will, you may disclaim the entitlement particularly if somebody else would benefit as a result of your disclaimer (eg your children). You may also disclaim an entitlement under the intestacy provisions. A disclaimer means that you give up your entitlement, it does not mean that you can re-direct your entitlement to a specific person.

Such a disclaimer will normally be effective for tax purposes provided:

(1)   you receive no payment for giving up your entitlement; and
(2)   you have not already received your legacy either expressly (ie you have started to enjoy the benefit) or by implication (which could occur if you delayed in making your disclaimer).

You should always seek legal advice before making a disclaimer.

Deed of variation

These (sometimes called 'deeds of family arrangement') differ from disclaimers in that, through a deed of variation, you can re-direct the property to a specific person.

The deed must be executed within two years of the death and an election must be filed within six months. In effect, the parties to the deed re-write the dead person's will, and the property is distributed as though the requirements of the deed were the will.

Certain conditions need to be satisfied and you should consult a solicitor:

(1)   The deed must be in writing and must specifically refer to the provisions of the will which are to be varied.

(2)   It must be signed by everybody who would have benefited under the original will.

(3)   Only one deed can ever be effective about a specific piece of property as far as inheritance tax is concerned, so it is important to get the wording right. There could be more than one deed of variation if each one refers to a different item of property in the will.

(4)   There must be no payment to a beneficiary as an inducement to enter into a deed of variation.

A deed of variation does not have any untoward implications for the beneficiaries as far as inheritance tax and capital gains tax are concerned. However, the income tax position is not so favourable; all the original beneficiaries will be liable for tax on any income that arises from assets in the will up to the time the deed is executed. Also, anybody giving up an entitlement in this way will be regarded as a settlor for income tax purposes (see 11.9).

The position in Scotland

Scottish law provides that a person must leave a set part of his estate to his children; their entitlement is called *legitim* (see 10.7.2). If the will does not take account of this, the children can have it set aside. In practice, children often decide to renounce their right to *legitim* particularly where this would result in a larger bequest to the widow. This renunciation does not form a chargeable transfer and the property is treated as passing to the widow under the terms of the will.

There can be potential problems if the children are minors, as children under the age of 18 do not have the legal capacity to renounce their entitlement. Any action taken on their behalf by the executors could have inheritance tax implications when the children reach the age of 18.

9.5   Life assurance in the mitigation of IHT

The problem for the executors

Although a certain amount of reorganising of our estates can prevent unnecessary inheritance tax liabilities falling on our children there is a limit to what can be done in this way. The most important requirement for many of us is to ensure that we have enough to live on until the date of our death -and this could mean retaining assets because they produce an income for us. Therefore, we still own some property and there could well be an inheritance tax liability on the death of the surviving spouse that is quite unavoidable.

For the beneficiaries, the first problem they may face is that inheritance tax is payable at the time the executors apply for a grant of probate (see 10.8.1). However, although the estate has a certain amount of cash and liquid assets, the executors cannot get their hands on them until they have obtained the grant of probate. This is a classic case of 'Catch 22'; no grant until the tax has been paid, no money to pay the tax until the grant has been obtained.

The problem might not be quite as bad as it seems because inheritance tax can be paid in instalments but only on certain assets, principally land and buildings, controlling shares in companies and certain other business assets. Rather than having to raise cash through a forced sale, it is possible to pay the inheritance tax by annual instalments over a period of ten years. Under certain circumstances, instalments are free of interest, provided they are paid on time. Similar rules also apply to agricultural property.

The need for cash

However, it is inevitable that some tax will still have to be paid before all the assets will be released. The beneficiaries may also have the problem that the total value of the liquid assets could well be lower than the inheritance tax bill. One way or another, if they want to settle the tax bill in total and avoid having to pay interest, they are going to be short of funds. They have three obvious choices:

(1)   They may have cash of their own available and be prepared to pay that to the Revenue.
(2)   They may be prepared to borrow the money.
(3)   They may not have the cash available and may have to sell some of the assets to raise the proceeds. However, it has to be borne in mind that the bill may have to be settled quite quickly and realising assets may take time.

There is, however, a fourth option and that is through a life assurance policy.

The use of life assurance

Life assurance is designed to provide a predictable sum of money at a totally unpredictable time in the future. It is relatively straightforward to look at today's position and estimate the potential liability to inheritance tax and then to take out a life assurance policy to cover it. The principal requirement is for a flexible policy. The tax rules can be guaranteed to change from time to time (as will your personal circumstances) and you will need a policy that is flexible enough to adapt to such changes.

For most married couples, the solution is to take out a 'joint life second death' policy. The policy is written in trust which means that when the second person dies, the proceeds are payable to the beneficiaries and so fall outside the estate. In this way, preparing for a potential inheritance tax problem can be arranged by your life assurance company. Writing a policy in trust can usually be arranged by them at no extra charge to yourself at all.

However, you may take the view that this life assurance policy cannot be afforded. You will have to pay the regular contributions out of income and you may well regard this as a high price to pay in order to protect your children. Your children may see things differently and, for them, a more attractive alternative might be for you to start using some of your capital (ie their potential inheritance) in a way which will protect the bulk of it.

Suppose in example 9.3.1, that the couple have not done any planning and have written their wills so that the entire estate passes to the survivor and is retained by the survivor until the second death. That means that there is a potential tax liability on a total net estate of £250,000, ie a potential tax bill of £40,000. That is 16 per cent of the capital and is also the required 'sum assured' currently required for the joint life second death policy.

If the man is in his late 50s and his wife is four or five years younger, the annual premium for such a policy is about £400, ie about one per cent of the potential tax bill. On that basis they would have to live for about 100 years to make paying the premiums a less attractive proposition than paying the inheritance tax.

Using capital to preserve capital is one of the most important and most popular ways for families to prepare for a potential inheritance tax liability.

Of course, what you are doing is paying contributions to a life assurance policy where your children will eventually benefit. Consequently, the regular contributions are regarded as a gift. Gifts are the third way in which the burden of inheritance tax can be reduced and these are covered in the next section.

9.6   Making gifts

The main impact of inheritance tax is felt by our beneficiaries when we die, measured as a percentage of our wealth that we leave behind us. One possible way of avoiding inheritance tax altogether, therefore, is to reduce our wealth by giving our property away while we are alive. Within reason, the Inland Revenue is prepared to go along with this, although you can expect the Revenue to take a keen interest in any large gifts that you make while you're alive.

Of course, there has to be a realistic approach to all of this. To check every single gift would be quite impractical (and unreasonable) and there are a range of exemptions that mean that many gifts will fall outside the net. However, even the smaller gifts do have to be watched and planned for, and the next sections cover some of the ways in which you can reduce your inheritance tax burden through your own generosity.

First, though, there are two key aspects to avoiding inheritance tax through gifts:

(1) Gifts with reservation of benefit.
(2) Potentially exempt transfers.

9.6.1 Gifts with reservation of benefit.

Any gift must be a real gift if it is to avoid inheritance tax; it must be 'absolutely irrevocable'. You cannot put strings on it so that you can ask for it back. For example, if you feel so generous that you are prepared to give away the family home to your children, you might think it sensible to make an arrangement under which your children will let you continue to live there rent free.

Unfortunately, for inheritance tax purposes, this is the equivalent of 'having your cake and eating it'. The technical term labels it as a 'gift with reservation'. You would have retained the right to live in the house (ie you have reserved a benefit) which means that you have not really given the house away at all. As far as the Revenue are concerned, it means that the property still belongs to you for inheritance tax purposes and it will be included in your estate when you die.

The Revenue can be expected to take an interest in any substantial gifts that you make where there is any possibility of your retaining some kind of benefit. If you give shares to your beneficiaries—but retain the right to receive the income from them—that is a 'gift with reservation' and the shares will be included in your estate for inheritance tax purposes.

In order to avoid any problems with gifts, it would be advisable if you were clearly seen to be receiving no benefit whatsoever as a result of your generosity; it must be a gift, pure and simple, with no strings attached. Nevertheless, there are some complex ways in which you can continue to receive some kind of benefit but these are for specific situations and beyond the scope of this book.

9.6.2 Potentially exempt transfers

If you suddenly receive grim news about your future life expectancy, you could well have left it too late to do anything much about inheritance tax planning. Although you might have a sudden fit of generosity and decide to reduce your estate in an attempt to reduce the inheritance tax burden, you may not succeed. Timing is all important.

There is one all embracing rule: if death occurs within seven years of making a gift, then all or a proportion of the inheritance tax will be payable as though the gift had been included in the estate on death.

'Tapering relief'

If death occurs within three years of making a gift then inheritance tax will not have been avoided at all; the tax will be charged at the full rate as though the value of the gift had been included in the estate on death. Provided the donor survives for seven years, the inheritance tax falls away completely. If he dies at any time between the third and seventh years after the gift, then a proportion of the inheritance tax is payable. This gradual reduction of the future tax bill is called 'tapering relief'.

An important point here is that, although the rate of inheritance tax applied to the gift will be that applying at the date of death, the value of the gift is the value at the date it was given. Any increase in value belongs to the new owner and is not included in any tax calculations if the donor is unfortunate enough to die within seven years. This can make the gifting of certain types of investment an effective 'hedge' against inheritance tax.

Because of this seven year rule, a gift which does not benefit from one of the exemptions (see below) carries the potential for an inheritance tax liability within seven years of the gift being made. Consequently, from the Revenue's point of view, the gift is never totally exempt from inheritance tax until seven years have lapsed. The technical term for such a gift, therefore, is a 'potentially exempt transfer' (PET for short) and there are essentially three principal type of gifts covered by this term:

(1)   Direct gifts to an individual.
(2)   Gifts to what are called 'interest in possession' trusts (which are defined as trusts under which an individual has the right either to the use and enjoyment of the trust assets or any income from them (see 11.3.1)).
(3)   Gifts to what are called 'accumulation and maintenance' trusts (certain kinds of trust which are set up for the benefit of your children or grandchildren, or for the future welfare of a disabled person (see 11.3.5)).

There are other forms of gift which are termed 'chargeable transfers' and these gifts may incur a liability to inheritance tax at the time they are made. Inheritance tax is charged at the time at half the rate payable on death; if death occurs within seven years of the transfer, then further tax may be payable subject to 'tapering relief'.

With considerable aplomb, the Revenue defines a chargeable transfer as anything which is not a non-chargeable transfer (ie not a PET or a transfer covered by one of the exemptions).

9.7 The main exemptions

There is a range of exemptions which will mean that, for most day-to-day gifts, there will not necessarily be a tax liability. These are as follows:

(1) Annual exemption
(2) Small gifts exemption
(3) Normal expenditure exemption
(4) Gifts on marriage
(5) Other exemptions.

9.7.1 Annual exemption

You may give away up to £3,000 in any one tax year. That applies equally to husband and wife who could between them give away up to £6,000 to their children without having to face any tax liability at all.

It is also possible to use up any unused amounts from the previous tax year, provided:

(1) it is given away in the current tax year, and
(2) you use up the full exemption for the *current* year first.

Suppose, for example, you have £1,500 left over from the previous tax year. Provided you give away at least £3,000 (ie the current year's exemption), you can make further gifts out of the held-over allowance ie up to a maximum of an additional £1,500. If you do not give away as much as £3,000, the whole of the held-over amount of £1,500 will be lost as it is not possible to hold it over into a subsequent tax year. If you give away less than £4,500, the balance of the held-over amount would be lost.

9.7.2 Small gifts exemption

You can give away as many small gifts as you like to as many people as you like, provided the total value of the gifts to any one individual does not exceed £250. If you have a thousand friends, you could give away £250,000 a year without the Inland Revenue asking you any questions about inheritance tax (though you might be asked where you got the money from in the first place).

9.7.3   Normal expenditure exemption

Many of us give money away on a regular basis. It comes out of our 'after-tax income' and has no overall impact on our normal standard of living. We regard this as 'normal expenditure'—and so does the Revenue—and there is no liability to inheritance tax.

A good example of this would be the life assurance premiums paid on a joint life second death policy—the policy written in trust to provide funds to meet your beneficiaries' inheritance tax liability (see 9.5). Because the policy is in trust, the regular contributions are technically a gift. However, because of their regularity and their relatively small size, they would generally qualify as 'normal expenditure'.

If they are more substantial and mean you have to draw on capital to provide the contributions then they will probably fall within the £3,000 limit. Either way, there is rarely going to be any liability to inheritance tax on the payments themselves.

Existing life assurance placed in trust

However, if you place an existing policy in trust, then you could be making a more substantial transfer. The value of the gift will be the greater of the gross premiums paid to date or the market value of the policy (which will usually mean the surrender value of the policy). If this value exceeds the exemptions then it will be treated as a PET.

9.7.4   Gifts on marriage

If one of your children marries, both husband and wife may each give the child up to £5,000 without incurring any liability to inheritance tax. If one of your grandchildren or great-grandchildren marries you may give them £2,500. If the person getting married is any other kind of relative, or even just a friend, you may give them up to £1,000 without any complications of inheritance tax to think about. However, these gifts are more correctly called 'gifts in consideration of marriage'; they should therefore be made *before* the marriage and should be conditional on the marriage taking place.

For the vast majority of us, therefore, all these exemptions provide a way of giving quite substantial gifts without falling foul of the inheritance tax rules.

It might be the case that the most substantial gift any of us wishes to make is to our children in the event of their marriage. The rules allow the parents of the bride or groom to make gifts of up to £22,000 without any need at all to be concerned about inheritance tax. All it needs is a little bit of careful planning and full use of all the exemptions that are available:

(1) Last year's annual exemption—£3,000 each
(2) This year's exemption—£3,000 each
(3) Marriage allowance—£5,000 each.

However, despite the fact that these exemptions are there to be used, it is prudent to keep records of exactly how you have calculated the gift in order to avoid any potential problems for you or your beneficiaries.

9.7.5 Other exemptions

In order not to discourage the spirit of giving, successive Governments have ruled that gifts such as gifts to charities, gifts for national purposes (eg, the National Trust, universities and libraries) and gifts of property for the national benefit are, to all intents and purposes, exempt from inheritance tax.

There is also a certain grim irony in the fact that gifts to the main political parties are also exempt.

9.8 Inheritance tax and businesses

Successive Governments have recognised that building up a business can be less than rewarding if its value is to be taxed at high rates when you die. Because of this, what is termed 'relevant business property' qualifies for business property relief, provided that you have owned it for at least two years.

The rules are complex but in broad terms 'relevant business property' includes shares in the business and land, buildings, plant and machinery used for business purposes. The effect of the relief it to reduce the value of that particular property for inheritance tax purposes by 100 per cent or 50 per cent depending on the type of property being transferred.

For example, if you are a sole proprietor and the business is transferred during your lifetime then it may be regarded as a potentially exempt transfer and business property relief (at 100 per cent) will be available if you die within seven years. However, this relief may be lost if the person to whom you give the property disposes of it before your death unless the proceeds are reinvested in qualifying business property within three years of the sale.

Agricultural property is treated in a similar way. Provided you have occupied the property for agricultural purposes for at least two years (or owned it for seven years with others farming it) at the time of transferring it, then agricultural property relief may be available. If the person making the gift has the right to vacant possession, the relief is 100 per cent. If the person making the gift does not have the right to vacant possession (eg, because it is let) then the relief is 50 per cent.

For gifts made within seven years of death, there are rules similar to those for business property.

There are slightly different rules for woodlands. If you have owned woodlands for at least five years or acquired them by gift or inheritance, there will not necessarily be an inheritance tax liability on your death. If, however, the recipient sells or gives away the timber, tax is charged on the proceeds or value of the gift. The relief applies only to the standing timber and not the land on which it grows (but the land may qualify for business property relief).

9.9   Pension plans and IHT

For inheritance tax purposes, the largest single element in a pension plan will be the death benefit. Although it is not possible to assign the *pension* benefits as such, it is possible to assign the *death* benefits under a retirement annuity or personal pension plan. There will be no adverse inheritance tax implications provided that the death benefit is paid out to the nominated beneficiaries within two years of death.

The same is true of the death benefits paid out by the trustees from an occupational scheme.

10 Making a will

It is estimated that fewer than three people in ten make a will. Each year a number of cases will come before the Courts to unravel the problems caused by someone having died 'intestate'. Even people who have taken the sensible step of making a will may leave behind unforeseen problems; the will may not be valid or may not do what they had intended.

In this chapter, wills are covered under the following headings:

(1)   The simplicity of a will
(2)   When there is no will
(3)   Getting advice
(4)   Drawing up a will
(5)   The formalities
(6)   Reviewing your will
(7)   The law in Scotland
(8)   Administering the estate
(9)   The enduring power of attorney
(10) Living wills.

One reason for writing a will is that it can play an important part in tax planning, particularly in relation to inheritance tax (see 9.4.1).

10.1   The simplicity of a will

In its most basic form, a will is nothing more than an expression of what you want to happen to your property when you die. Wills have no effect whatsoever during a person's lifetime. This means that a will can be revoked or changed at any time up to the time of death. It also means that as the will only takes effect on death, you are not making any form of gift during your lifetime.

Making a will does not restrict what you can do with your property during your lifetime, nor does it mean that you will alter your tax position before the date of your death. In this way, a will is very different from a declaration of trust (see 11.1.1) which *is* effective during your lifetime. This can give rise to some confusion as it is also possible to create a trust in your will. However, any trust that is set up by a will only takes effect on death and, until then, can be revoked or altered, just like any other part of the will.

A will ensures that property passes to someone (the executor) who will look after it and distribute it to the people entitled to benefit under the will (the beneficiaries) in accordance with the instructions of the person who drew up the will (the testator). The role of the executor is generally a temporary one, limited to distributing the assets of the testator and paying the testator's debts and any tax bills.

Wills can be revoked by deliberately tearing them up and in some cases by marriage or divorce (see 10.6.1). It is also possible to add to or delete part of a will by means of a codicil (see 10.6.8). The important thing to remember is that a will is not necessarily a 'once and for all' decision and should be reviewed on a regular basis.

10.2   When there is no will

Anyone dying intestate will have his affairs administered according to a set of rules laid down by law. These intestacy rules are quite arbitrary and make assumptions about what the majority of people would want to happen to their property on their death. The rules take no account whatsoever of personal choice.

The rules depend on how much your estate is worth and the kind of relatives you leave behind; the rules differ for larger estates and depend on whether you leave behind a spouse or children. There are separate rules for Northern Ireland and also for Scotland.

Their principal impact can be looked at under five headings:

(1)   Who looks after the estate?
(2)   Who gets what?
(3)   Who looks after the children?
(4)   Personal bequests
(5)   The tax position.

10.2.1   Who looks after the estate?

If someone dies intestate, the law sets out a list of people who can apply to the Courts to do the job of administrator (in Scotland the equivalent is called an 'executor-dative').

In order of priority, the list of potential administrators is as follows:

(1) The surviving spouse.
(2) Any child (or grandchild if the parent has died).
(3) The father or mother (just the mother if the deceased was an illegitimate child).
(4) Any brother or sister (or nephew or niece if the parent has died).

The list then goes on to include more distant relatives. Eventually it includes any creditors of the deceased and even the Treasury Solicitor, who can apply if there are no surviving relatives at all. In Scotland the list of potential executors-dative is different (see 10.7.1).

Of course, there will often be a surviving spouse who will be entitled to apply to become the administrator, but this may not always be desirable. For example, the survivor may be unable to take on the burden of dealing with financial matters so soon after the death. Equally, the surviving spouse might even have been separated from the deceased at the date of death.

Where there is no surviving spouse, disputes may arise about who is to be the administrator. The right to be administrator can be very important, especially if there are shares with voting rights in a family company which forms part of the estate or there is a valuable asset which some beneficiaries wish to sell and others do not. If there is more than one child, all the children can apply but the first to do so can be appointed as administrator ahead of the others. While there are rules to prevent the administrator taking advantage of the position and to prevent unsuitable people being appointed, disputes usually mean escalating legal costs.

On a practical note, until the uncertainty over who is to take charge is resolved, no one can do anything in relation to the deceased's assets. This can cause considerable difficulties if money is needed urgently or an asset is to be sold.

10.2.2 Who gets what?

Perhaps the largest misconception that people have on this subject is about who gets what if there is no will. Many married couples assume that the surviving spouse will receive all the family property but this is often not so. The following tables set out the position.

INTESTACY TABLE—ENGLAND AND WALES

MARRIED COUPLE—WITH CHILDREN

Spouse receives:	°	All the personal belongings (car, furniture, jewellery, etc.)
	°	£125,000 absolutely*.
	°	A 'life interest' (ie the income only) in half the balance, for the rest of her life.
Children receive: (shared equally):	°	Half the balance when they attain the age of 18 or marry, if earlier.
	°	The remainder of the estate when spouse dies

MARRIED COUPLE—NO CHILDREN

Where there is a living parent, brother, sister, nephew or niece:

Spouse receives:	°	All the personal belongings.
	°	£200,000 absolutely.
	°	Half the balance absolutely.
Relatives receive:	°	Half the balance to parents but, if no living parent, to brothers and sisters (with nephews and nieces stepping into their parent's shoes if the parent is dead).

Where there is no living parent, brother, sister, nephew or niece:

Spouse receives:	°	Everything absolutely.

SINGLE PERSON

Estate passes to:	°	Children; but if none:
	°	Parents; but if none:
	°	Brothers, sisters (nephews and nieces step into parent's shoes); but if none:
	°	Grandparents; but if none:
	°	Uncles and aunts (cousins step into their parent's shoes); but if none:
	°	The Crown.

*Absolutely = without condition or limitation.

INTESTACY TABLE—NORTHERN IRELAND

MARRIED COUPLE—WITH CHILDREN

Spouse receives:	°	All the personal belongings (car, furniture, jewellery, etc.).
	°	£125,000 absolutely.
	°	Half the balance, where there is one child, or one-third of the balance, where there is more than one child.
Children receive: (shared equally)	°	Half or two-thirds of the balance depending on whether one or more child survives.

MARRIED COUPLE—NO CHILDREN

Where there is a living parent, brother, sister, nephew or niece

Spouse receives:	°	All the personal belongings.
	°	£200,000 absolutely.
	°	Half the balance absolutely.
Relatives receive:	°	Half the balance to parents, but if no living parent to brothers and sisters (with nephews and nieces stepping into their parent's shoes if the parent is dead).

Where there is no living parent, brother, sister, nephew or niece

Spouse receives:	°	Everything absolutely.

SINGLE PERSON

Estate passes to:	°	Children; but if none:
	°	Parents; but if none:
	°	Brothers, sisters (nephews and nieces step into parent's shoes); but if none:
	°	Next of kin; but if none:
	°	The Crown

There are separate rules for England and Wales and for Northern Ireland; the position in Scotland is dealt with later (see 10.7). Which rules apply depends upon the person's domicile (see 12.3.2) at the date of death.

The intestacy rules represent different attempts at an 'average' which is suitable for the majority of cases. The rules are updated periodically, the last changes having been made in England and Wales in 1993 (the time before that was 1987). The changes are normally to the monetary limits rather than the basic principles. In England and Wales, these principles have remained largely unchanged since 1925 (although a fundamental review did take place in Scotland as recently as 1964). The rules do not take account, for example, of any tax advantages that can be achieved by writing a will in a particular way, nor indeed do they reflect the social changes that have occurred in recent years. For example, it is much more common nowadays to leave property to a widow outright than it was in 1925.

10.2.3   Example—Intestacy rules

A has died, leaving behind his widow, B and two teenage children, a daughter aged 13 and a son aged 16. At the date of his death, A owned the following assets:

Family home (half share)	£80,000
Share portfolio	60,000
Life assurance (not in trust)	75,000
Building society account	15,000
Car	10,000
Investment property	25,000
Bank accounts	4,000
Total	£269,000

There was a mortgage of £75,000 on the family home but this will be repaid by another life assurance policy assigned to the mortgage company.

The house was held as a 'joint tenancy' (see note below) so that it now passes automatically to B and can be left out of the calculations. Removing the half share of the family home (£80,000) leaves a figure of £189,000. Out of this the car (£10,000) and any other personal effects will pass to B along with £125,000. This leaves a balance of £54,000 which is divided into two halves. One half will be held in trust and invested so that B will receive the income for her life with the capital passing to the two children when she dies. The remaining £27,000 will be divided between the children and held in trust so that they will each receive £13,500 (plus any investment growth) when they reach eighteen.

All this may appear reasonable until you analyse it in more detail. First, a large part of the investments are now tied up in trust so that B does not have complete control over those assets. Second, the children will receive a large sum of money at an early age, which may not be what A would have wanted. If the son decides to spend some of his £13,500 on a powerful motorcycle on his eighteenth birthday, B will be powerless to stop him. In addition, A's favourite charity, which had been receiving a regular amount each month under a covenant, will not receive a penny because the covenant has been cancelled by his death.

Joint tenancy

This is the most common way of owning a property but it is not always used. Sometimes the property is held by a couple as 'tenants in common' so that it does not go to the surviving spouse. Where this applies, the deceased's share in the property forms part of his estate and, if no will has been left, will be subject to the intestacy rules. If you do not know which applies to your home you should check with the person who did the conveyancing when you purchased the property; alternatively your lender or a solicitor will be able to advise you.

Simultaneous deaths

Statistically, the likelihood of a husband and wife dying at the same time or within a brief period is very small. Unfortunately, however, such tragedies do happen and when a couple leave behind young children the consequences can be serious.

The rules that apply in these situations are complicated. This is especially true where it cannot be established which of the couple died first, as occasionally happens in car accidents, for example. The general rule in such cases is that the younger is treated as the last to die with the assets of the elder first of all being subject to the intestacy rules and then passing to the younger's estate with the intestacy rules applying again if the younger one has left no will.

One effect of this is that, in England and Wales, the rules which apply to the estate can exclude entirely the parents and other relatives of the spouse that dies first (or is treated as having died first). In this case, all the property could pass to the other set of parents, for example. In Scotland, this problem is avoided by presuming that, in the case of a married couple, neither survives the other with the rules applying to each estate separately.

10.2.4 Who looks after the children?

If you have children under the age of 18, making a will is a 'must', if only to appoint a guardian to look after the children should both you and your wife die. Few people even think of this and those that do often assume that the grandparents will be there to look after the children. They may be willing to undertake the job but if they are elderly they may not be a suitable choice. Without a will, the matter may be left to the authorities to determine.

If there is no will the Courts have the power to appoint a guardian (called a 'tutor' in Scotland). In choosing the most suitable person, the Courts must have regard to the best interests of the child and, in many cases, there will be an obvious candidate, perhaps the grandparents or an aunt and uncle with children of a similar age. However, this may not always be the case and the only option may be for the children to be placed in the care of the local authority.

Another problem which can arise as a result of the operation of the intestacy rules is the possibility of relatively large sums of money passing to the children at an early age. Few eighteen year olds have the maturity to deal with large sums of money and this, together with the loss of their parents' stabilising influence, can be a cause for concern.

10.2.5 Personal bequests

If you wish to make specific gifts to individuals or to charity on death, the only means of doing this is by a will—the intestacy rules do not stretch to individual gifts to your family or friends or to charities. If you die without leaving any living relatives, your estate can pass to the Crown; hundreds of thousands of pounds are 'given' in this way every year.

10.2.6 The tax position

The final point about dying intestate is that many of the ways of avoiding inheritance tax (see 9.4.1) are totally lost. Not only could your family suffer emotionally as a result of your failure to leave a will, they could also eventually find themselves paying a larger than necessary inheritance tax bill to the Inland Revenue.

10.3 Getting advice

10.3.1 Do you need advice?

The answer to this is inevitably 'Yes' although there is no law preventing you from drafting your own will. However, there are sound reasons why you should seek advice from someone who can give clear guidance on the contents.

(1)   If your will is not correctly witnessed (see 10.5.4) it may be completely invalid so that none of your wishes can be carried out.
(2)   Even comparatively simple words can lead to complex legal disputes. For example, in two instances that led to Court cases, the word 'pictures' was given two different meanings in relation to a stamp collection.

(3)   If you choose words that are not sufficiently certain there could be an unexpected tax bill to pay. This can happen where, for example, property is given to charity and the words used to describe the charity are not clear, with the result that the charity does not benefit and the tax man does.

(4)   If you are divorced, you might still have obligations to a former spouse and this can affect what must go into your will.

(5)   You may want to leave your Porsche to your son but, if you replace it with a Ferrari at a later date, the gift could lapse.

DIY wills are possible, but are not to be recommended.

10.3.2   Where to get advice

Solicitors

A solicitor is a common choice for someone thinking of making a will. As cost is a consideration for many it is wise to obtain quotations from several solicitors before committing yourself.

Will writing companies

Recently, a number of companies have started to provide wills. They normally charge about the same as solicitors for simple wills, although in general they are not able to deal with the more complicated wills that only a solicitor should handle. Most of these companies use a computer program (similar to that used by many solicitors) to produce the will based on information that is supplied in response to a questionnaire.

In recent times, a number of insurance companies have begun to offer a will writing service. These offer the advantage of a visit to your own home to discuss your requirements; the company may also offer a storage facility so that your will is always kept in a safe place.

Will kits

For the brave, there are a number of books and 'will kits' that will provide you with guidance on how to draft a will. In very simple situations it should be possible to use this type of book to draw up an adequate will. However, the leading legal textbook on the subject runs to two volumes and over 1,700 pages so, unless you have *some* legal experience, it is probably best to get professional help.

10.4   Drawing up a will

The first step is to make a list of the people whom you wish to benefit and the type of gifts that you wish to make.

10.4.1   Who must benefit?

English law, unlike the law of many other countries including Scotland, does not impose too many rules regarding those to whom you must make gifts. In many countries, you are obliged to make gifts to your children and your spouse and these must be a certain percentage of your estate. Under English law, you are not obliged to make gifts of any specific amount, but the law does attempt to ensure that your family and dependants are reasonably provided for.

This arises under the Inheritance (Provision for Family and Dependants) Act 1975, which allows members of your family to apply to the Courts if they consider that they should have received more from your estate than your will provides. Those who can apply include your spouse, an unmarried former spouse, any of your children (including any who, although not strictly your children, you treated as such) and any person whom you maintained immediately before your death. In drafting your will, you should think carefully about how much you want to give to members of your family, because the Court can override your will if you have not made reasonable financial provision for them. When considering the case, the Court will look at all the relevant factors, such as the claimants' other resources and their ability to take care of themselves.

The law in Scotland is very different (see 10.7).

10.4.2   The appointment of executors, guardians and trustees

Executors

You will have to appoint executors to administer your estate. It is sometimes thought that a solicitor (or a firm of solicitors) must be appointed to act as executor, but this is not a legal necessity. It is perfectly acceptable to appoint a spouse, relative or friend, and although the role of an executor can be quite demanding, especially in complicated cases, the advice of a solicitor can still be obtained if needed at the time. If the will leaves everything to the surviving spouse, it is normally advisable to appoint her as the sole executor (though the will can also make provision if the surviving spouse is unable or unwilling to act for any reason).

Guardians

If you have children under the age of 18, the most important decision is your choice of guardian for your children, should both you and your wife die. Normally, two people are appointed as joint guardians and a couple of similar age to yourselves would be considered preferable if it is felt that the child needs the support of a 'normal' family.

Trustees

If your will is one which sets up a trust (see 11.1.3), perhaps for your minor children, you will have to consider who are to be the trustees. One point to note is that the trustees do not have to be the same as the executors although this is the normal position. However, if your trust is for a minor child, you might want to appoint someone other than the child's guardian as the trustee, as this separates the responsibility for the financial affairs from the day-to-day welfare of the child.

10.4.3   Drafting the will

The next step is for your will to be drafted. If it is to be drafted by a solicitor or a will drafting company this may take a few days; more if the will is complicated.

You should read the will carefully and check that everything is in order. Pay particular attention to names and addresses because mistakes in these are easily made. If you do not understand why a particular clause is in the will, you should ask the person drafting it for an explanation of what it means.

A 'model' will is included at the end of this book as Appendix A.

10.5   The formalities

A will has to satisfy certain formalities before it is valid. These are intended to reduce the risk of a will being forged or fraudulent alterations being made to it and to help reduce the chances that a person could be forced to make a will against his wishes.

The main legal requirements for wills are as follows:

(1)   They must be in writing.
(2)   They must be signed.
(3)   The testator must intend to make a will and must be of sound mind.
(4)   They must be validly witnessed.

10.5.1   Wills must be in writing

A will must be written, but under English law (the position is slightly different in Scotland) they do not have to be handwritten. You can use any language (including English or the odd piece of Latin if you are legally inclined), although you should be careful that there is someone who will be able to understand the significance of the will when it comes to light after your death.

If your will consists of more than one page, the pages should be firmly stapled or preferably bound together so that they do not become separated. You must not add a new page after the will has been executed because this will not be valid. You should not staple anything to the will because this could cause problems later.

10.5.2 Wills must be signed

You should sign with your normal signature but there is no need to write your full name as long as you use your usual signature. If you cannot sign, perhaps because of some physical incapacity, you can ask someone to sign on your behalf as long as you are physically present when they do so.

If there are any minor alterations (eg to correct spelling mistakes) these should be signed and witnessed, but this should only be done *before* the will is finally signed. If there are any major alterations, a completely new will is probably best. A will should not be altered in any way once you have signed it; the proper course is to amend the will using a suitable codicil (see 10.6.4) or to have a completely new will drawn up.

In Scotland, if you cannot sign the will personally, it must be notarially executed before a notary public, a solicitor, justice of the peace or the local parish minister. Also, except in the case of a 'holograph' will (one which is in the testator's handwriting or is typewritten or printed but signed as 'adopted as holograph' by the testator), the testator must also sign each page of the will if it is written on more than one piece of paper.

10.5.3 The testator's intentions must be clear

Normally, there is no doubt that in signing a will the testator intends to validate the *entire* will. However, there can be situations where there is some doubt. For example, if the signature does not come at the end of the will, there can be doubt whether the testator intends that all the will is to be valid, or just the part before the signature.

A valid will can be made only if the testator is of sound mind. If the testator is incapable of understanding that he is signing a document which gives property to certain beneficiaries after death, the will is invalid. In addition, the will can be challenged if it can be proved that the testator was acting under the undue influence of another person, for example, where the testator is very elderly and influenced by a person who was looking after him.

10.5.4 Wills must be validly witnessed

This is the area that causes most of the problems in practice and it is particularly important to meet all the requirements. In outline, the normal rules are as follows:

(1)   There must be two witnesses.
(2)   The testator must sign the will in the presence of both witnesses.
(3)   The witnesses must sign the will intending to witness the signature of the testator.
(4)   Except in Scotland, the witnesses must sign in the presence of the testator and each other.
(5)   The witnesses or their spouses must not receive any benefit under the will.

In Scotland there is a special rule that holograph wills do not need to be witnessed at all (although the normal case is for the will to be witnessed).

Most of the problems arise from the rule that a witness (or spouse of a witness) must *not* benefit from the will. The safest way to ensure that the will is executed properly is to have two completely independent witnesses who are not mentioned in the will in any way, (whether as executors, trustees or beneficiaries). The witnesses do not need to know what is in the will and it is quite common for the will to be witnessed by neighbours or members of the solicitor's staff. If a will is witnessed by a person who takes any benefit under the will, it is still valid, but the witness will *not* be able to receive his gift.

10.5.5   Challenging the will

If the will is properly drafted, signed and witnessed and any dependants entitled to a claim on the deceased's estate have been adequately provided for, there should be little danger of the will being challenged. However, challenges to wills do occur and are sometimes successful.

There are several grounds on which a will can be challenged. The main ones are as follows:

(1)   A claim under the Inheritance (Provision for Family and Dependants) Act by a dependant or relative for whom reasonable provision was not made in the will (this does not apply in Scotland.)
(2)   A claim that the testator was not mentally capable of making a will.
(3)   A claim that the testator was forced to make the will against his wishes or was subject to undue pressure at the time the will was made.
(4)   In Scotland, a child born after the will was made but not included in it may claim that the will is invalid.

It should be possible to avoid all these pitfalls by taking proper advice at the time the will is made. For example, it will be more difficult to claim that someone was pressurised into making a will if that person was advised by a solicitor of his own choosing. Similarly, if there is likely to be any doubt that the testator was mentally capable, it may be desirable to have the will witnessed by the person's doctor, who could later testify that the person was capable at the time.

10.6   Reviewing your will

The best advice is to review your will on a regular basis. If tax is a concern to you, then the annual Budget speech will often be a good time for a review of the way you intend to leave your property (particularly as the impact of inheritance tax will be according to the tax rules at the date of death, not the date you drew up your will). Apart from that (and apart from the fact that you may wish to amend your will simply because you have changed your mind) the events that should trigger off a review of your will are as follows:

(1)   Marriage and divorce
(2)   Changes to people mentioned in your will
(3)   Disposal or acquisition of assets.

10.6.1   Marriage and divorce

Marriage

Except in Scotland, the general rule is that the entire will is revoked by the marriage of the testator after the will was made. This does not apply where the will is made 'in expectation of marriage' ie where an engaged couple make wills which clearly envisage that they are to get married. To be certain, it must state clearly that it is made in anticipation of the marriage *to a specific person* and that it is not to be revoked by the marriage.

Divorce

For divorce a slightly different rule applies. Again with the exception of Scotland, the will remains valid but any gift to the former spouse will lapse. The former spouse's appointment as an executor will also lapse. However, the need to review the will remains for two reasons.

(1)   The effect of the lapse of gifts may mean that the will does not deal with who is to receive any property left to the former spouse.
(2)   There could be a liability to make reasonable provision for a former spouse who is a dependant, perhaps because they are receiving maintenance.

The position in Scotland is dealt with later on (see 10.7.5).

10.6.2 Changes to people mentioned in your will

Birth of children or grandchildren

The will may be drafted in such a way as to refer to all future children and grandchildren, but it is wise to check that the will covers all the children and not just those named specifically. In Scotland the law goes further than this and a will which does not provide for children born after the will was made may be challenged by any child who was born subsequently.

Death of a beneficiary

The effect of the death of a beneficiary of the will depends upon the way in which the gift to them is drafted. If the will makes a specific provision for what is to happen, no change may be required. If it does not cover the situation, the will should be reviewed and a new one drafted or a suitable codicil made.

Changes to executors, trustees or guardians

You should review regularly whether the people you have chosen as executors, trustees or guardians are still suitable and available to act. Again, any changes can be made by a suitable codicil.

10.6.3 Disposal or acquisition of assets

If you make a specific gift of property in your will and then sell that asset, the gift will not be valid, even if you use the proceeds of the sale to purchase new assets (unless the will includes a specific clause which says this is to happen). Similarly, if you acquire new assets, the general rule will be that the assets will pass to the person entitled to the residue of your estate and, unless this is what you intend, you will need to revise your will.

10.6.4 New will or codicil

Whatever the reason for the change to the will, you have a choice of using a codicil or making a new will. A codicil would be suitable where the change is relatively simple; for example, if you want to change your executors or make a further specific gift of some property you have recently required. However, in most cases, a new will is preferable as it ensures that all your wishes are contained in one document. In either case you will need to get advice on the contents.

If you decide to add a codicil you will need to go through the formal process of signing and witnessing again because the rules are identical to those for a new will, except that the existing will remains valid subject to any changes that are made.

10.7   The law in Scotland

The law in Scotland differs substantially from the law in the remainder of the United Kingdom and these differences are particularly marked in the areas of wills and the laws of intestacy.

10.7.1   What happens when there is no will?

The first question is who will deal with the estate and see to the payment of debts and the distribution of the estate. This person is called an executor-dative and the list of potential claimants for this role is broadly as follows:

(1)   The surviving spouse (who has the sole right to be executor where she is entitled to the entire estate by virtue of 'prior rights'—see below)
(2)   Any child, grandchild or great grandchild
(3)   The father or mother
(4)   Aunts, uncles and nieces and nephews.

The full list also includes remoter relatives and also creditors, judicial factors (in the case of a bankruptcy) and the procurator-fiscal. The key point is that, in the absence of a will naming the person to administer the estate, the choice is very wide.

10.7.2   Prior rights and legal rights

A key element of the Scots law relating to wills is the system of 'prior rights' and 'legal rights'. These are the rights of a person's spouse and children to a specified share of the estate after death. These rights apply not only to the estates of persons who die without making a will but also act, with certain modifications, to supplement or, indeed, override the terms of any will that has been made. The effect of these rules is to restrict the freedom of testators to make a will in the way that they choose and to ensure that provision is always made for the spouse and children.

Prior rights

Prior rights are the rights of the surviving spouse to certain property, furnishings and money from the deceased's estate. These rights have, as their name suggests, priority over all other claims over the estate other than debts and expenses. They apply where there is no will or if the will does not cover all of the deceased's property.

Legal rights

These are the rights of the deceased's spouse and the children to a share of the deceased's property (the children's legal rights are known as *legitim*). They apply not only where there is no will but also where there is a will. Legal rights apply only to the deceased's 'movable property' (basically any property, including investments and life assurance policies, other than land and buildings) and cover the value of the moveable property after prior rights have been paid.

10.7.3 The free estate

Once the prior rights and the legal rights have been paid, the balance of the movable estate, is added to the deceased's 'heritable property' (any land or buildings that belong to the deceased). This balance is called the free estate and passes in the following order:

(1) Children (including illegitimate and adopted children, but not stepchildren)
(2) Parents, brothers and sisters
(3) The surviving spouse
(4) Uncles and aunts
(5) Grandparents
(6) Brothers and sisters of the grandparents
(7) Remoter ancestors
(8) The Crown, if no relatives can be found.

It is worth noting that the spouse (being protected by the system of prior rights and legal rights) only appears third in the list of potential beneficiaries of the free estate.

10.7.4 Effect of wills

Unlike the law in the remainder of the United Kingdom, a Scots-domiciled person who leaves a spouse or other dependants is restricted in the way that he can write a will. The will can only apply to a person's free estate, ie a Scots testator can only have a will that deals with any land or buildings (his heritable property) and the share of his movable estate which is not affected by the legal rights (prior rights do not apply where there is a will unless the will does not deal with all the deceased's property for some reason).

10.7.5 Reviewing wills

Reviewing a will is just as important in Scotland as elsewhere in the United Kingdom but there are important differences in the law.

The first difference is that a will is not revoked by a subsequent marriage. This is because the system of legal rights automatically ensures that the spouse is provided for at least to some extent. In addition, there is no rule that gifts to a divorced spouse lapse. Although the divorced spouse's legal rights cease to apply, gifts in the will are still valid after a divorce unless it is made clear in the will that the gift to the spouse is conditional on the marriage existing at the date of death.

Perhaps the most significant difference between English and Scots law is the rule that a will which does not include children born after the will is made can be ruled invalid. There is no equivalent rule elsewhere in the United Kingdom but, in Scotland, unless it is clear from the will or the surrounding circumstances that the will is to remain in force, the birth of a child who is not provided for in the will could mean that the child could challenge the will at a later date. In all cases, the birth of a child should prompt a review of your will to ensure that it is kept up to date.

A final point is that many people overlook the importance of ensuring that the will can be found when it is needed. In Scotland this is doubly important as a lost will is presumed to have been revoked unless it can be proved that the loss of the will was not due to its destruction by the testator.

10.8   Administering the estate

All deaths must be registered (with the local Registrar of Births, Deaths and Marriages) within five days (eight in Scotland) by a relative or the person who is making the funeral arrangements. The Registrar will issue a Certificate of Registration of Death for social security purposes, and a Certificate for Burial or Cremation which needs to be given to the funeral directors before the funeral can proceed. He can also issue, for a fee, as many copies of the death certificate as the executors will need for probate, pension claims, insurance policies etc.

10.8.1   Paying inheritance tax and obtaining the grant of probate

The grant of probate (or confirmation in Scotland) is the formal authority that is needed to allow the executors to deal with the assets of the deceased. The grant is obtained by an application to the appropriate Probate Registry (or, in Scotland, to the local sheriff court), and involves the completion of various forms which give details about the will and the assets of the estate. Without the formal authority of probate or confirmation, banks, insurance companies, company registrars etc who hold the deceased's assets are perfectly within their rights to refuse to deal with the executors.

Sometimes, especially where the estate is small, insurance companies and banks etc may be prepared to make small payments without a formal grant of probate. However, before a grant of probate can be obtained, the executors must pay any inheritance tax that is due on the value of the estate. This may mean that the executors have to borrow the money to pay the inheritance tax unless there are funds readily available elsewhere, such as from an insurance policy that was written in trust (see 9.5).

10.8.2 Duties of the executors

The executors have an important role to play. In short, their duties are to pay the deceased's debts and any tax and then distribute the balance of the estate in the way specified in the will. The exact duties of the executors will vary from will to will.

(1)   The first task is usually to find out exactly what the deceased owned and whether there are any outstanding debts that need to be paid. This information is also needed by the Inland Revenue to assess any tax that may be payable. All of the deceased's debts and liabilities will also need to be identified as part of the inheritance tax calculation and they will need to be paid before the estate is wound up.

(2)   The next step is to collect in all the assets of the estate. For example, with shares, the executors can apply to the company registrars for the estate to be registered as a shareholder or, if the will provides, for the shares to pass to a beneficiary. The grant of probate or confirmation will allow the executors to close accounts and transfer the proceeds to a special bank account which should be set up for this purpose in the name of the executors.

(3)   The debts of the deceased, including any unpaid income and capital gains tax, must be paid before the final balance of the estate is transferred to the people entitled to the residue. Once it is clear that there is sufficient in the estate to pay all the debts, the executors can pay out any specific gifts of money or assets that are provided by the will. Where gifts of money are concerned, this is usually done by selling assets to raise the money. If the beneficiary consents, assets can be transferred rather than being sold to pay cash.

(4)   The next stages are to formalise the accounts of the estate and to ascertain how much money is available to be paid to the beneficiaries who are entitled to the residue. This may result in an adjustment to the inheritance tax bill that was previously paid if new assets have come to light during the administration of the estate or if any assets have fallen significantly in value before the date of death. The final accounts will also deal with the expenses of the administration such as the funeral and any solicitors' or other costs incurred. There may also be some income tax to pay in respect of any income received during the period when the estate is being administered. Once the accounts have been finalised and all remaining debts settled, the residue of the estate can be transferred to the beneficiaries (or to the trustees if the residue is to be held in a trust).

10.8.3   Intestacy

If no will can be found and there is no evidence that a will was drawn up, then the deceased will be assumed to have died intestate. In this case, if you are entitled to administer the estate under the intestacy rules (see 10.2.1), you may apply for a grant of letters of administration.

The position in Scotland is different (see 10.7.1).

Letters of administration have the same authority as a grant of probate, but it is the *only* authority held by an administrator. An executor, on the other hand, derives authority from the will itself and can, even before the grant is issued, perform certain acts which do not require proof of his authority (eg pay debts or put a house on the market).

10.9   The enduring power of attorney

Mental disability can affect anyone, whatever his age. It can arise as a result of illness, such as a stroke, or accident, and is not confined to those in extreme old age. Whatever the cause, the effects are the same, with the sufferer left incapable of dealing with the financial and other matters that most of us would take for granted.

People who are mentally incapable of dealing with their business affairs are legally prevented from taking any action in relation to their property and investments. While there are special legal procedures to deal with the problems, these are by no means always satisfactory.

10.9.1   What happens when mental disability strikes?

In practical terms, the effect is very similar to the position on death. At death, the law provides that someone will take over the administration of the estate and, if there is no will, there are always the intestacy rules to fall back on. Where mental disability strikes there are several possibilities. One is that dealings with the property are simply suspended until the person dies, at which point the person's executors or administrators can take over and distribute the assets in accordance with the will or the intestacy rules.

A further alternative is that an application is made to the Court of Protection, a special court that looks after the affairs of people who are incapable of looking after their own affairs because of mental disability. The procedure is usually for the Court to appoint a receiver to administer the estate. This will mean that the receiver (normally a near relative or a solicitor or accountant), will be able to receive the person's income, pay debts and deal with most day-to-day matters. Larger transactions, such as the sale of the family house or significant investment decisions, will require specific approval from the Court, who will then need to be satisfied that they are in the best interests of the individual before letting the transaction go ahead.

Although there are special procedures for smaller estates of less than £5,000 in total value, the costs can be very significant. In addition, the limited personal attention is one reason why the Court of Protection may often not be suitable.

10.9.2   Powers and enduring powers

A power of attorney is simply an authority to a named individual, called the attorney, which allows the attorney to act on behalf of the person who is giving the authority, called the donor. Normal powers of attorney are quite commonplace but have the disadvantage that they come to an end if the donor ceases to be able to look after his own affairs as a result of mental incapacity.

The enduring power of attorney was introduced in England in 1985. It allows people to choose someone to look after their affairs should they become unable to do so themselves. As its name suggests, it endures *after* the donor becomes incapable, and may even be worded in a way that it only takes effect once incapacity strikes. (The position in Scotland is slightly different. Anybody appointed to act on your behalf since 1 January 1991 can continue to do so even if you become unable to look after your own affairs as a result of mental illness.)

10.9.3   What are the advantages of enduring powers?

Compared with an application to the Court of Protection, an enduring power of attorney offers many advantages.

(1)   They are inexpensive. The only fee is a small registration fee if the power has to be used and there are no annual fees.

(2)   They enable you to choose who is to be your attorney, rather than having to rely on a Court-appointed receiver. You are free to choose whoever you want, usually your spouse, a relative or friend, or a professional adviser.

(3)   A degree of advance planning is possible. You are able to execute an enduring power at any time, as long as you are able to understand the nature and effect of the document.

(4)   There are standard forms for enduring powers and a solicitor will be able to help you with these. The documents are relatively simple with detailed explanatory notes and require only to be signed, by both the donor and the attorney, and be independently witnessed. In the standard form, the attorney can be given wide powers that are usually enough to cope with most situations that arise.

(5)   Once the power needs to be used, the procedures are very simple. When the donor becomes incapable of managing his affairs, the attorney must give notice to the donor and to certain relatives of the donor and any co-attorneys. If no objection is made, the attorney can register the power with the Court of Protection, allowing it to be used.

10.9.4   Wills and enduring powers

It is advisable to consider executing an enduring power at the same time as you make a will. One thing that the attorney cannot do for you is to make or amend your will, except with the approval of the Court of Protection. However, the combination of a will and an enduring power will cover most situations that could arise, ensuring that your affairs will be looked after in all eventualities.

10.10   Living wills

A living will is a statement, in writing, made by an adult outlining the steps that should or should not be taken in the event of terminal illness. Essentially they are an expression of a wish that medical treatment should be withdrawn if there is no hope of improvement or if the treatment becomes a burden.

They are not legally binding and can only be an expression of your wishes. In the final event, your doctor has the right to decide whether treatment is withdrawn. The benefit of having a living will drawn up is that your doctor is at least aware of your wishes.

There is, of course, a considerable difference between, on the one hand, the withdrawal of treatment which is keeping somebody alive and, on the other hand, actively helping somebody to die (which is technically murder). However, doctors are allowed to withdraw treatment in certain cases where recovery is impossible and this was confirmed by the Government in May 1994. Despite this, there is no specific legislation on living wills and there is no reference to living wills in any existing legislation.

Nevertheless, it is important that a living will is drawn up in a legal form not only to make sure your wishes are clear and unambiguous but also to give protection to those people whom you expect to respect your wishes and withdraw treatment when the time comes. Details of a suitably drafted living will can be obtained from the Voluntary Euthanasia Society.

11 Trusts

Among the great military adventures of the last thousand years were the Crusades. For any wealthy land-owning knight, setting out from England on such a hazardous mission, a worry had to be what would happen to his land whilst he was away and, more importantly, if he were killed. It became the custom for the knight to leave his land with trustworthy friends and ask them to look after it for the benefit of his son until he returned. If he were killed, the friends could continue to use the land for the son's benefit until the son reached 21, at which point the land would become his.

As the alternative was for the land to go to the Lord of the Manor, you can see that trusts (or 'uses' as they were called) were an early but effective form of tax planning. From such simple beginnings, trusts have evolved to become a very useful way of arranging your affairs so that things happen in the way that you want them to happen. That was true for the knights of the Crusades and it is true for a great many people today

This chapter looks at trusts under the following headings:

(1)   What is a trust?
(2)   Why trusts can be a good idea
(3)   The principal types of trust
(4)   Setting up a trust
(5)   The appointment, retirement and removal of trustees
(6)   The duties and responsibilities of trustees
(7)   The rights of beneficiaries
(8)   Trusts in practice
(9)   Anti-avoidance legislation.

11.1   What is a trust?

11.1.1   The basic workings of a trust

A will is a straightforward statement of your wishes regarding what happens to your property when you die. If you want your nephew to receive £1,000 then you put that in your will and it will happen. A trust is similar to a will in that it allows you to dispose of your property in the way that you wish. One difference, however, is that a trust allows you to give your property away while you are alive and, at the same time, retain a degree of control over it.

Suppose you would prefer your nephew to get the money while you are alive. If you give him £1,000 in cash for him to spend, it is an outright gift. You have immediately handed over the £1,000 and you have no further say in what happens to it. In legal terms, you (the donor) have made a gift to your nephew (the beneficiary) absolutely.

But you may not wish to make an absolute gift; your nephew may be young and unused to handling money. Trusts allow you to make a gift now in such a way that the full benefit may not take effect until some time in the future. Instead of making an outright gift to the beneficiary, you give it instead to a person or group of people who will look after the property on behalf of the beneficiary. These people (the trustees) have to follow your instructions regarding the eventual handing over of the property, and its treatment in the meantime and those instructions (the trust deed) will be carefully drafted to eliminate doubts as to what you want to happen.

The obvious question, of course, is why not wait until the nephew *is* old enough and give him the money then? Tax could play a part in this, particularly inheritance tax. You might wish to make use of the annual exemptions to make gifts (see 9.7.1) but you might not wish to make an outright gift.

11.1.2   A simple example

A couple have been married for some years and have two teenage children. The husband has invested with some success and has built up a portfolio of shares and unit trusts. He keeps a close eye on these and manages his portfolio as best he can. His wife isn't particularly interested in the detail of this type of investment but the income from them is a useful addition to the household budget.

The husband wants to ensure that his children eventually benefit from his investment success. However, he has to think of what would happen if he died first:

(1)   Will his wife want to look after the portfolio?
(2)   If the children inherit the portfolio while they are still young:
    (a)   how will they know what to do with it?
    (b)   will his wife miss the income?

His solution is to set up a trust and hand over his portfolio to a person or group of people he can trust (the trustees) to look after the portfolio (and there is no reason why he can't appoint himself as a trustee for as long as he is alive). The trustees have to act at all times in the interests of the beneficiaries (the people who will benefit from the trust) and he will make quite sure that the trust deed spells out what they can and cannot do—and he will use a solicitor to get the words right.

The basis of this particular type of trust is that, on his death, his wife receives the income from the portfolio for as long as she is alive. On her death, (or later, if they are still young), the portfolio passes to the children and the trust will be 'wound up'.

11.1.3 Wills versus trusts

A key point about trusts is the difference between a trust and a will. They are both concerned with giving away property but wills only take effect on death. You can change a will as often as you want while you are alive. Trusts, on the other hand, take effect as soon as they are set up and can be very difficult (or even impossible) to change.

Will trusts

Wills and trusts can be combined. It is possible, for example, to make a gift via a will that is not an outright gift but one which is controlled until the beneficiary is of a suitable age. This is what is called a will trust and, in effect, gives you the best of both worlds. You can look after and enjoy your property while you are alive but you can make the necessary arrangements to make sure that, in the event of your death, the interests of your beneficiaries are looked after until they are old enough to look after themselves. In fact, this is probably what the husband would have done in the previous example.

11.1.4 Setting up a trust

When you set up a trust (or, as it is often put, 'declare' a trust) you are making a gift; you are transferring the property. However, it is not a simple gift, as would be the case where, for example, you give some property to your son. In this case, your son would be the outright owner of the property or assets and could do with them whatever he wished. If you make a gift of the same property or assets through a trust, the arrangements would be somewhat different.

There are, in fact, two types of ownership of property: legal ownership and beneficial ownership. If you own something absolutely, you have both legal and beneficial ownership and this, for most of us, is the usual state of affairs. However, it is possible to separate legal from beneficial ownership and this is what happens when a trust is set up.

For example, if you make a gift of property or assets to your child through a trust, your child becomes the *beneficial* owner of the property or assets but there would be a new body of people, the trustees, in place as the *legal* owners. The trustees must always act in the child's best interests and their actions will usually be controlled by the terms of the trust deed.

11.2 Why trusts can be a good idea

11.2.1 The general advantages of trusts

There are a number of general advantages of making large lifetime transfers by putting money into trust rather than making outright gifts. The main ones are:

(1)   Trusts are a very effective way of giving property away 'with strings attached'. You may want to make sure that the capital you give away is applied for specific purposes or, at any rate, is not frittered away. You must, however, be wary of making a gift under which you could benefit yourself (although there are a few *limited* circumstances in which you can benefit under the terms of your own trust without falling foul of the Inland Revenue).

(2)   You can retain a measure of control either by appointing trustees who will pay due regard to your views and wishes, or even by being a trustee yourself.

(3)   You can make provision for your spouse to benefit at some time in the future after your death should her financial circumstances change for the worse.

Trusts also enable you effectively to have control over the management of your assets after your death.

11.2.2 Typical uses of trusts

The following are typical ways in which trusts are put to everyday use:

Giving property away

Rather than leave a large amount of money in your will which could have inheritance tax implications you could give away smaller sums of money over a number of years (see 9.7.1). By declaring a trust you can dispose of the money without making outright gifts of it to a particular individual. In this way, trusts can be an important part of your long-term tax planning.

Looking after your beneficiaries

Your intended beneficiary could be too young to hold the property or assets. There is no objection, however, to property or assets being held on trust for such a beneficiary. The beneficiary might not be considered responsible or mature enough to hold the property or assets outright, so you might not wish to make an irreversible decision as to who is going to get the benefits. You could even give the trustees discretion as to the amount which they would be allowed to pay over to the beneficiary or beneficiaries at any given time.

Benefiting future generations

A trust could be used to ensure that your property will benefit certain persons in succession. If you were to make an outright gift to a married son or daughter, you could not be certain that, on their death, the property would go to your grandchildren. If you were to make a gift to trustees to hold upon trust for that parent for life, with the property going to the children on the parent's death, you would know that your grandchildren will ultimately benefit from the gift.

Life assurance in the right place

Trusts can be very flexible indeed. You may wish to leave the proceeds of a life assurance policy to your heirs without giving rise to any inheritance tax liability and without any probate delay. If the policy was written under a suitable trust it would not form part of your estate (thereby avoiding inheritance tax) and the proceeds could be paid to the trustees (for them to pay to the beneficiaries) without any need to wait for the grant of probate (see 9.5).

11.3   The principal types of trust

From the above ways in which trusts can be used, it is clear that they can be extremely flexible. Quite simply, you can make a trust do more or less exactly what you want it to do and there are different kinds of trusts for different purposes. However, there are three particular types of trust that crop up over and over again:

(1)   Interest in possession trusts.
(2)   Discretionary trusts.
(3)   Accumulation and maintenance trusts.

Of course, there is nothing so certain as death and taxes, and trusts do not escape. Consequently, it is important to have a basic understanding of the way trusts are taxed. However, it is a complex area, and the following notes are not intended to be anything other than an introductory guide.

Trusts involve a transfer of property (so there are inheritance tax implications), the assets may earn income (so there are income tax implications) and assets may be bought and sold (with implications for capital gains tax). Furthermore, there could be tax implications for the settlor (the person setting up the trust), the beneficiaries and the trustees.

11.3.1   Interest in possession trusts

In the example in 11.1.2, the husband put his investments into trust so that:

(1)   he could look after them while he was alive;
(2)   after his death, his wife received the income for as long as she was alive; and
(3)   his children inherited the capital when his wife died.

This is an interest in possession trust and the basic principle behind this type of trust is that the income is treated separately from the capital. Under such trusts, one or more of the beneficiaries enjoys the right to any income arising from the trust fund for a certain period; usually during their lifetime. These beneficiaries are the 'life tenants' and are said to have a 'life interest' under the trust. After the death of the life tenant (or the last surviving life tenant, if there is more than one) the capital then passes to those people that you wish to benefit from the capital. These people (the 'remaindermen') are said to be entitled to the reversion and have a 'reversionary interest' in the trust.

You could also write such a trust under the terms of a will. You might be concerned about leaving capital to your surviving spouse when you die. By setting up an interest in possession trust under the terms of your will, you can ensure that your surviving spouse receives the income from the capital but not the capital itself (unless, of course, the trustees have the power to distribute capital and decide to exercise that power).

11.3.2   The taxation of interest in possession trusts

Inheritance tax

When you set a trust up during your lifetime, the life tenant is regarded as receiving a gift of the value of the trust fund; he or she has the benefit of the fund which is producing an income. The inheritance tax position depends on the relationship between you and the life tenant:

(1)   If the life tenant is your spouse, there will be no inheritance tax payable because of the inter-spouse exemption (see 9.4.1).
(2)   If the life tenant is anyone else, the gift will be a potentially exempt transfer (see 9.6.2).

The death of the life tenant will give rise to inheritance tax implications for the life tenant's estate (as it will include the value of the trust property) and there will also be inheritance tax implications if the life tenant renounces her entitlement to the income (as the property will be handed back to the trustees and this will be a potentially exempt transfer).

If you include yourself in the class of beneficiaries, the property transferred into the trust will still be included in your estate on your death for inheritance tax purposes under the gifts with reservation of benefit rule (see 9.6.1). This should not prevent your spouse from benefiting under the trust after your death.

Income tax

The trustees are liable for income tax (at the basic rate) on any income earned by the assets of the trust. This income (after deducting any expenses incurred by the trustees) is then paid to the life tenant. Any tax paid may be reclaimed by the life tenant if she is a non-taxpayer. If the life tenant is a higher rate taxpayer she may be liable to pay an additional 15 per cent (at current rates).

If you or your spouse (or your minor children) could benefit under a trust set up by you, the trustees' income will be taxed as if it were yours. This could mean your facing a liability to higher rate tax even though the income is actually paid to someone else. You are allowed to claim the tax back from the trustees but the underlying point is that the tax due will be based on your overall financial position and not that of the trust (ie there is no overall tax advantage). There are details of further anti-avoidance provisions in 11.9.

Capital gains tax

Capital gains tax (at the rate of 25 per cent) is payable by the trustees on the trust's total gains for the tax year after deducting the annual exemption, which for trusts is usually half the individual exemption (see 8.6). If either you or your spouse could benefit under the trust, now or in the future, the trust gains will be treated as your gains, though you have the right to recover the tax paid from the trustees.

11.3.3 Discretionary trusts

Stripped of legalese, a discretionary trust usually provides something like this:

> The trustees will hold the trust fund until [a fixed day in the future] and will use the income to make payments to any one or more of a defined class of beneficiaries as they shall, in their absolute discretion, decide. The trustees may also distribute capital if they wish. At the appointed day, the trust fund will be distributed as follows . . .

Discretionary trusts can therefore be extremely flexible. The appointed day may often be a date up to 80 years after the trust was created. The class of beneficiaries may be very narrowly defined (eg, 'my wife and daughter') or it may be very widely defined (eg, 'any lineal descendant of my great grandfather'). The trustees have the power to accumulate income for a limited period (ie not to pay it out but to reinvest it) and they may or may not have power to distribute capital before the appointed day.

Such a trust requires careful thought. On the one hand, it is a very flexible vehicle giving the trustees wide powers to apply your money to meet changing circumstances and needs. On the other hand, it is giving considerable powers to the trustees and you have to choose them carefully.

11.3.4   The taxation of discretionary trusts

Discretionary trusts are known as 'settlements without an interest in possession'. The tax position is quite different from that of interest in possession trusts.

Inheritance tax

Because of the wide powers given to trustees, they can delay the distribution of capital almost indefinitely. In order to prevent this delay of potential inheritance tax, there are special rules designed to collect it 'on account'.

(1)   There is an immediate liability to inheritance tax (at 20 per cent) whenever property in excess of the nil rate band is transferred to a discretionary trust.
(2)   There is a ten-yearly 'periodic charge' (at reduced rates) on property remaining in the trust.
(3)   There is a proportionate 'exit charge' when property is transferred out of the trust.

Income tax

The trustees are normally liable to income tax at the basic rate plus a surcharge of ten per cent on all the income which the trust receives, making a tax rate of 35 per cent in total. Where dividends are received, the trustees will face a surcharge of 15 per cent (as the tax credit on dividends is 20 per cent).

Where the trustees distribute income to beneficiaries, the amounts received by the beneficiaries are treated as being net of tax at 35 per cent. The beneficiaries may reclaim part or all of this tax if their incomes are low enough. If the beneficiaries are higher rate taxpayers, however, they may be liable to a further five per cent tax (at current rates).

If you or your spouse is named as a beneficiary of a trust set up by you, you yourself will be assessed for income tax on all the income of the trust at both basic and (where appropriate) higher rates, though you will be able to claim the tax paid back from the trustees.

The position with your minor children is slightly different. The trust may have been set up for them and, as the underlying structure is that it is a 'settlement without interest in possession' (ie the income is generally accumulated, not distributed), you will only face a tax liability if the income is distributed to your minor children.

Capital gains tax

The trustees will normally be charged to capital gains tax at the special rate of 35 per cent on any gains arising within the trust. The annual exemption is half the individual exemption (see 8.6). Once again, if either you or your spouse could benefit under the trust, now or in the future, the trust gains will be treated as your gains, though you will be able to claim back the tax from the trustees.

Overall, discretionary trusts offer you considerable flexibility in arranging your financial affairs and looking after the family money but this has to be balanced to some extent by the rather more complicated tax position.

11.3.5 Accumulation and maintenance (A & M) trusts

An accumulation and maintenance trust is a special type of discretionary trust set up for a stated class of beneficiaries. They are popular trusts for family purposes as the trustees are given a fair amount of control and discretion and, at the same time, the tax treatment is considerably more favourable than for normal discretionary trusts.

There are four conditions which must be satisfied:

(1) The trust must have a life of not more than 25 years or it must be a trust for the benefit of grandchildren of a common grandparent.

(2) All the beneficiaries must be below the age of 25 when the trust commences. There must be at least one beneficiary alive when the trust is set up but the beneficiaries could include unborn children (eg future grandchildren).

(3) One or more of the beneficiaries must become entitled to an interest in possession (ie the income) on or before reaching a specified age not exceeding 25 years. In practice, these trusts often provide that the beneficiaries become entitled to the income at the age of 18 or 21.

(4) Prior to this, the income must be either accumulated or distributed for the maintenance, education or benefit of one or more of the beneficiaries.

The trustees can postpone applying the *capital* for the benefit of the beneficiaries almost indefinitely. This makes these trusts popular because, although the beneficiaries are bound to benefit from the income, the trustees decide when they may benefit from the capital.

11.3.6 The taxation of accumulation and maintenance trusts

Inheritance tax

A transfer of property into such a trust will be a potentially exempt transfer (see 9.6.2). Unlike a normal discretionary trust, there is no immediate liability to inheritance tax and there are no periodic or exit charges. Also, there is no inheritance tax liability:

(1)   when a beneficiary becomes beneficially entitled to an interest in possession in the trust property; or
(2)   on the death of a beneficiary before attaining the specified age; or
(3)   when a beneficiary becomes absolutely entitled to trust property.

Income tax

Income received by the trustees is subject to tax at the basic rate plus a surcharge of ten per cent (15 per cent in the case of dividends). When a beneficiary becomes entitled to the income, the rate of tax goes down to the basic rate. The beneficiary may reclaim tax (if a non-taxpayer) or be liable for additional tax (if a higher rate taxpayer).

Capital gains tax

The trustees are liable for capital gains tax (at the special rate of 35 per cent) on any chargeable disposals. The annual exemption is half the annual exemption for individuals. If you or your spouse could benefit under the trust now or in the future, the trust gains will be treated as your gains, though you will be able to claim any tax paid back from the trustees.

There may be a deemed disposal for capital gains tax purposes when:

(1)   a beneficiary becomes entitled to an interest in possession; or
(2)   when the trustees make an advance of capital to a beneficiary; or
(3)   when a beneficiary becomes absolutely entitled to trust property.

The significance here is that, with an A & M trust, the actual or effective transfer of property to a beneficiary gives rise to a liability to capital gains tax, not inheritance tax.

11.3.7 Other types of trusts

The three types of trust described above are those most commonly found in practice and the majority of financial planning situations can be resolved by one or other of these. However, they are not the only types available.

Bare trusts

A bare trust (also known as a simple trust) arises where a trustee simply holds the trust property but has no active duties to perform. For example, if property is left to a minor by way of gift, that property will be held by a bare trustee (usually a parent or guardian) until the child reaches the age of 18.

Special trusts

A special trust is one where the settlor appoints a trustee to carry out specific purposes. For example, the trustee might be asked to collect the income arising from the trust property and pay such income to a life tenant.

Precatory trusts

A precatory trust is one where the trust instrument uses such phrases as 'I hope' or 'I wish'. Precatory trusts are not legally binding and would be appropriate where you are undecided as to who should receive your property after your death but have full confidence that one person will carry out your wishes. With a legally binding trust, you would need to execute a new will or codicil every time you changed your mind. With a precatory trust, one supreme beneficiary can be chosen to distribute the property in accordance with your wishes, with your instructions being amended from time to time by informal notification to the beneficiary.

Offshore trusts

A trust will be treated as UK-resident unless the general administration of the trust is carried on outside the United Kingdom and the trustees (or at least the majority of them) are not resident or ordinarily resident in the United Kingdom (see 12.3.1). Offshore (or non-resident) trusts may provide tax advantages for UK expatriates; however, anybody who is considering sheltering their investments from the Revenue must consider very carefully the anti-avoidance legislation which is complex and beyond the scope of this book.

11.4   Setting up a trust

Declaring a trust is a significant step. Unlike a will (which only comes into effect on your death and which can be changed as often as you like while you are alive), a trust takes effect immediately. If you subsequently find that it is not achieving its purpose, it can be very difficult indeed to change. It is therefore vital to obtain competent legal advice.

11.4.1   The three certainties

In order for a trust to be valid, it must fulfil requirements known as the three certainties:

(1)   The words used in the declaration must express sufficiently clearly the intentions of the settlor. The word 'trust' is not absolutely necessary if the settlor's intention is clear.

(2)   The beneficiaries should be clearly ascertained even if the list of beneficiaries includes as yet unborn beneficiaries.

(3)   The property which is going into the trust must be clearly identified: for example, you need to specify which shares, how much money, which life assurance policies etc.

11.4.2   Capacity to declare a trust

Any individual over the age of 18 and of sound mind is able to declare a trust. A minor could declare a trust but such a trust would be voidable by the individual when he reached the age of 18 (ie he could declare that the trust no longer exists).

11.4.3   Choice of trustee

The choice of trustee is of great importance to everyone involved with the trust. Unless you have appointed yourself as trustee (or otherwise reserved powers for yourself in the trust deed), you will have handed complete control over the property to the trustees. It goes without saying, therefore, that the trustees must be honest, be prepared to look after the trust property, understand your wishes and understand the terms of the trust. Unless the trust specifically permits the payment of fees to the trustees, they must act without any payment.

If you wish to appoint an individual as trustee, you might consider appointing someone who knows you and your financial affairs, such as your accountant or solicitor. If you are considering appointing a friend or relative as a trustee, somebody with no experience of financial matters at all is not likely to be a suitable choice.

The location of your trustees is also important. Your trustees should be readily accessible—a delay in obtaining a trustee's signature might prejudice the interests of the beneficiaries.

People often choose their spouse as trustee; after all, your spouse is the person who knows and probably understands your wishes better than anyone. In the majority of cases there is no doubt that this is a wise choice. Nevertheless, some marriages do fail and, if the split is acrimonious, life is not made any easier by your spouse being the trustee or co-trustee of a trust that you have set up. After all, the trustees can only act unanimously, a trustee cannot be forced to resign, and legal action (which is usually expensive) would need to be taken to have an unco-operative trustee removed. It is, however, possible to include, within the trust deed, the power to have a trustee removed in certain circumstances.

11.4.4   Who can be a trustee?

Any individual, limited company or other corporation may be appointed as trustee. There is nothing to prevent a beneficiary being a trustee, although it would perhaps be sensible to ensure that a beneficiary was not a sole trustee.

Trust corporation

A trust corporation is a company that is empowered to act as a trustee; it is likely to charge a fee for accepting the appointment, and for managing the trust and may also charge a fee when assets are withdrawn from the trust.

Public trustee

The Public Trustee is a public corporation whose main function is to administer private trusts; it can be appointed to act in the same way as a private individual. The Public Trustee will always impose a charge for acting, its remuneration being based on the value of the trust property.

Custodian trustee

A custodian trustee's function is simply to hold the legal title to trust property, leaving the administration of the trust in the hands of managing trustees. A custodian trustee (eg a bank) is usually appointed so that there is no need for any further appointment of new trustees to look after the trust deeds and securities.

11.5   The appointment, retirement and removal of trustees

Statutory provision is made in the Trustee Act 1925 for the appointment and removal of trustees.

11.5.1   The appointment of trustees

Trustees must be appointed on the creation of a new trust and may also be appointed during the continuance of an existing trust. The appointment of trustees is always made by deed (ie it is not sufficient merely to write a letter appointing someone as trustee). Sometimes the Court will have to make the appointment itself when there is no-one else capable of making the appointment.

You, as the settlor, will usually appoint the first trustees. You could declare yourself the sole trustee of the trust or you could appoint yourself and others to be the first trustees. Also, you may want to retain the right to appoint future trustees.

If new trustees need to be appointed, there may be provision for this within the trust instrument itself; if not, there is statutory power within the Trustee Act.

The total number of trustees must not exceed four. Where a trustee wishes to retire, but there is no proposal to replace him as trustee, he can retire if there are at least two trustees remaining. As a rule of thumb, a minimum of two trustees is desirable, to give the beneficiaries adequate protection.

11.5.2 Retirement of trustees

It is possible for trustees to retire from office. They could do so under the terms of the trust itself, under the statutory powers of the Trustee Act, by obtaining the consent of all the beneficiaries (who must be over 18 and absolutely entitled to the trust property), or by obtaining the consent of the Court. Trustees may retire provided there remains a minimum of two trustees (or a trust corporation) after their retirement and provided they obtain the consent of the remaining trustees.

11.5.3 Removal of trustees

A trustee may be removed from office either under a power within the trust itself, under a statutory power within the Trustee Act or by the Court. A statutory power of removal can be used where trustees remain outside the United Kingdom for more than 12 consecutive months, where they refuse to act, or where they are either unfit to act or are incapable of acting.

11.6 The duties and responsibilities of trustees

If you accept an appointment as a trustee, you are bound to participate in the administration of the trust and you will, of course, have to take on certain responsibilities:

(1) You must become familiar with the terms of the trust. If you under-

take a transaction which is not permitted under the terms of the trust, this would constitute a breach of trust. It is clearly important, for example, that you do not distribute trust funds to the wrong beneficiary.

(2) Where you are a new trustee appointed to an existing trust, you must be satisfied that there has been no prior breach of trust. Although you cannot be held to be liable for such a breach, you could be acting in breach of trust yourself by not enquiring.

(3) In the administration of the trust, (as an unpaid trustee), you must use as much care as any prudent person would use in the management of their own affairs.

(4) On occasions, the trustees may not be sure how they should act. In such cases, they should apply to the Courts for guidance or direction.

(5) All acts and decisions of the trustees must usually be unanimous— unless the trust specifically allows it, it is not possible for a decision of the majority to bind all the trustees (although this is the case in Scotland).

(6) Trustees are responsible for keeping the Inland Revenue informed about the trust and for making annual returns.

11.6.1 Investment policy

On matters of investment policy, the trustees' bible is the Trustee Investments Act 1961 (although its provisions are often expressly varied by the trust itself). The main principles laid down by the Act are:

(1) Trustees must consider the interests of the beneficiaries at all times. If, for example, there is a life tenant and remaindermen then, as well as taking steps to preserve the income of the life tenant, trustees must also take account of the need to preserve the capital for the remaindermen.

(2) Trustees could be in breach of trust if they do not take all practicable steps to reduce risk by diversification.

(3) Trustees must take proper advice about specific investments.

(4) The Act states that at least half the trust fund should be invested in 'narrower range' investments (eg bank and building society deposits, gilt-edged securities, most National Savings products and certain debentures) with the balance in 'wider range' investments (such as unit trusts and also ordinary shares that meet certain criteria).

Usually, trust deeds give express powers of investment overriding the provisions of the Act but that does not remove from trustees a duty of care over the investments in the trust ie the principles in the Act still hold true. If the terms of the trust do not override the provisions of the Act then the only investments you may consider are those certified as 'trustee investments'.

11.7   The rights of beneficiaries

Generally speaking, as a beneficiary, you cannot interfere in the administration of the trust; all you can do is anticipate the benefits which the trustees will eventually forward to you. However, that is not the final word as the law does give beneficiaries some rights outside the strict wording of the trust.

(1)   Beneficiaries often wish to have some say in the control of the trustees' discretion, particularly in the field of investments and the allocation of discretionary trusts. The trustees are bound to take note of any representation that is made to them by the beneficiaries, although ultimately any decision will have to be taken by the trustees alone.

(2)   It is possible, in certain circumstances, for the beneficiaries to bring a trust to an end. Put simply, if there is a sole beneficiary under the trust who is of a sound mind and over the age of 18, or if there are two or more such beneficiaries who are all in agreement, they can bring the trust to an end irrespective of the wishes of the trustees or the settlor.

(3)   If you consider that the trust is not being properly administered, you may apply to the Courts either for the determination of a specific question or for an action for general administration of the trust.

(4)   You are entitled to inspect deeds and documents relating to the trust and to be provided with information about the trust including copies of the accounts.

11.8   Trusts in practice—an example

A couple have three adult children and seven grandchildren. Their house is worth about £200,000, they have investments (mainly in shares and unit trusts) totalling approximately £40,000 and they have about £20,000 in a building society deposit.

The husband is a successful businessman who has built up a small printing business of which he is the principal shareholder; the company is worth something in the region of £500,000. He has a good pension plan and a lot of personal life assurance.

He has decided that he would like to make arrangements for the following:

(1) To make effective provision for his wife on his death (she has already made it clear that she is not interested in the business).
(2) To prepare for any inheritance tax that might be payable on his death.
(3) To ensure that his business is divided fairly between his children in a tax-efficient way.
(4) To help with the education and future careers of his grandchildren.

Providing for the family

He has agreed with his wife that, in view of the amount of personal life assurance already arranged, she will only require the income from the investments and capital that he was going to leave. He therefore creates a trust in his will giving her the right to receive the income from the total investments for as long as she is alive and then, on her death, for the portfolio to pass to the children. This will come into effect on his death; until then, he continues to own the investments outright.

The type of trust is an interest in possession trust with the life interest belonging to his wife and the reversionary interest belonging to the children.

Preparing for inheritance tax

He intends to provide the funds to pay any eventual inheritance tax bill in the future, rather than gifting all of his property during his lifetime (he also has to take account of the fact that his life assurance will provide capital on his death and this will almost certainly increase the estate of his wife on *her* death). He arranges this through a joint life, second death, whole-of-life policy on the lives of himself and his wife and, to ensure that the proceeds do not fall into the deceased's estate at the second death, the policy is written in trust with the children as beneficiaries.

Looking after the business

A large part of the husband's wealth consists of his shares in his business. He understands that one way of reducing his inheritance tax bill (and at the same time helping his family) would be to transfer some of his shares to his children now. However, like many proprietors of family businesses he does not wish to relinquish control.

He puts the shares into a discretionary trust for the benefit of his children, appointing himself and/or his professional advisers as trustees. Provided the value does not exceed the nil rate band, there will be no inheritance tax liability at the time. Of course, as trustee, he must act in the interests of his beneficiaries and not just himself (this is doubly important to avoid any suggestion that he has retained an interest or is deriving some benefit from the shares).

Educating the grandchildren

He is also keen to help with the education and future career developments of his grandchildren. By transferring a block of his shares in his company to an accumulation and maintenance trust of which his grandchildren are the beneficiaries, the dividends received by the trustees could then be used to cover their school fees. The personal allowances of the grandchildren may well mean that no income tax is ultimately paid on these dividends. The shares will, of course, become the property of the grandchildren at some time in the future but the trustees have absolute discretion over when that happens.

11.9   Anti-avoidance legislation

Setting up a trust can be very beneficial from the point of view of tax planning, particularly in relation to inheritance tax. There may also be some benefits from the point of view of income tax and capital gains tax. Here, however, there is a range of anti-avoidance provisions in place to make sure that the trust is a genuine settlement and not one from which you may benefit. It is an area where you need professional advice; the broad thrust of the provisions is as follows.

(1)   If you set up a trust where you and your wife *may* benefit, then you may be liable to income tax on income earned by the assets of the trust. If the trust wording is not clear on whether or not you may benefit, the Revenue may well tax you on the income if it believes you *could* benefit. The effect of this legislation is that the benefits of independent taxation (see 8.5) are not obtained by putting capital in trust for your wife. The legislation also has implications for deeds of variation (see 9.4.5).

(2)   Setting up a trust for your unmarried minor children, including adopted and illegitimate children, will mean that, in most cases, you will be liable to income tax on the income (though this does not apply in the case of bare trusts if the income is not distributed before the child reaches the age of 18).

(3)   You may also be liable for income tax (even if you are expressly excluded from benefiting from the income) if you receive capital payments from a trust set up by you which has undistributed income.

(4)   If you set up a trust where there are any circumstances whatsoever whereby you or your wife could benefit from capital or income then you will be liable for paying the capital gains tax on any gains made by the trust. This could have a significant impact as the retention of only a very small interest in the trust could make you liable for tax on possibly considerable gains that you did not (and perhaps could not) enjoy.

In the vast majority of cases, you will be able to claim back any tax that you have paid from the trustees. The underlying point is that the tax will be based on your personal circumstances (eg it will take your allowances and other income into account) with the overall objective being to ensure that you cannot set up a trust in order to 'shelter' income or capital gains from tax.

12 Retiring abroad

The growth in foreign travel over the last 30 years has led to an increasing number of people buying property abroad, usually for holidays. This became a veritable flood when exchange control restrictions were lifted in 1979. Today, a considerable number of people own property abroad, with France and Spain being two particularly popular areas. Many of these people are retired; for them, the opportunity to get away from the long British winters has proved to be irresistible.

There is, of course, considerably more to retiring abroad than indulging in a warmer climate. This chapter looks at the following areas:

(1)   The emotional factor
(2)   Buying property abroad
(3)   Domicile and residence
(4)   UK taxation
(5)   Pensions
(6)   Tax in a foreign country
(7)   Investment considerations
(8)   Health and social security
(9)   Returning home
(10) Conclusions.

12.1   The emotional factor

This might seem a slightly odd way to start this chapter but the fact is that some people do seem to make decisions about living abroad or buying property abroad for entirely emotional reasons without really considering any of the practical problems. After a pleasant holiday or two in an area with which they have become familiar, people have been known to make, in the warmth of the afternoon sun, a decision which will affect their lifestyle for some years to come and over which they would deliberate for many weeks if they were at home. The decision to sell up and move to another part of the United Kingdom would be a long and carefully thought-out process. The decision to sell up and move to say, Spain, has been taken over a few drinks.

Many people do successfully transport themselves to another country and adapt to a new way of life. Others do not and discover that they have made an expensive mistake, finding themselves unable to come to terms with a different culture, different laws, different taxes, different standards, different health systems and different attitudes towards retired people—all conducted in a different language. After many years of experience, they know how the United Kingdom works. They know how to get things done, how to complain if things go wrong and how to sort out an incorrect gas bill or electricity bill. In a foreign country, they have to learn new tricks of social survival and a fair proportion of them find that it is too much hassle.

The overall message is to explore your own thoughts about why the prospect of retiring abroad is so attractive. If you are really enthusiastic about learning new skills and absorbing new ideas, then you may well be suited to life in a warm climate. But if it is just the climate that attracts you, then it might be an idea to think again.

12.2 Buying property abroad

The growth in overseas property buying in recent years has been quite staggering and not just from the point of view of the United Kingdom. The general increase in prosperity throughout Europe has meant that more and more people from northern Europe are looking for a holiday or retirement home in the sunnier parts of southern Europe. The Mediterranean coastline is now dotted with apartments and villas, with Spain being a favourite spot.

Compared to buying property in the United Kingdom, buying property abroad seems to be simplicity itself. There are no end of people in the United Kingdom eager to sell you property abroad and they may even fly you out there and put you up in an hotel at their expense. Provided you are prepared to limit your search in this way, there are a number of reputable agencies that will provide you with an excellent service. But be warned; buying a property in, for example, Spain, may appear to be little different from buying property in England when you are having it explained to you at an hotel seminar in Tunbridge Wells. However, the reality is:

(1)   You are buying a house in a foreign country.
(2)   The contract may be in a foreign language.
(3)   The legal system is totally different.
(4)   The bureaucracy in some foreign countries can seem almost medieval at times.
(5)   Different countries have different tax systems.

Provided you follow the rules, you will have no problems but you can more or less guarantee a layer of extra complication which will occasionally make buying a house in the United Kingdom look like child's play. Things will obviously be easier if you learn some of the local language.

The golden rules are not to cut corners and be prepared to pay for expert advice and help. If you were buying a house in the United Kingdom, you would expect to pay a solicitor to ensure that all the legalities were tied up, but some people still buy houses abroad without a thought for the legal niceties. It would be beyond belief if it didn't happen all the time.

12.2.1   A home for retirement

It is not at all uncommon, of course, to buy property now with a view to using it as a retirement home when you finally do retire. The important thing to bear in mind, if this is your aim, is to ensure the property is suitable for you when you do retire. On the rushed inspection flight, it is all too easy to buy the perfect property now but one which could well become a problem for you in the future. If you intend to buy property in the sun for use as a home when you retire, you should consider it from all manner of viewpoints to make sure it is going to be the kind of property that will suit you when you retire.

Two very important considerations are the weather and maintenance. If you go out to look for your retirement home in the fine weather, it is tempting to believe that it is fine all the time. But the coastline at the western end of the Mediterranean, whilst it can have fine warm days in winter, can also have some very cold days, some very wet days and some very windy days. People who have built houses in more exposed positions (eg on hillsides to get those wonderful views) have found to their cost that log fires, and even central heating, to keep warm in the winter have been of more value than air conditioning to keep cool in the summer.

Also, do keep a very careful eye on future maintenance. Don't believe that just because you have a home in the sun, it won't require looking after. Those white houses look lovely in the sunshine, but they soon get dirty and start to look shabby. They are going to need painting about once every three years.

On the plus side, membership of the EC has meant a general raising of building standards and houses throughout the EC tend to be of much better quality than, say, ten years ago.

12.2.2   The key steps

Unless you know the area where you are going to look for property, you will probably do what most buyers do and go and look 'on spec'. The choice of property is often very wide and, if you are buying new property, you may well find the sales pitch more than enticing. Clearly, you will be able to make your own mind up about the property itself but you should also reassure yourself about the nearest shops, the access to English speaking doctors and dentists, local bus and taxi services, likely future development in the area and so on.

Having decided that you like the area and that the property is also to your liking, you can then start thinking about the steps to be taken in actually purchasing the property.

The first thing to do is to engage a lawyer and the general advice is to find a solicitor in the United Kingdom who has experience in property transactions in the area in which you wish to live. The Law Society will be able to advise you on solicitors who can do this. This is a significantly better option than using a local lawyer because there is no guarantee that they will do the job with anything like the attention to detail you are entitled to expect from your United Kingdom solicitor. Your powers of redress in the event of problems may be limited and very difficult to pursue.

Do not be tempted by the deals which appear to save you money, the most popular one being to organise the purchase in such a way as to save you tax. The chances are it will not save you tax in the long run and the immediate benefit may be to the seller.

Do not over commit yourself on the purchase price or running costs. Remember that in addition to coping with domestic inflation you now have to cope with a fluctuating exchange rate and a foreign inflation rate which could well be higher than that in the United Kingdom.

Do not overlook the tax and rates position. If you own a second house in the United Kingdom you will have to take due regard of capital gains tax, inheritance tax and, if you let your property, income tax. The same will probably be true in a foreign country so you will need to make yourself fully familiar with their tax rules as well. You will almost certainly have some taxes to pay when you buy your property and also when you own it.

Finally, do take care and don't sign anything or pay over any money at all until you have sought professional advice. A number of people have lost money in overseas property deals and not just at the hands of foreign companies. Your legal title to property in some foreign countries is considerably weaker than it is in the United Kingdom and the only way to prevent yourself from falling into the many traps is to use competent legal advice.

12.3 Domicile and residence

As soon as you decide to spend any length of time outside the United Kingdom, you will be faced with questions of your domicile and residence. These are important because they will decide the basis on which you are to be taxed. Throughout this chapter, residence will refer to your *tax* residence ie to which Inland Revenue you will be obliged to make tax returns. This is a quite separate concept to your *legal* residence ie gaining the necessary authority to live in the country of your choice. It would, for example, be perfectly possible, in any one tax year, for you to be a legal resident of Spain (because you comply with their requirements to live there permanently) and be a tax resident of the United Kingdom (because of the amount of time you have spent in the United Kingdom in the tax year in question). It may also be possible to be a tax resident in more than one country at a time.

For the purposes of UK taxation, the 'United Kingdom' means England, Scotland, Wales and Northern Ireland. It does not include the Channel Islands or the Isle of Man.

12.3.1 Residence and ordinary residence

These concepts are not defined anywhere in tax law. There are a number of factors which are regularly taken into account when the Inland Revenue determines your tax status but, in complex cases, a final decision will depend on the facts of the case in question.

Residence

You will be resident in the United Kingdom if you fulfil one of two basic requirements.

(1) If you are physically present here for 183 days or more in the tax year. There are no exceptions to this rule. It does not matter if the time is taken up in one long visit or several visits (though the days of arrival and departure are normally not counted).

(2) If you average 91 days or more here *per annum* over a period of four tax years.

Ordinary residence

If you are resident in the United Kingdom year after year (ie you regard the United Kingdom as your habitual home) then you are ordinarily resident here. It is quite possible to be ordinarily resident here but resident elsewhere eg by going on a long holiday and not setting foot in the United Kingdom for a complete tax year.

If you claim that you are no longer resident or ordinarily resident, then it will be up to you to prove it. Inland Revenue booklet IR 20 (*Residents and non-residents—liability to tax in the United Kingdom*) states as follows:

> ... you will normally be asked for some evidence that you have left the United Kingdom permanently—for example, that you have taken steps to acquire accommodation abroad to live in as a permanent home, and if you continue to own property in the United Kingdom, the reason is consistent with your stated aim of permanent residence abroad. If you can provide this, you may be treated as *provisionally* not-resident and not-ordinarily resident from the day after the date of your departure. Normally, this provisional ruling is confirmed after you have lived abroad for a whole tax year, as long as your visits to the United Kingdom since leaving have averaged less than 91 days a tax year.
>
> If you do not have this evidence, a decision is postponed for up to three years. The decision will be based on what has actually happened since you left the United Kingdom. Until then you are provisionally treated as remaining resident in the United Kingdom. You continue to receive tax allowances and reliefs. Your tax bill may be adjusted when the final decision has been made.

12.3.2 Domicile

The implication of domicile is that if you are of UK domicile, you are liable to inheritance tax on your worldwide assets, *regardless* of your residence or ordinary residence (as distinct from income tax and capital gains tax where your liability depends on your residence and ordinary residence).

Domicile is a concept of general law and is determined by a range of factors. Broadly speaking, domicile is where you have your permanent home. It is distinct from nationality or residence. You can only have one domicile at a time. You normally acquire a domicile of origin from your father when you are born, though this may have changed if the person on whom you were dependent at the time changed his domicile before you were aged 16.

Women who married before 1974 automatically acquired their husband's domicile, though they may now change it to a domicile of their choice.

Anybody over the age of 16 has the legal power to apply for a new domicile of choice. However, it is not easy to do and will usually require proof that you have severed all connections with your existing country and intend to settle permanently in a new country.

12.4   UK taxation

The UK income tax system is very wide-ranging. If you are resident in the United Kingdom for tax purposes, then it sets out to tax you on any investment income that arises in the United Kingdom or that is remitted to the United Kingdom. 'Arising' income is income that is actually earned in the United Kingdom, eg interest on a bank account. 'Remitted' income means it could arise outside the United Kingdom but is actually paid into the United Kingdom. Even non-residents are liable to UK income tax on investment income that arises in the United Kingdom.

The most common types of investment income are:

(1) Interest from banks and building societies
(2) Interest from government securities
(3) Rental income
(4) Dividends.

Pensions are regarded as earned income, not investment income. They are dealt with in section 12.5.

12.4.1 Double taxation relief

As a tax resident of a foreign country, you will also have to make tax returns to the Inland Revenue of that country for any income you receive. However, it is not generally the purpose of governments to tax people twice and so the UK government has entered into agreements with the governments of other countries for the purpose of preventing double taxation in respect of the same income. Under double taxation conventions, certain types of income are taxable in only one of the countries and that will generally be the one in which you live.

Even where there is no double taxation agreement, the UK authorities will generally give you a credit (called 'unilateral relief') for any foreign tax which has been deducted from income which you have earned. Fortunately, the United Kingdom has concluded double taxation treaties with the principal countries which people retire to. However, the terms and the taxes covered vary considerably from country to country so it is essential to check on the rules for your particular country of interest.

12.4.2 Income tax

Personal allowances

Under normal circumstances, you are entitled to claim certain allowances that can be deducted from gross income to arrive at the actual level of income on which tax will be levied. The most important of these are personal allowances which are of particular interest to the retired expatriate as it is possible to continue to claim them even though you are no longer resident in the United Kingdom for tax purposes. This is particularly useful if you have income arising in the United Kingdom that you cannot or do not wish to rearrange.

Independent taxation

There could be a good case for dividing up income-producing UK assets in order that both husband and wife can fully offset their individual personal allowances against income arising in the United Kingdom.

Interest from banks and building societies

If you are not ordinarily resident in the United Kingdom and receive interest from a UK bank or building society, you can apply to have the interest paid gross without deduction of tax. You will have to provide a declaration to your bank or building society that you are not ordinarily resident and all future interest will be paid gross (declarations cannot be backdated). If you have a joint account, both account holders must be able to sign the declaration for income to be paid gross.

You should note that the fact that you are receiving gross interest does not of itself mean that you are not obliged to pay tax. You are (because of your domicile) but, by concession, tax is not charged if you are non-resident for the whole of any tax year for which you received gross interest.

Another point to bear in mind is that the need for compliance with Inland Revenue rules is an extra responsibility for the banks and building societies and this is occasionally reflected in high minimum levels of deposits or lower rates of interest for non-residents with on-shore accounts. Some even refuse to pay gross interest and always deduct tax.

Offshore accounts avoid all this as the interest is paid gross anyway.

UK government securities (gilts)

Interest paid on certain British government securities is exempt from income tax provided you are neither resident nor ordinarily resident in the United Kingdom. This applies *only* if you hold a stock at the date that the interest is actually paid (ie it does not apply if you have sold the stock even though the sale may have been 'ex-dividend'). The Inland Revenue is understood to apply a strict interpretation of this rule.

Rental income

If you are living abroad, but own property in the United Kingdom which is being let, there are tax implications for both you and your tenants. Anybody who rents UK property is required to deduct basic rate tax from any rents paid to a non-resident landlord and pay the tax to the Inland Revenue. This is the case even if the rent is paid into a UK bank account. In addition, the obligation to deduct basic rate tax applies to the gross amount of the rent so that if the landlord incurs expenses, he is obliged to make a repayment claim.

The only way of avoiding these problems is for the rent to be collected by a UK agent. Rent paid to an agent is paid gross and the agent then becomes liable for assessment. However, the assessment is on the net amount after deducting allowable expenses, so this provides a valuable cashflow benefit.

The usually allowable expenses would be agent's fees, ten per cent of the net rents for wear and tear to furniture, and interest on mortgages and similar loans (but not overdrafts). The relief on mortgage interest is not limited to interest on the first £30,000 only of the loan provided the property is let for six months of the year and is available for letting all year round.

Dividends

If you are resident in the United Kingdom, you are entitled to a tax credit when you receive dividends (see 6.4.6). If you are a non-resident, you will only get the benefit of the tax credit if you are claiming your UK allowances. If you are not in this position, you will not get the tax credit even though the tax has been withheld from the dividend payment. As the income is potentially liable to tax in the country where you are now a tax resident, there is the real chance of double taxation.

This can be avoided if the other country has a double taxation treaty with the United Kingdom as, under these circumstances, you may be entitled to a tax credit.

12.4.3   Capital gains tax

You will be liable to capital gains tax if you are either resident or ordinarily resident in the United Kingdom, ie the rules are tighter than for income tax. If you leave the United Kingdom during a tax year and cease to be resident and ordinarily resident then, by concession, you are not taxed on gains you make after your date of departure. Provided you remain a non-resident and non-ordinarily resident for the whole of the following 36 months, you will only be liable for capital gains made after you return to the United Kingdom.

The net effect is that if you have assets that are 'pregnant' with capital gains, moving abroad for at least three years will potentially remove all liability to UK capital gains tax (though you still have to abide by the residence rule see 12.3.1). However, this depends on the Inland Revenue applying the terms of the necessary extra-statutory concession and the general view of the Inland Revenue is that such concessions will not be applied in cases where people seek to take advantage of them for tax avoidance. The Revenue practice is, therefore, to charge tax on certain gains realised very shortly after an individual moves abroad if those gains fall in the same tax year.

You may, of course, have a liability to capital gains tax in your new country of residence but you could avoid that if you time your arrival correctly (see 12.6.1).

Double taxation agreements also cover capital gains tax to prevent you being taxed twice on the same disposal. You will generally be taxed in the country where you were resident at the time.

Sale of property

If you are intending to sell your home when you retire abroad, there will not usually be any implications for capital gains tax (on the basis that it is your main residence). However, if you have other property to sell then it will be beneficial to time the sale to take place after your departure and, preferably, in a different tax year. Bear in mind that it is usually the date contracts are exchanged that is the crucial date, not the completion date.

Sale of a business

You will face no liability if you dispose of your shares in a private limited company after you have ceased to be resident or ordinarily resident. However, if you are a sole proprietor or a partner, you may find it more difficult. The chances are you will want to sell it as a going concern which means that the price may well contain a sizable element of goodwill. Unfortunately, even if you are neither resident nor ordinarily resident in the United Kingdom, you are still liable to capital gains tax if you dispose of business aspects whilst the business is still active. You may be unable to convince the Revenue that the business is not active if it is being sold as a going concern in order to maximise the price and the end result might be that you just have to pay the tax.

12.4.4 Inheritance tax

Domicile can have a major impact on your liability to inheritance tax. If you are UK-domiciled then all of your assets, wherever they are situated in the world, fall into the UK inheritance tax net. This is a major liability and needs to be quantified rather than trusting to luck that you will not have a problem. Even if you become non-domiciled, you will still have a liability to inheritance tax on assets that are physically situated in the United Kingdom such as property or investments.

Writing a will

Under international law, where there is a will, the passing of assets from your estate to your heirs is governed by the law of your country of domicile in the case of 'movable' property (such as bank deposits or securities) and by local law in the case of 'immovable' property (such as a house). It is therefore quite possible that the decision of, say, an English Court relating to your overseas home will not be effective in the other country until it has been approved by a Court there. A further point to bear in mind about overseas assets is that not all countries will allow you complete freedom to dispose of your property as you please. In many countries, your children are entitled to inherit a minimum portion of your estate (and will often get priority over your wife) and it is often the case that the incidence of estate duties is according to the kinship of the heirs and the value of their existing assets.

From all this it follows that the administration of an overseas estate can be very complex. One thing is certain; the trouble and expense (in the way of legal fees payable both here and elsewhere) incurred in sorting matters out properly in advance will be a fraction of the time, trouble and expense your heirs might be put to if you don't make a will in the country where you intend to retire to.

12.5   Pensions

The tax treatment will depend on the type of your pension and the country you have chosen to retire to.

State retirement pension

This is always paid to you gross and it will form part of your worldwide income on which you will normally have to pay tax in your country of residence. Living abroad will not normally affect the amount of your pension (but see 12.8).

Occupational pension or personal pension

This will normally be paid to you net of tax at the basic rate but once you have been accepted as a non-ordinarily resident pensioner, you can apply to the Inspector of Foreign Dividends (the address is in chapter 16) to receive your pension gross (or net at a lower rate of tax) when it will be taxable solely in your country of residence. However, if you move to a country that does not levy taxes, you may well find that the Inland Revenue will tax your pension at source.

Your decision to move abroad could also have an impact on the timing of taking benefits if you have not already done so by then. Some countries, for example, do not recognise the concept of the 'tax-free' lump sum and will tax it along with your pension.

Government pensions

Civil service, NHS and armed forces pensions etc are always paid net of UK tax regardless of your country of residence. If there is a double taxation agreement between that country and the United Kingdom, there will usually be no further tax to pay.

12.6 Tax in a foreign country

The main purpose of this chapter is to help you with the UK considerations you must take into account when planning to retire abroad. However, it is clear that tax and investment considerations in your chosen retirement country are equally important. Clearly, a book of this nature cannot deal in any detail with taxation in even the most popular retirement countries but the following are some general principles which will hold good for most countries. If your affairs are complex, you should get advice from a competent financial adviser.

Many countries on the European mainland, principally Spain and Portugal, used to be tax havens. This was not only because tax rates were low but also because the administration was somewhat inefficient. Tax evasion was a way of life and almost to be encouraged. This is no longer the case. Although some tax rates are still lower than their UK equivalent, others are more severe. Also, the authorities are significantly more efficient than they used to be and now insist that you pay your dues.

In addition, the British practice of paying a tax bill some months after the tax return has been filled in is often unheard of abroad. The forms are often designed to be filled in by the taxpayer or his representative and, from the form, it is usually possible to calculate your tax liability. Consequently, when you send in your forms, you send in your cheque at the same time.

12.6.1 Tax status

Domicile

There is no direct equivalent of the UK concept of domicile in most other countries. In inheritance tax matters, your nationality often (though not always) stands in its place. This is certainly the case in most of Europe where, if you are a national of the country concerned, you will be subject to inheritance tax on your worldwide assets but, if you are a non-national, you will be subject to the tax on your locally sited assets only.

It follows that if you are UK-domiciled and therefore subject to UK inheritance tax on your worldwide assets, you will probably be liable for both British and foreign inheritance taxes on your foreign assets. The burden is alleviated slightly by the fact that unilateral relief (see 12.4.1) may be granted in the United Kingdom for that part of your estate which has already been subjected to foreign taxation. This does not mean, of course, that foreign inheritance taxes can be ignored.

Residence

Most countries in the world operate a 'six month rule' so that if you spend 183 days or more in that country during the tax year, you will be resident there for tax purposes. However, you should remember that although the UK tax year runs from April to April, in most other countries the tax year is the same as the calendar year. This means that it is perfectly possible to be resident in two countries at the same time by virtue of the same rule, although the potentially damaging effects of this are usually alleviated by double taxation treaties.

It could also be that timing your departure and your arrival could work to your advantage because the same rule could mean that you are not tax resident in either country for a period of time. By leaving the United Kingdom before April 5 means that you have given yourself the means to be non-resident in the United Kingdom for the whole of the following tax year. By not arriving in your new country until after 1 July, you will also not be regarded as a resident there for the tax year ending on 31 December.

You should also find out if the definition of residence is covered by other factors. Until recently, for example, you would have been regarded as a resident of the United Kingdom if you had accommodation 'available for your use' here (and 'available' was given a very liberal interpretation by the Inland Revenue). This rule was dispensed with in 1993 but other countries are starting to introduce it.

Ordinary residence

There is no direct equivalent to ordinary residence in most foreign tax systems though many have some provision for recognising a degree of permanency in your residence arrangements.

12.6.2   Tax liabilities

Income tax

Unlike the United Kingdom, which taxes resident foreigners differently from (and sometimes more favourably than) its own citizens, most countries make no distinction in their tax treatment between locals and immigrants. Quite reasonably, the tax authorities take the view that if you decide to live in their country, you must expect to be asked to pay the same taxes as their own citizens. As a result, once you move abroad, you can expect to be asked to pay tax on your worldwide income (and usually your capital gains also) whether remitted to that country or not, though you will, of course, be protected by any double taxation treaties.

Capital gains tax

As is now the case in the United Kingdom, it is common in many tax regimes to tax capital gains as income in the year that they are made. Most will also take account of the effects of inflation to ensure that only 'real' gains are subject to taxation. This means, that in the majority of cases, redemption of a capital holding will give rise to a lower overall rate of tax than would the equivalent income.

However, not many countries follow the UK practice of allowing you to realise a proportion of your annual gains free of capital gains tax.

Inheritance tax

In many countries (particularly most continental countries), inheritance tax applies to lifetime gifts as well as transfers at death. More importantly, there is often no inter-spouse exemption as we have in the United Kingdom. This means that if you keep substantial assets abroad, your death could result in your partner receiving a sizable tax bill at a time when there are likely to be problems enough. The rate of tax levied usually depends on the blood relationship between you and the recipients of your estate, with the lowest rates applying to your immediate family and the highest to remoter relations and friends.

You may be able to mitigate the effects of the tax if you keep as much of your estate as possible outside the country by arranging your investments elsewhere ie in one of the offshore 'tax havens' for example.

12.7   Investment considerations

The overall investment strategy outlined in chapter 6 will still be valid regardless of where you live. The position on living abroad is, however, complicated by the interplay of three factors:

(1)   UK taxation
(2)   Foreign taxation
(3)   Exchange rate movements.

With Britain's departure from the Exchange Rate Mechanism and the consequent reshaping of the ERM (ie a widening of the bands to the extent that it is largely ineffective), we have returned to a situation where currency movements are an important factor in planning retirement income abroad. As all your living expenses are going to be in a currency other than sterling, there is something to be said for perhaps increasing the amount of short-term cash and have rather more of it immediately accessible so that you can convert it quickly into your local currency if exchange rates move in your favour.

A number of banks and building societies operate expatriate accounts which enable you to have the benefits of a bank or building society account and to receive the interest gross (but see 12.4.2).

With your other investments, you will want to organise these in the most tax-efficient way. You will be able to make use of some of the tax-efficient short to medium term investments (eg TESSAs and National Savings) with the one exception of personal equity plans which are only available to UK residents.

If you wish to invest in gilt-edged securities, then it may be appropriate for you to invest in one or more of the exempt gilts.

If you decide to invest in any form of asset-backed, income-producing investments, then there would be some merit in investing in UK-based funds but only up to the extent that you are able to claim back tax paid on any income arising from them (ie up to the extent of your personal allowances). In all other cases, it could be more appropriate for you to invest in offshore funds so as to avoid the problems of withholding tax.

In the same way, it might be beneficial to set up an offshore bank account (in the Channel Islands or Isle of Man) as the means of receiving all income. This will then enable you to control the flow of money into your new country without having to reclaim tax paid on UK bank or building society deposits. Clearly, you are also going to require a bank account in your new country but you may find it helpful to arrange that through a bank with offices in both your new country and your offshore choice.

Finally, don't forget that you will have to make tax returns in your new country. Some people find it simpler to engage a local accountant to do this for them (although, in Spain, for example, you can use the services of a *gestor*—literally a 'form filler'—to do the job for you).

Do be advised that the tax collection agencies of most countries to which you are likely to retire to are very much stricter than they may have been. Don't be tempted to cut corners, no matter how much the locals tell you it is the done thing.

12.8   Health and social security

Social security payments (particularly pensions) and medical treatment (particularly the availability of free medical treatment) are important considerations for anybody planning to retire abroad. For the purposes of your entitlement to the various benefits, the world is divided into three areas:

(1)   The European Community, which currently consists of the United Kingdom, Belgium, Denmark, France, Germany, Greece, the Republic of Ireland, Italy, Luxembourg, The Netherlands, Portugal and Spain.

The United Kingdom (for the purpose of health and social security benefits only) includes Gibraltar, but not the Channel Islands or the Isle of Man.

From 1 January 1994, members of the European Free Trade Area are also covered. These are Austria, Finland, Iceland, Norway and Sweden (and eventually Liechtenstein).

(2)   Countries with which the United Kingdom has reciprocal agreements. These are currently Australia, Bermuda, Canada, Cyprus, Israel, Jamaica, Jersey and Guernsey, Malta, Mauritius, New Zealand, the Philippines, Switzerland, Turkey and the USA.

(3)   Any other country.

12.8.1   The European Community

Pensions and social security benefits

As with everything else in life, the position is not particularly simple. If you are drawing any kind of benefit in the United Kingdom, you should get specific advice on the implications of a move to another country.

In general terms, if you retire to a country covered by the EC requirements, you will be under the same obligation to pay national insurance contributions as though you had retired in this country. This would mean that if you took early retirement, it could be in your best interests to pay Class 3 voluntary contributions (see 2.2).

When the time comes for you to receive your pension, you should claim this in the normal way. It will be paid to you in the usual way but normally only either four weekly or quarterly. Payments can either be sent direct to you, or paid into a foreign bank account (or UK bank or building society).

You will qualify for indexation increments and also increased payments for dependants (see 13.2).

In general terms, if you have been receiving any special allowances (for example, attendance allowance and invalid care allowance) then these will not continue to be paid, but you may be able to qualify for a similar benefit in your new country. If you are widowed in your new country, you will be able to claim widow's benefit in your new country. (A full description of all relevant UK social security benefits is given in chapters 13 and 14.)

Health

If you are below State retirement age, you will not automatically qualify for free medical help in your new country (though you may qualify if you are receiving certain allowances in the United Kingdom). You may be able to contribute voluntarily to the state sickness scheme of your new country; alternatively, you may have to take out private medical insurance in the United Kingdom before you leave (some countries insist on this anyway).

Once you qualify for your retirement pension (or widow's benefit), then you and your dependants will generally be entitled to the health services of the state sickness insurance scheme of your new country.

In all cases, you only qualify for health care in the United Kingdom if you are living in the United Kingdom. The fact that you continue to pay UK national insurance contributions does *not* entitle you to health care in your new country at UK expense.

Most important of all, you should consider what will happen to you if you become seriously ill. Clearly, hospital treatment is available but, for more elderly people, nursing and residential homes may be both limited and expensive in other countries.

12.8.2   Non-EC countries

Pensions and social security benefits

You will be obliged to continue to pay Class 3 national insurance contributions in order to qualify for your full benefits. An important point (for men) to note is that you will not get any contributions credited to you when you reach age 60 for any tax year you are a non-UK resident, ie you may have to pay contributions up to age 65.

Your pension can be paid to you in the usual way but you will not get any cost of living increases unless you remain ordinarily resident in the United Kingdom or you go to live in one of the countries with which the United Kingdom has reciprocal agreements (with the notable exceptions of Australia, New Zealand and Canada).

In the case of other social security benefits or allowances, you may be able to continue receiving these if there is a reciprocal arrangement with the country concerned.

Health

It is most inadvisable to rely on the health services of any country outside the EC and you should always make private arrangements in the United Kingdom before you leave. There is no claim against the NHS for any treatment you receive abroad.

12.9 Returning home

If it was odd to start this chapter on the emotional aspects, it may seem even odder to end it with a section on returning home. In many ways, however, facing up to the problems of returning home is one of the most important aspects of taking the decision to go abroad in the first place.

For all its faults, Britain is home to most of us. It is the place where we feel most comfortable, particularly when things start to go wrong. Increasing frailty, old age and illness can turn a foreign idyll into a nightmare, and in all the advertisements for overseas property, there will always be a fair sprinkling of 'distress' sales, instances where the dream has gone sour and the people concerned want to get home literally at any price.

Living abroad does present problems in particular for your family if you suddenly need their help. A 100-mile car drive may be a nuisance; a 1,000-mile flight may be impossible. The general advice on housing is to think the next stage well in advance. If your current house is getting too big, it makes sense to move into a smaller house while the move is still a relatively simple problem. This is even more true for overseas property. There are plenty of advertisements for overseas property but most of them are developers selling new property. Selling second-hand property in a foreign country is never easy and it is extremely difficult indeed to do it successfully from the United Kingdom.

Plan your departure carefully—but plan your return with even greater care and give yourself both time and room to manoeuvre.

Many people, for example, really do pull up their roots and move away only to wish they had retained a base in the United Kingdom to which they could return. It is no good relying on sons and daughters to keep a room open for you—a new arrival in their family may mean the room being taken up for more immediate purposes. Retention of property may well be the best option; even a small property in the United Kingdom is likely to maintain its value in real terms. If you sell up and move away completely, you might find it very difficult to return at a later date and get back into the property market.

12.10 Conclusions

Overall, moving from the cold winters of the United Kingdom to the warmth of, say, the Mediterranean, has a lot of attractions for many people—but it is certainly not a decision which should be taken hastily. If you have been going on holiday to the same part of Europe for many years, you will have grown used to it and it could just be the place for you to retire. But retiring there and living there full time is significantly different from spending a few weeks once a year there. Providing you can cope with the overall changes, life in a warm climate can be very motivating and extremely pleasant. But if you are just going for the cheap drink and low taxes, it might be best to think again.

Useful reading matter

The Allied Dunbar Expatriate Tax and Investment Guide gives more detailed information on investment and other matters affecting expatriates. It can be obtained through any bookshop.

Inland Revenue leaflet IR 20 (Residents and non residents) gives detailed guidance on the taxation implications of living abroad. A copy can be obtained from your local tax office.

DSS booklets SA 29 and NI 38 give information on social security matters within the European Community and outside the Community respectively.

13 The payment of State pensions

In this and the next two chapters, the topics to be covered will be those affecting people approaching or at retirement age. This particular chapter looks at the various factors that can affect the amount of State retirement pension that may be claimed by people of State retirement age, and the way in which certain other State benefits may have an interaction with their State pension. The subject is dealt with under the following headings:

(1)   Introduction
(2)   Increases to State pensions
(3)   Deferring your State pension
(4)   Married women
(5)   Widows and widowers
(6)   The impact of other benefits on your pension
(7)   Summary table.

13.1   Introduction

When the time comes to draw your State pension, there are a number of factors which could have an influence on the amount you are eligible for. There are even circumstances under which you may decide not to start drawing your pension or even to stop it once you have started to draw it and to restart it at a later date. In addition, you may be claiming certain other State benefits as you approach retirement age and you will have to decide whether to continue with these other benefits or to stop them and start drawing your pension instead.

As with everything else in the social security system, the position is not at all straightforward and it will take some digging around to find out all the relevant facts. Some benefits will affect your entitlement to other benefits, your entitlement to some benefits will be affected by your level of other income (and, in some cases, the income of your wife or partner) some benefits will be taxable, others not and so on.

What follows can only be taken as an outline guide to the benefits on offer and the conditions that have to be fulfilled if you are to claim any of them. What is important are the options that may surround what appears to be, at first sight, a straightforward situation. It may, for example, seem obvious to take your State pension when you can. However, in certain circumstances, that may not be the best thing to do because, by doing so, you may lose other benefits that are of better value.

This is certainly an area where you will have to ask the way and, such is the complexity of the system, the DSS have had to ensure that a small army of people is gainfully employed, up and down the country, in doing nothing more than answering questions. You may also find the answers to most of your questions in the array of booklets and brochures published by the DSS. You may well need a handful to answer more complex questions because the level of cross-referencing and cross-dependency between benefits is quite high. Age Concern also publish a useful booklet which helps to explain the benefits entitlement of older people.

13.1.1 The terminology and other background points

Category A pension

At retirement age, you will entitled to the basic retirement pension and, possibly, an additional pension (eg SERPS). The basic pension (plus, if relevant, the additional pension) is called the 'category A' pension. It is based on your own contributions.

In addition, if you have been contracted-out of SERPS at any time, you will receive a pension from your contracting-out scheme coupled, of course, with a correspondingly lower additional pension. (Throughout this chapter, there will be a number of references to the effect of contracting-out of SERPS and the influence of either the guaranteed minimum pension or the 'contracted-out deduction' on any additional pension you might be eligible for. All these are defined in sections 2.8 and 2.9.2.)

Category B pension

Married women, widows and widowers may also qualify for a basic pension (and, where relevant, an additional pension) based on someone else's contributions, ie those of their husband or wife. This is called the 'category B' pension.

In short, your category A pension is based on your own contributions; your category B pension is based on those of your spouse.

13.2 Increases to State pensions

Increases to State pensions can occur in one of five ways:

13.2.1 Indexation

All State pensions (with the exception of the age addition—see 13.2.5) are reviewed annually in line with any increase in the rate of inflation. The increase takes place in April of each year.

13.2.2 Graduated pension

If you are eligible for this benefit (see 2.5), you will receive an extra pension dependent on the number of units you have accumulated. The total weekly benefit is the number of units multiplied by the unit price and this price is also re-valued each year.

13.2.3 Dependency increases

Children

If you are responsible for a child, and claiming child benefit (see below), then you may claim an addition to your category A or B pension. Any increases will be affected by the earnings of your wife or partner living with you if these earnings exceed certain prescribed limits. In this context, 'earnings' includes any occupational or personal pension.

There are also certain limited circumstances when you can get an increase if someone is looking after the child on your behalf.

Child benefit is a tax-free weekly cash payment for anyone who is responsible for a child (or children) regardless of income or national insurance contribution record. It is payable for any child under 16 (or up to 19 if they are in full time education). The rates for second and subsequent children are slightly lower than the rate for the first child.

Being responsible for a child means that, in normal circumstances, the child is living with you and is dependent on you. This would mean, for example, that child benefit could be claimed by grandparents.

Your wife

You can get an increase in your category A pension for your wife. The amount will depend on whether or not she herself gets a category A pension (or any other State benefits), whether or not she is living with you, and also whether she has earnings of her own above the prescribed limits.

If you are unable to claim a dependency increase for your wife because her earnings are too high, it might be that you would still be better taking your pension so that she can claim her category B pension on your contributions.

Your husband

You can get an increase in your category A pension for your husband, but only if his earnings are below the prescribed limits and you were getting an increase of sickness benefit, unemployment benefit or invalidity pension (see 13.6) for him immediately before you qualified for your pension.

In all the above three cases, the prescribed limits on earnings levels are different.

13.2.4 Invalidity allowance

If you are getting invalidity allowance shortly before you reach pensionable age, your basic retirement pension will be permanently increased (see 13.6.3).

13.2.5 Age addition

At the age of 80, you will qualify for an additional 25p a week. This has been the same for many years and is not indexed.

13.3 Deferring your State pension

There is no obligation on you to start drawing your pension when you reach State retirement age and there is even a facility to stop drawing your pension and restart it at a later date. In both situations you will eventually get a higher pension as a result of 'increments'.

13.3.1 Delaying your State pension

If you put off drawing your State pension beyond State retirement age, then it will be increased by 'extra pension increments'. You must put off receiving your pension for at least seven weeks; your pension will increase by one-seventh of 1p for every £1 of benefit for every six days (not including Sundays) that you do not claim it. You will not, however, be credited with increments for any period during which you are claiming any of the other regularly paid benefits covered in this chapter. Increments do not apply to the age addition or for any increases for dependants (see 13.2.3).

The overall rate of increase is about 7.5 per cent for each full year that you do not claim it. You may not defer drawing your pension beyond age 70 (for men) or age 65 (for women) which means a total maximum increase of around 35 per cent. The level of increments is due to change in 2010 to coincide with the move to equalise State pension age (see 2.11.1). The rate will rise to around ten per cent a year and it will be possible to defer your pension indefinitely.

You will also be able to delay taking any pension you are entitled to as a result of contracting out of SERPS. You may be entitled to certain increments, except in the case of money purchase schemes where your eventual pension will depend on the value of the underlying fund.

13.3.2 Stopping and starting your State pension

Once you have started to draw your pension, you may give it up temporarily and start again at a later date. You will earn increments during this period, but you may only stop and restart your pension once (and you may not back-date your request). If your wife receives a category B pension as a result of your past contributions, you will need her written permission to give up your pension because she will have temporarily to give up her pension as well (although she will get increments).

It will not usually be possible to suspend any pension you are receiving as a result of contracting out. However, if you are receiving a guaranteed minimum pension from your employer and you return to work with the same employer, it may be suspended and will benefit from increments.

If you temporarily give up your pension because you have returned to work, you will not lose your entitlement to sickness benefit, invalidity benefit or unemployment benefit if you subsequently fall ill or lose your job.

13.4 Married women

Married women can qualify for a category A pension in their own right and may also be able to claim (at some point) a category B pension based on their husband's contributions. What you actually receive and when depends on your respective ages and when you decide to claim your pension.

You will not be able to claim a pension until you reach age 60. If you are not entitled to a category A pension or graduated retirement benefit, you will not get any benefit at all until your husband reaches 65 or until he actually decides to take his pension.

If you are only entitled to claim a category B pension on the basis of your husband's contributions, you may put off drawing your pension and get increments even though your husband decides to draw his category A pension. If, however, your husband decides to defer his pension then you will be unable to draw your pension in the meantime, though you will, of course, qualify for increments. It was taken by the DSS that you would disqualify yourself from increments if you started to draw any graduated retirement benefit to which you were entitled but the Courts have ruled that this is not the case.

If you are entitled to a category A pension in your own right, you may take it, but your category B pension will not be payable until your husband decides to take his own pension and will not benefit from any increments in the meantime. If your own pension is small, therefore, it might make sense to forgo it, so that you can earn increments on the category B pension based on your husband's contributions.

If you wish to give up your pension temporarily, you must give up all your pension, including any category B pension (although your husband will not need to give up his category A pension).

13.5   Widows and widowers

In considering the potential benefits for a husband and wife, there is a range of conditions that could exist.

(1) Either could qualify for a basic retirement pension in his or her own right though the exact amount will depend on their past contribution record.

(2) Either could qualify for an additional pension and either may at some time in the past have contracted out of SERPS and so be eligible for a guaranteed minimum pension or the benefits from a money purchase scheme.

(3) Either could potentially qualify for a category B pension based on the contributions of the other.

(4) Either could qualify for graduated retirement benefit.

If one of them dies, then the pension payable to the survivor could be a mixture of all these elements. The legislation sets out to ensure that the survivor does not lose out on any benefits but is also designed to ensure that they do not profit. The effect is that some, but not all, of the deceased's benefits will go to the survivor with the greatest impact being on any additional pension that they might be eligible for.

13.5.1   Widows

Widows will be entitled to a basic pension, but the precise rules depend on whether they were widowed before or after age 60. They will also be entitled to additional pensions and benefits not only from their own past contributions but also from their husband's past contributions. There is a range of benefits payable to widows (see 13.6.4) but none of these will usually be paid if you take your retirement pension.

Widowed before age 60

At age 60, you have a choice of doing one of three things:

(1) You may claim your pension; or
(2) You may continue to receive any widow's benefit until you wish to claim your pension (or until you reach age 65); or
(3) You may put off your pension, give up widow's benefit and get increments on your pension until you do decide to claim it (or until you reach age 65).

You may be entitled to your own category A pension and also a category B pension from your late husband's contributions. You can qualify for both but only up to the amount of a single person's pension.

You will also be eligible for an additional pension if either you or your husband had contributed to SERPS. If, in the past, you have contracted out of SERPS you will get your own benefit from your own contracted-out scheme and you will suffer a contracted-out deduction from your additional pension.

If your late husband had contracted out of SERPS, you will get a benefit from his scheme as follows:

(1) If he was a member of a scheme paying a guaranteed minimum pension, you will get half the guaranteed minimum pension to which he would have been entitled.
(2) If he was a member of a money purchase scheme, you will get the widow's pension from that scheme. If you yourself are a member of a contracted out scheme, the value of the benefit you receive from your husband's scheme will be added to your own contracted-out deduction, ie your own additional pension will be reduced.

You will get your own graduated retirement benefit, if relevant, and half of your late husband's entitlement, if relevant.

You will also qualify for a widow's payment (see 13.6.4).

Widowed after age 60

You will be entitled to a category B pension based on your late husband's contributions. If you are also entitled to a category A pension in your own right, the two basic pensions will be combined but may not exceed the single person's basic pension.

You will also be entitled to the relevant proportion of your husband's entitlement to any contracted-out benefits or graduated retirement benefit (see above).

If your husband was not entitled to a pension when he died, you will get a widow's payment (see 13.6.4).

13.5.2 Widowers

If your wife died before you were aged 65 (or after you were aged 65, but before your wife was aged 60), and your own category A pension is not at the full rate, it may be possible for your late wife's contributions record to be taken into account. You will also be entitled to a proportion of her benefits from a contracted-out scheme. Normally, these benefits will not be deducted from your own additional pension.

If your wife died when both you and your wife were of pensionable age, you may be entitled to a category B pension (based on your wife's past contributions) in addition to your own category A pension but only up to the level of a single person's pension. You will also be entitled to half of any of her graduated retirement benefit.

If she was receiving benefit from a contracted-out scheme paying a guaranteed minimum pension, you will be entitled to half the benefit and this will be added to your own contracted-out deduction. If she was receiving benefits from a money purchase scheme, you will be entitled to a pension from the scheme but the amount will not be included in your contracted out deductions.

13.6 The impact of other benefits on your pension

There is a range of other State benefits that you may be receiving when you reach State retirement age and that could be affected if you start to take your State pension. Under certain circumstances, you may be better off not taking your pension immediately. This position may not last for very long as the Government is reviewing unemployment benefit, sickness benefit and invalidity benefit.

The benefits covered in this section are as follows:

(1) Unemployment benefit
(2) Sickness benefit
(3) Invalidity benefit
(4) Widows' benefits
(5) Invalid care allowance
(6) Miscellaneous aspects.

13.6.1 Unemployment benefit

This is a taxable weekly cash payment, payable for up to a year. It is paid to people who normally work for an employer but who have lost their jobs. It is related to the number of Class 1 national insurance contributions you have paid or been credited with. To get unemployment benefit, you must be capable of, available for and actively seeking work.

If you are over pensionable age, and working but have become unemployed, you can claim unemployment benefit. You cannot, however, claim it more than five years after pensionable age. You will also lose benefit when you claim your pension.

If you are over 55 and receiving an occupational or personal pension of more than £35 per week, unemployment benefit is reduced by 10p for every 10p that your private pension exceeds £35. From April 1994, that would eliminate unemployment benefit if your private pension was over £92 a week.

Unemployment benefit is due to be replaced in April 1996 by a 'job-seeker's allowance' which will be paid for only six months.

13.6.2 Sickness benefit

This is a tax-free benefit payable if you are unable to work due to illness or disability for at least four days in a row (not including Sundays). It is related to the number of Class 1 National Insurance contributions you have paid or been credited with. If you do not have a contribution record that would entitle you to a full basic pension, you will not get full sickness benefit.

If you are employed, your employer will normally pay you statutory sick pay (SSP) for up to 28 weeks. If you are not entitled to SSP, or it stops, and you are still sick, you can claim sickness benefit for the balance of the 28 weeks.

If you are still sick after 28 weeks, you will become eligible for invalidity benefit (see below).

You would also be eligible to claim sickness benefit if you are self-employed, non-employed or unemployed (but not if you are claiming unemployment benefit).

If you are over State retirement age, you will remain eligible for sickness benefit if you defer your pension, or if you temporarily stop drawing your pension.

You may go on claiming sickness benefit if you are entitled to a retirement pension, but decide not to draw your pension. However, if the basic pension to which you are entitled would be less than the benefits you are claiming, then you will get a reduced rate of benefit, ie there is no specific advantage to be gained by not taking your pension.

Two factors that should be taken into account in your thinking are that, on the one hand, sickness benefit is tax-free (unlike your retirement pension) but, on the other hand, you will not get any increments to your pension while you are claiming sickness benefit.

13.6.3 Invalidity benefit

This is a tax-free benefit and is made up of four factors:

(1) Basic invalidity pension
(2) Additional invalidity pension
(3) Invalidity allowance
(4) Dependency increases.

Basic invalidity pension

This is the crucial benefit because, if you do not qualify for it, you will not qualify for any of the other parts of invalidity benefit.

In simple terms, if you have been entitled to sickness benefit (which, in turn, depends on your contribution record) during a total of 28 weeks and you are still unable to return to work, sickness benefit stops and you become eligible for the basic invalidity pension. If you receive statutory sick pay from your employer for any period of time, that will count towards the 28 weeks.

Once you become eligible, basic invalidity pension (at the same rate as the basic retirement pension) will be paid for as long as your incapacity lasts but will technically end when you reach State retirement age. However, you may continue to claim basic invalidity pension for a further five years or until you decide to start your pension, if earlier.

There are special rules for some widows and widowers.

Additional invalidity pension

This is an earnings-related pension based on your earnings above the level needed for a basic retirement pension during the period April 1978 to April 1991. If you continue with your basic invalidity pension beyond State retirement age then the additional pension will be reduced by any benefits you receive as a result of membership of a contracted-out scheme.

Invalidity allowance

You may qualify for invalidity allowance in addition to invalidity pension if you were more than five years from State retirement age when you first became unable to work. The allowance is payable at one of three rates depending on your age when you became incapacitated; the amount will be offset by any additional invalidity pension you are receiving plus any guaranteed minimum pension you are eligible for.

When you start to draw your State pension, the amount of any invalidity allowance you are entitled to will be permanently added to your retirement pension provided you were receiving the allowance during the eight weeks leading up to State retirement age. When invalidity allowance is paid with your pension, it is taxable.

Dependency increases

In the same way that you may qualify for increases to your basic retirement pension (see 13.2.3), you may also qualify for increases to your basic invalidity pension, subject to certain prescribed limits on earnings.

Interaction with the retirement pension

You may go on claiming invalidity benefit if you are entitled to a retirement pension, but decide not to claim your pension. However, if the basic pension to which you are entitled would be less than the benefits you are claiming, then you will get a reduced rate of benefit, ie there is no specific advantage to be gained by not taking your pension.

The factors that should be taken into account in your thinking are that, on the one hand, invalidity benefit is tax-free but, on the other hand, you will not get any increments to your retirement pension while you are claiming it.

Changes on the way

In his November 1993 Budget, the Chancellor announced that sickness benefit and invalidity benefit were to be phased out and replaced by a new incapacity benefit. The change will start in April 1995 but there will be transitional arrangements for people claiming benefits at the time. The new benefit will be taxable. The proposals are that incapacity benefit will be in two forms:

(1)   Short-term incapacity benefit will be payable for the first 52 weeks of incapacity. The rate for the first 28 weeks will be equivalent to the basic rate of sickness benefit with a higher rate being paid for the following 24 weeks. Payment will continue beyond State retirement age only if the incapacity started before State retirement age.

(2)   Long-term incapacity benefit will be payable after short-term incapacity benefit but not beyond State retirement age. The basic rate will be equal to invalidity benefit but the additional pension is to be withdrawn for all new cases.

The first 28 weeks of incapacity will be based on incapacity for your own occupation; after that, eligibility will depend on your incapacity to carry out any occupation.

The overall effect is a tightening of the rules for eligibility and a general reduction in the amount of State help for longer-term incapacity. This reduction will be most marked in the 24 weeks following the initial 28 week period.

13.6.4 Widows' benefits

The overall range of widows' benefits depends on whether you were widowed before, or on or after, 11 April 1988.

Before 11 April 1988

If you are currently widowed, and were widowed before 11 April 1988, you could well be claiming either the widowed mother's allowance or widow's pension (you cannot claim both at the same time). Both benefits depend on your late husband having paid or having been credited with the required number of Class 1 national insurance contributions at the date of his death.

You qualify for the widowed mother's allowance by having at least one child on whom you are entitled to claim child benefit (see 13.2.3). Once you cease to qualify because you no longer have a dependent child then, provided you are under the age of 60, but not under the age of 40, you will qualify for a widow's pension.

The widow's pension is payable when you are widowed or when you cease to be eligible for the widowed mother's allowance provided you are over 40 at the time. You will get the full rate of pension if you were 50 or older when your husband died and a reduced percentage if you were between 40 and 49.

Both the widowed mother's allowance and widow's pension are taxable.

In addition to these benefits, you may also be receiving an additional pension based on your late husband's earnings from employment since 1978. This will be reduced if, because of your age, you qualify for only a reduced rate on widow's pension.

On or after 11 April 1988

If you are widowed on or after 11 April 1988, you may qualify for widow's payment and either the widowed mother's allowance or the widow's pension. All the benefits are dependent on your late husband having paid or been credited with the required number of Class 1 national insurance contributions at the date of his death or if his death was caused by industrial accident or disease.

The widow's payment is a single tax-free lump sum benefit payable if you are under the age of 60 when your husband dies or if he was not entitled to a category A pension when he died.

The widowed mother's allowance is payable if you have a child for whom you are entitled to claim child benefit or if you are expecting a baby. Once you cease to be eligible for the widowed mother's allowance then, provided you are under the age of 60 but not under age 45, you may be eligible for a widow's pension.

The widow's pension is payable when you are widowed or when you cease to be eligible for the widowed mother's allowance provided you are at least aged 45 at the time. You will get the full pension if you are 55 or over at the date of your husband's death. You will get a reduced percentage if you were between 45 and 54.

You may also qualify for an additional pension based on your husband's earnings from employment since 1978. This will be reduced if, because of your age, you qualify for only a reduced rate of widow's pension.

13.6.5   Invalid care allowance

Provided you qualify for invalid care allowance when you reach State retirement age, you can continue to claim it for a further five years (and sometimes more). It will be reduced by the amount of your basic pension, but not by any additional pension or graduated retirement benefit.

If your wife or partner is receiving a basic invalidity pension (see 13.6.3), he or she will be entitled to a dependency increase for you, but not if you are receiving invalid care allowance. Under these circumstances, and depending on the figures, it might be worth both of you not drawing your pension and also giving up invalid care allowance. Your wife or partner will then get an increase in the basic invalidity pension and, in the meantime, your retirement pensions will be benefiting from increments.

Invalid care allowance is covered in more detail in chapter 14.

13.6.6   Miscellaneous benefits

Reduced earnings allowance

This is a special allowance to which you may be entitled if you cannot return to your regular type of work because of disablement due to an accident which occurred before 1 October 1990. If you take your pension, you will lose your entitlement to it, but you may qualify for a retirement allowance, equal to 25 per cent of the reduced earnings allowance that you were previously entitled to.

Severe disablement allowance

This is a tax-free benefit payable to people who cannot get sickness benefit or invalidity benefit because they have not paid enough national insurance contributions. You can go on claiming this provided you are still entitled to it, but it will be reduced by the amount of any basic pension you receive. It will not be affected by any additional pension or graduated retirement benefit.

Other aspects

Normally, any benefits you receive from the DSS or any other government department will have an impact on your basic pension. In the same way:

(1)   Any benefits paid to dependants will affect any increases you might claim on your pension; and
(2)   Any benefits paid to you will have an effect on any increase to the pensions of those on whom you are dependent.

In every case, it is worth doing the figures because it might be better to claim the dependency increases and leave the pension to gain increments until it is needed.

13.7   Summary table

The table below summarises all the benefits referred to in this chapter and shows whether or not they are taxable or tax-free and whether or not they are dependent upon a satisfactory record of national insurance contributions.

	Taxable	*NIC dependent*
Child benefit	No	No
Unemployment benefit	Yes	Yes
Sickness benefit	No	Yes
Invalidity benefit	No	Yes
Widows' benefits		
Widow's payment	No	No
Widowed mother's allowance	Yes	Yes
Widow's pension	Yes	Yes
Invalid care allowance	Yes	No

	Taxable	NIC dependent
Reduced earnings allowance	No	No
Retirement allowance	Yes	No
Severe disablement allowance	No	Yes

Useful reading matter

The following DSS booklets contain more information on taking State pensions.

FB 6—Retiring? Your pension and other benefits

NP 45—A guide to Widow's benefits

NP 46—A guide to Retirement Pensions

14 Help at home

Many elderly people living at home, often without the income from an occupational or a personal pension scheme, have, as their sole source of earnings, a State pension and the income from their savings. This is not always enough and, particularly if they start to succumb to the physical problems of old age, they may start to need increasing levels of financial assistance.

In addition, as they get older, they are going to require practical help and they may well become increasingly dependent on you. Planning for your own retirement may, therefore, be tinged with increasing demands from others for help in their retirement and you need to know the ground rules.

This chapter looks first at the range of financial and other benefits that are available either from the State or from local government to support people on low incomes and then looks at the position of the carer. The following topics are covered:

(1) Sources of financial help
(2) Income support
(3) Housing benefit and council tax benefit
(4) The social fund and other sources of help
(5) State benefits for the disabled and housebound.
(6) Caring for the elderly
(7) Financial help for carers.

14.1 Sources of financial help.

14.1.1 Introduction

The three main benefits available to people of limited means and whose income is below a level set by Parliament are income support, housing benefit and council tax benefit.

In addition, certain help can be obtained from the social fund.

All the three main benefits are non-taxable and do not depend on the past record of national insurance contributions. They are all means-tested benefits. The general way in which they all work is as follows:

(1) If the individual believes himself to be eligible, he submits a detailed claim containing information about his personal circumstances.
(2) His weekly income needs are expressed as a combination of allowances and premiums for various circumstances. Each person applying for benefit is individually assessed to see which allowances and premiums are applicable in his case. The total of these premiums and allowances (the 'applicable amount'—see 14.1.4) is his weekly assessed need.
(3) The individual's savings are taken into account. If they are above a certain limit, he will get no benefit. Savings below a certain level are ignored; saving between the lower and upper levels will be taken to produce a level of notional weekly income (called the 'tariff income'—see 14.1.5).
(4) The individual's total income (including any tariff income) can then be calculated. If his total weekly income is above the applicable amount, he will get no benefit; if it is below, he will get weekly benefit to make up the difference.

However, nothing is straightforward and the detailed rules covering eligibility for benefits are extremely complex. In addition, the various benefits inter-relate with one another and claiming one may rule out a claim to another. The following pages contain an overview of the key benefits; fuller details can be found in the various DSS leaflets and booklets.

14.1.2 Making a claim

Claims for income support are made to the local office of the DSS; if housing benefit and council tax benefit are also being claimed, they are claimed at the same time. If income support is not being claimed, claims for housing benefit and council tax benefit are made direct to the local council.

All claims will require the disclosure of a good deal of information about the claimant, particularly his financial circumstances. A claim may also involve an interview. All claims are assessed and a decision made; there is an appeals procedure for disputed decisions.

The period covered by a claim for benefits will normally begin on the date the claim is made but, in some cases, claims can be backdated. Benefits will be paid for as long as the claimant is eligible and there is an absolute responsibility on the claimant to notify any changes in his personal circumstances that would increase or reduce his entitlement to benefit.

14.1.3   Who can claim?

The family

The group of people in a claim is called 'a family'. This will include the claimant, his spouse or partner, and any children under the age of 19. If a claimant is unmarried, he will be treated as a single claimant. If he is married, or lives as though he were married with someone of the opposite sex, they are regarded as a couple. Only one person in the family can claim benefit.

Non-dependants

Non-dependants are people who normally live with the claimant. These will usually be relatives but the term does not include members of the family as defined above. Some benefits may be affected if a non-dependant lives with the claimant.

14.1.4   The applicable amount

The total amount of assessable needs (the applicable amount) is a combination of allowances and premiums.

The personal allowance is an amount towards day-to-day living expenses and will be determined by the claimant's age and whether he is single or has a partner.

Premiums are additional amounts paid to people with special needs:

(1)   A carer premium is paid to people who are caring for people and who qualify for invalid care allowance (see 14.7.2).

(2)   The pensioner premium is paid to people aged 60 and over (or to a couple, where one of them is age 60 or over) and is paid at three rates:

    (a)   a basic rate if either person is aged 60 to 74;

    (b)   an enhanced premium if either person is aged 75 to 79;

    (c)   a higher premium if either person is over age 80. This is also paid if either person is over 60 and claiming certain disability benefits.

(3)   There are also certain disability premiums for people claiming disability living allowance or attendance allowance (see 14.5.3).

14.1.5   Capital and income

The assessment of any of these benefits takes into account any resources owned by the claimant and, where relevant, his partner. These resources are split into capital and income.

The first major test is on the total amount of capital:

(1)   If it exceeds £8,000, it rules out any claim to income support.
(2)   If it exceeds £16,000, it rules out any claim for housing benefit or
       council tax benefit.

Tariff income

Any capital or savings between £3,000 and the upper limit is taken to
produce a weekly 'tariff income' of £1 for every £250 of capital or part
of £250. For example, capital of £4,000 is taken to produce an income of
£4 a week, capital of £6,000 is taken to produce an income of £12 a week,
capital of £6,000.01 is taken to produce an income of £13 a week and so
on.

Capital includes all money held in whatever form (but does not include
the surrender value of life assurance policies). It does not include the value
of a home lived in by the claimant unless part of the premises could reasonably be sold off. 90 per cent of the value of any second home (including overseas property) will count as capital unless it is occupied by the
claimant's partner, family member or elderly, sick or disabled relative.

If the claimant is owed money, this may also count as capital as will any
capital that has been disposed of for a purpose not connected with the
claimant's personal welfare. Any capital given away to bring the
claimant within the benefit levels will be taken into account. Personal
possessions will also normally be disregarded unless items have been
bought specifically to reduce the amount of capital for the purposes of
claiming benefits.

Realisation of the impact of the level of savings on notional income
usually induces a sense of outrage. People who see their savings
increased by £250 ask how it is possible that their income can possibly
increase by £50 a year, particularly at a time when interest rates have
fallen so sharply.

This, of course, ignores the fact that the first £3,000 is not taken into
account and also overlooks the fact that the whole purpose of the rules is
to get people to part with their savings, rather than rely on a steady
subsidy from the State when their savings are relatively high. Within that
requirement, the would-be claimant should not dispose of his savings in
the 'wrong' way (eg by giving money to his grandchildren) as such gifts
will be discounted for the purposes of claiming benefits.

Total income

The assessment of total income is not at all straightforward. It is the
money coming in from all sources but, depending on the type of income,
some of it will be ignored totally, some of it is ignored partially (the 'dis-
regards') and some is taken fully into account.

Most social security pensions and benefits are taken fully into account (with the exception of the three benefits being covered here and certain disability benefits). Occupational and personal pensions are also taken fully into account. Any earnings from part-time or casual work will generally be taken into account if they exceed the disregarded level.

Actual income from savings and capital is ignored; instead, the tariff income is taken fully into account (and any income arising from the capital is regarded as capital when it is due).

14.1.6   Hospitalisation

If the claimant (or his partner, or both) has to go into hospital, there is a potential claim to additional allowances to help with continuing household costs such as standing charges. There will generally be no impact on benefits for the first six weeks of hospitalisation but there may be adjustments to benefits paid for up to the following 46 weeks.

After 52 weeks, the claimant will generally be reassessed and treated as a single claimant.

There are different rules for residents in a residential care or nursing home (see 15.7).

14.2   Income support

Income support is generally available to a wide range of people whose resources are below certain levels. For the purposes of this chapter, however, income support will be covered in the context of people aged over 60 and also for people who have to stay at home to look after elderly relatives (see 14.7). The important aspect of this is that the claimant does not have to sign on as being available for work.

Income support is paid only to UK residents but it will continue to be paid during temporary absences abroad, eg for a holiday.

In addition to the allowances and premiums, the applicable amount for income support can also take into account housing costs not covered by housing benefit. These are generally related to mortgage interest payments (ie not capital repayments nor premiums on endowment policies or pension plans) and interest on loans taken out for essential repairs and improvements (eg damp proofing, insulation etc). Benefits may be reduced if it is considered that the housing costs are excessive, for example, that the house is unnecessarily large or located in a particularly expensive area.

Any allowance for housing costs may be reduced if there are non-dependants living with the claimant. The amount deducted will depend on the number and age of non-dependants but no deduction will be made if the claimant or partner are getting either attendance allowance or the care component of disability living allowance (see 14.5.3).

14.3 Housing benefit and council tax benefit

These are social security benefits schemes to help pay for rent and council tax. They are assessed and paid by local councils. They are similar in treatment to income support but the capital levels are different. Someone who is not entitled to income support because of the level of their savings may still be able to claim for housing benefit or council tax benefit.

Conversely, if the claimant does qualify for income support, he will usually qualify for the maximum housing benefit and council tax benefit.

14.3.1. Housing benefit

Housing benefit helps with the cost of rent for accommodation lived in by the claimant. It does not cover mortgage interest payments—these are covered by income support.

The form that housing benefit takes is determined to some extent by the type of accommodation. For private rented accommodation it would be paid as an allowance; for council accommodation, it will result in a reduction in the rent.

In general terms, housing benefit does not apply to owner-occupied houses though some assistance may be granted towards ground rent and service charges on leasehold properties if the original lease was for less than 22 years.

It does not just apply to fixed property, it can also apply to houseboats, mobile homes and caravans.

Housing benefit can only be claimed if rent has to be paid to a landlord; it will not apply if the landlord is a close relative and lives in the same property.

Eligible rent

Housing benefit can be claimed on the amount of rent paid for living accommodation. The local council will want to assure itself that the accommodation is suitable and that the rent is reasonable. If it decides that the house is too large than it may regard it as unsuitable and restrict the amount of benefit. Benefit may also be reduced if the council believes the rent to be excessive.

'Eligible rent' is the money the council regards as being paid for actually occupying the house, ie it would not include any fuel costs and would also exclude certain service charges. Housing benefit is always related to eligible rent and can never exceed 100 per cent of eligible rent.

14.3.2   Council tax benefit

Council tax benefit is a rebate scheme to provide help with up to 100 per cent of the council tax.

14.3.3   How the benefits are worked out

The maximum benefits that may be applied for are 100 per cent of the eligible rent and 100 per cent of the council tax. If the claimant is on income support, he will qualify for the maximum levels of housing benefit and council tax benefit.

The applicant's total needs (the applicable amount) and assessable income are calculated in the usual way. If the total assessable income from all sources (including any tariff income from savings) is less than the applicable amount, then housing benefit and council tax benefit will be paid in full.

If his assessable income is greater than the applicable amount, then lower benefits will be paid. The reduction is based on the difference between the assessed income and the applicable amount and a percentage of this difference is deducted from the maximum benefit. It follows that, above a certain level of assessed income, no benefit will be payable.

Housing benefit

If the assessable income is less than the applicable amount, then the eligible rent will be paid in full. If the assessable income is greater than the applicable amount, then the amount of benefit will be reduced by 65 per cent of the difference.

For example, if the applicant pays eligible rent of £15 per week, has a total assessable income of £87 per week and an applicable amount of £70 per week, then his maximum housing benefit of £15 a week would be reduced by £11.05 (65 per cent of £17). The applicant would receive no housing benefit if his assessable income exceeded £93 per week.

There may be an impact on housing benefit if a non-dependant is living in the same property. If the council believes that arrangements have been made to take advantage of housing benefit and that the non-dependant has greater resources, then it will be the non-dependant's resources that are taken into account. There will be no impact on housing benefit due to non-dependants if the claimant or partner is receiving either attendance allowance or the care component of disability living allowance.

Another important point is that, in certain circumstances, the net income from a home income plan (see 6.11.3) may be regarded as part of the claimant's assessable income.

Council tax benefit

If the claimant's assessable income is higher than the applicable amount, then the amount of available benefit will be reduced by 20 per cent of the difference.

For example, if the applicant is liable for council tax of £6 per week, has a total assessable income of £87 per week and an applicable amount of £70 per week, then the maximum council tax benefit would be reduced by £3.40 (20 per cent of £17). The applicant would receive no council tax benefit if his income was £100 per week or more.

As with housing benefit, council tax benefit may be affected if non-dependants are sharing the same accommodation (but not if the claimant or partner are receiving disability benefits). There would be a non-income related reduction of council tax benefit equal to £1 per week if there are non-dependants living in the same accommodation rising to £2 per week if they are in remunerative work (defined as working for 16 hours a week or more).

14.4 The social fund and other sources of help

14.4.1 The social fund

This exists to help people with exceptional expenses which are difficult to pay out of regular income.

Cold weather payments

These are special payments made to people on income support and qualifying for the pensioner premium. They are paid automatically.

Community care grants

These are discretionary grants available to a range of people who are trying to rehabilitate themselves in the community. They are, for example, occasionally granted to people who are trying to move back into the community after a period of residential care; they could even be granted to help people try to avoid having to go into residential care in the first place.

The grants are not easy to obtain and the means testing is tighter than that for income support (only capital under £500 will be totally disregarded).

Budgeting loans

These are interest-free loans obtainable by people on income support to help spread the payment of large one-off expenses over a longer period.

Crisis loans

These are interest-free loans available to cover emergency short-term expenses. They are also available to people not receiving any other social security benefits and could, for example, cover the period while a claim for income support was being assessed.

14.4.2   Other sources of help

People on income support are eligible for the following NHS benefits:

(1)   Free prescriptions
(2)   Free dental treatment
(3)   Free eye test, prescription and vouchers toward the cost of glasses
(4)   Free travel to hospital
(5)   Free NHS wigs and fabric supports.

Unless they are on income support, people of State retirement age qualify only for free prescriptions. They may also be able to qualify for a whole range of local services available via their local social security office, but there will normally be a charge for these (see chapter 15).

14.5   State benefits for the disabled or housebound

The two principal benefits that are payable to disabled or housebound people are either disability living allowance or attendance allowance. The qualification is essentially based on age. Both benefits are tax-free, are unaffected by the past record of national insurance contributions and are normally unaffected by the level of income or capital resources.

Both also offer a basis of self-assessment in that a medical examination will not normally be necessary to support a claim. However, in assessing a claim, information may be required from the claimant's doctor.

14.5.1   Disability living allowance

This allowance is for individuals who are either under 65 years of age or who are over 65, who started to require help before they were 65 and who claimed before their 66th birthday. It consists of a care component (for people who need help with personal care) and a mobility component (for people who need help in getting around).

To qualify for the allowance, the need for help must have existed for at least three months and must be expected to continue for a further six months. Once granted, the allowance can be paid for as long as the conditions of entitlement are met.

The waiting period is usually waived for people with a terminal illness.

The care component

The care component would be paid to someone who is so severely disabled (physically or mentally) that he is unable to carry out some of the essential tasks of daily living without assistance. There are three rates (lowest, middle and highest) depending on the level of attention or supervision required. Somebody unable to cook themselves a main meal, for example, would be on the lowest rate; somebody requiring frequent attention, day and night, would be eligible for the highest rate.

Terminally ill people automatically qualify for the highest rate.

The mobility component

The mobility component would be paid to someone who is either totally or virtually unable to walk without restriction either because of a direct incapacity (such as physical disability) or because of an indirect incapacity (such as being both blind and deaf). There are two rates (lower and higher). The lower rate will be payable to someone needing assistance in unfamiliar places. The higher rate is payable to someone who is unable to walk, an amputee, deaf and blind or mentally impaired and qualifying for the highest rate of the care component.

Hospitalisation

The mobility component of disability living allowance is not affected by hospitalisation but the care component may be withdrawn after 28 days.

For the position relating to residential or nursing home care, see 15.7.

14.5.2   Attendance allowance

This allowance is for individuals whose need for care begins after their 65th birthday, or who do not claim for assistance until after their 66th birthday. An important point is that the benefit is potentially payable to people who can demonstrate that they have a *need* for help with personal care; they will not be disqualified from benefit if they are not actually receiving the help they need.

To qualify for attendance allowance, claimants must be so severely disabled that they either need frequent attention throughout the day in connection with their bodily functions or need prolonged or repeated attention at night. Also, they must have needed help for at least six months. People with a terminal illness can get financial assistance immediately.

There are two rates of allowances; the lower rate is paid to people who need frequent help with personal care day *or* night, the higher rate is paid if help is needed both day *and* night.

14.5.3   Impact on other benefits

Disability living allowance

If a person claiming income support, housing benefit or council tax benefit is also receiving disability living allowance, his applicable amount will include the higher pensioner premium.

If he is a single claimant, and qualifies for the middle or higher care component of disability living allowance, he will also qualify for the severe disability premium. Couples can only get the severe disability premium if both fulfil these requirements. A person receiving the care component of disability living allowance will not have his housing benefit (or any housing costs incorporated with income support) affected if he shares his house with a non-dependant (see 14.1.3).

Attendance allowance

If a person claiming income support, housing benefit or council tax benefit is also receiving attendance allowance, the applicable amount will include the higher pensioner premium. If he is a single claimant, he will also qualify for the severe disability premium but only if:

(1)   nobody is claiming invalid care allowance for him (see 14.7.2); or

(2)   there are no non-dependants living with him.

If he has a partner, they will only get the severe disability premium if both qualify.

Any reduction in housing benefit (on housing costs incorporated as part of income support) due to non-dependants will not apply if the claimant is receiving attendance allowance.

14.6   Caring for the elderly

14.6.1   Helping the elderly to care for themselves

Many elderly people would prefer the independence and quality of life available through living in their own home and there is a range of services and resources to help them do this. Indeed, the workings of the Community Care Act (described in more detail in chapter 15) means that, if care is required, local authorities set out to provide as much help as possible at home, with residential care being very much a last resort.

The level of help varies across the country, so that first port of call is the local social services office to find out what help is available. Home help, meals on wheels, chiropodist services etc are usually available (although, nowadays, at a cost). Elderly people with specific medical problems might also be able to get access to district nurses and health workers, physiotherapy and occupational therapy. In particularly serious cases, nursing (even night nursing) facilities may be available.

If alterations to the home are needed for people with mobility problems, there may well be advice available through the local authority on how the alterations might best be done.

If substantial alterations are required to a home to make it suitable for an elderly person to remain living there, the local authority may be able to help in a number of ways:

(1) Home improvement grants may be awarded to help people with mobility problems adapt their home to make it more suitable (eg installing a stairlift or wheelchair ramps).
(2) Some councils (and building societies) offer interest-only loans to help with home adaptation with the capital being repaid when the house is sold.
(3) Some councils will install relatively minor safety aids themselves (eg safety rails for baths, or light fittings at low level).
(4) Elderly people receiving income support or housing benefit can apply for grants to cover the cost of fitting insulation or draught proofing to their homes.

14.6.2 Caring at home

It is estimated that over five million people in the United Kingdom provide long hours of care for someone, usually a relative, who is elderly or disabled. Carers tend to come from the age range of 45-65, tend usually to be women and most of them look after people of 75 or older.

Help for carers is much more readily available than it used to be. There are specific social security benefits aimed at carers and there is a growing band of support groups and organisations set up to help.

However, it scarcely needs saying that the decision to take a dependent person into your home and provide them with full-time care is not an easy one to make. The government is, of course, trying to increase the level of help from within the family and to make people less dependent on State resources; the Community Care Act is evidence of this. However, any decisions you take in this regard have to be looked at from the emotional and physical viewpoint as well as the financial.

The emotional implications

If your elderly relative has become so frail that he needs constant care, your immediate reaction may be that home care is preferable to residential or nursing home care and not just from the financial viewpoint. However, that immediate reaction does need to be tested against a fairly objective review of the implications.

Whilst you may get on extremely well with your relative on the basis of infrequent meetings and visits, that is not the same as having someone living in your home for 24 hours a day, seven days a week. Also, he will be there, not on the basis of a visit or holiday, but because he needs care and attention and probably on an increasing basis.

Even close relatives draw apart in terms of their likes and dislikes and having to take a middle course can be stressful to both sides. Your loss of independence won't help.

You will also need to think about the impact on your own family. Their needs can often be overlooked, yet the strain on them could be almost as great as the strain on you.

The physical implications

Your decision on whether or not to accept an elderly relative into your home could hinge on purely physical aspects. Your home may simply not be suitable, due to lack of space, or it could be that changes have to be made. Many elderly people have difficulty with stairs or getting in and out of the bath.

You will also have to consider your own physical limitations. You have to be sure that you are strong enough to help an elderly person, possibly with mobility problems, and that you can cope with the inevitable disruption to your sleeping patterns. Also, whilst there are resources available to help with aspects of personal care, you will have to face the fact that, at sometime or other, you may be called upon to provide a level of personal care that you last faced with your own infant children.

14.6.3   Help for carers

When you come up against the problem of caring for an elderly relative, it is often surprising just how much help is available. The first step is to talk it through with your local Social Services Department—your GP will be in a position to give you an introduction if you need one. Many of the resources available to elderly people will be available regardless of whether they are living on their own or living with you.

The **Carers National Association** is a nationwide organisation which gives help and advice to carers through a network of branches and carer support groups. It has been established for nearly 40 years and has been active in promoting the needs of carers at local and national level. They produce a bi-monthly journal and operate CarersLine, a telephone advice and information service.

Help the Aged sets out to provide support to the elderly, particularly those who are frail or living on limited means. They help with the funding of day centres and hospices (to give respite to carers) and they are also active in home safety and community alarms for elderly people living on their own. They run a SeniorLine telephone information service for elderly people, their relatives, friends and carers.

Counsel and Care provides a nationwide service for older people and their carers. They offer a free advice and information service and issue a series of fact sheets. In certain cases, they are able to offer financial assistance to elderly people who require care and may be able to help with one-off payments for such things as telephone installation, household goods and respite care.

14.7 Financial help for carers

14.7.1 Introduction

The financial implications of living with an elderly person are more than just an extra mouth to feed. Old people need more resources and money and their needs increase as they get older. You will be faced with extra fuel costs, more travel costs and so on.

In addition, a relative moving into your home may end up costing more overall because his entitlement to any social security benefits will be reassessed and your financial circumstances may be taken into account.

14.7.2 Invalid care allowance

Invalid care allowance is paid to those people who are 'regularly and substantially' engaged in looking after a disabled person and who are not gainfully employed (and who are unable to get a job because of their commitment to the disabled person).

You may be able to qualify for invalid care allowance if you meet all of the following conditions:

(1)   The person you are caring for is getting either attendance allowance (see 14.5.2) or the care component of disability living allowance at the middle or highest rate (see 14.5.1).

(2)   You are under 65

(3)   You spend at least 35 hours a week looking after the person

(4)   You normally live in the United Kingdom.

The benefit is taxable. You will be unable to claim invalid care allowance if you earn more than £50 a week after allowance for certain expenses (and this would apply if you were being paid to look after the disabled person).

Once you have received the allowance for 22 weeks, occasional weeks of non-caring will not disqualify you from receiving the allowance, ie you (or the disabled person) could go on holiday for up to four weeks in every 26 without the allowance being stopped.

The allowance will stop once the person you are caring for goes into hospital or residential care and ceases to receive attendance allowance or the care component of disability living allowance.

14.7.3   The impact on other benefits

If you yourself are receiving income support, housing benefit or council tax benefit, then your benefits will be affected if you start to receive invalid care allowance, ie they will be reduced as invalid care allowance counts as your income. However, you will also get the benefit of the carer premium in assessing your applicable amount.

If the person you are caring for qualifies for the severe disability premium, then they will lose this when you start to receive invalid care allowance.

Your maximum entitlement to invalid care allowance will also be affected if you are claiming certain other benefits (eg invalidity benefit or widow's benefit) However, it may still be worth claiming it. If, for example, the other benefit is a widow's pension, you will be credited with national insurance contributions for each week you are claiming invalid care allowance (though not if you have kept the right to pay reduced rate contributions).

14.7.4   Home responsibilities protection

Home responsibilities protection (HRP) is a system for reducing the number of qualifying years you need to work in order to qualify for a basic retirement pension (see 2.3). It applies to both men and women who are carers.

If you are a carer, you will get HRP if you fulfil one of the following two conditions for at least one complete tax year:

(1) You have stayed at home for at least 35 hours a week to look after a person who, for a minimum of 48 weeks in the year, got either attendance allowance or the middle or highest rate of the care component of disability living allowance.

(2) You are able to claim income support on the basis that you are looking after a sick or disabled person.

In the first case, you will have to apply for home responsibilities protection; in the second case, you will qualify for it automatically.

If you are a married woman or widow, you cannot get HRP for any tax year when you have exercised the right to pay reduced contributions, though you may cancel this right if you still have it.

Useful reading matter

The following DSS booklets provide more information on the topics covered in this chapter.

FB 2—Which benefit? A guide to Social Security and NHS benefits

IS 20—A guide to income support

RR 2—A guide to housing benefit and council tax benefit.

FB 31—Caring for someone?

CF 411—Home Responsibilities Protection

15 Caring for the elderly

With increasing age and frailty, the need to turn to residential care of one sort or another for the future support of an elderly person becomes ever more likely. Although there is a wide choice of residential care and nursing homes, finding the one that suits a particular individual is not so simple. Added to that, there is the matter of cost. Residential care is not cheap and the introduction of the Community Care Act has meant that anybody looking to the State (or, more likely, their local authority) for help will find some rigorous means-testing in place. This chapter covers the following topics:

(1)   Introduction
(2)   Care in the community
(3)   Financial aspects of community care
(4)   Sheltered housing
(5)   Residential care homes and nursing homes
(6)   Long-term care insurance
(7)   State benefits and residential care
(8)   Sources of help.

15.1   Introduction

One of the biggest social changes in the United Kingdom is taking place right before our eyes. It is often called the 'demographic time bomb' which, although now something of a cliché, underlines the extent of the change. The balance of the UK population is slowly changing as, with increased standards of health care, more and more people are living into their 80s and 90s. The projected shift over the next 30 years means that, by the year 2025, there will be a 25 per cent increase in the number of people of State retirement age, ie age 65 and over.

One measure of the changing balance of the population is the 'age dependency' ratio. This is the proportion of the population aged 65 and over (ie those most likely to be looking for State help) expressed as a percentage of the population aged 15 to 64 (ie those earning the income out of which the State help is funded). At present, it is 23 per cent. It will dip slightly over the period to 2010 but will rise to over 25 per cent in the year 2020 and to over 30 per cent in the year 2030. At present, the United Kingdom has one of the highest age dependency ratios and this almost certainly is one of the reasons which has led to the intended equalisation of State pensions at age 65 (see 2.11.1). Other countries fare better at the moment but stand to do less well in the future (in Germany, for example, the age dependency ratio could be nearly 45 per cent by the year 2030).

What is even more significant is the proportion of people aged over 85 and their expected rate of increase. At present it is one in 60 of the population. By the year 2010, it will be one in 45.

This has considerable implications for some people planning for retirement as they may well face, not only the problem of providing for their own long-term future, but also the prospect of elderly parents or other relatives becoming increasingly dependent on them as well.

Changes in financial support

Hand-in-hand with this development has gone the realisation by the government that it cannot continue to fund long-term care out of the public purse. In recent years, the level of support for the payment of residential care and nursing home fees has simply exploded; it is estimated that in the ten years up to 1993 (ie the implementation of the Community Care Act), the level of support increased by a factor of 100, from £2.5 million a year to over £2 billion. The Community Care Act pushes the responsibility for this funding on to local authorities and it is quite clear that, in future, the resources are going to have to come increasingly out of our own pockets with public funds providing only a safety net.

In simple terms, the *automatic* provision of services for those people who are too frail to look after themselves is a thing of the past. Some services may not be there and, if they are, they may only be available at cost. The fact that the service is available is no guarantee that it will become available in any specific case; needs are now assessed by local authorities and their decision is final. If an alternative level of care is felt to be desirable, we may have to arrange it ourselves and pay the full cost.

The financial implications are covered in more detail in the next section but, in broad terms, if there is a need for residential care, support from the local authority will only start to become available if the resident's income (including any pension) doesn't cover the fees and their total capital (which may well include the value of their home) is below £8,000.

15.2   Care in the community

Broadly speaking, community care covers the following areas:

(1)   Providing accommodation and welfare services for disabled people (which would include the blind, the deaf and the mentally ill).
(2)   Promoting the welfare of older people, mothers and young children.
(3)   Providing certain after-care and home help services.

The Community Care Act (or, to give it its full name, the National Health Service and Community Care Act 1990) introduced a new regime for the care of needy people with effect from 1 April 1993. The underlying philosophy of community care, in the eyes of the present Government,' means providing the right level of intervention and support to enable people to achieve maximum independence and control over their own lives'.

The practical implications of the new Act are that the responsibility for arranging community care for vulnerable people now lies with local authorities. Local social service departments now have financial control over expenditure incurred in arranging this care and it is they who decide on the type of resources to be provided in any area and for deciding who qualifies for help. This means that those in need, and of limited means, no longer have the right to automatic State support. The provision of care is now dependent on local budgets and the type of care offered may, at times, depend on the political persuasion of the local party in power.

Added to that, the new regulations are a major change for local authorities and, as with any new rules, they take time to settle down and are not always applied in a fair and consistent way.

15.2.1   Local authority assessments

As all care services are to be provided by local authorities, it is they who will decide who is in need of these services. The local authority has the power to assess someone whom it believes has needs, but it has no legal obligation to assess anyone who asks to be assessed. There are circumstances where the local authority would be within its legal rights to refuse an assessment (eg some authorities may decline to assess somebody who does not habitually live in the area). This, of course, is not the same as saying that nobody applying for an assessment will get one. In most circumstances they will, but a local authority is within its rights to refuse an assessment it has not initiated.

A key part of the Act is that the assessment of needs and the provision of services to meet those needs are quite separate. If a local authority is made aware that someone may have special needs, it is obliged to assess those needs. However, it is not obliged to provide the services that will meet those needs (unless the needs fall into an area where the local authority is legally obliged to provide services).

An equally important point is that the financial resources of the claimant or his family are not relevant at the assessment stage. The local authority must first establish the need and then decide whether they can provide the service to meet the needs. If they can, then and only then do the financial resources of the claimant come into contention.

The overall approach of local authorities will be to find the most cost-effective package of services that meets the need, taking into account the personal preferences of the claimant or carer. The route followed is to look first at providing the service in the claimant's own home wherever possible and then to consider other alternatives as follows:

(1) A move to other accommodation, such as sheltered housing
(2) A move to another private household, eg with relatives or an adult fostering scheme
(3) Residential care
(4) Nursing home care
(5) Long-stay hospital care.

15.2.2 The assessment procedure

Generally speaking, you can expect that your local authority will publish guidelines of the criteria it will use for eligibility for assistance and the way it carries out assessments. It will also publish details of the needs for which it accepts responsibility, the type of service available and its charging policy.

The claimant or his representative should always be involved in the assessment though the local authority cannot insist on this. The 'assessment decision' is usually given in writing and will always define the individual's needs in relation to community care services regardless of whether or not those services are available. The 'service provision decision' follows on from the assessment decision by stating what services the local authority will provide in meeting the assessed needs, either in whole or in part.

There is an appeals/complaints procedure for contested assessments.

15.3   Financial aspects of community care

15.3.1   Local authority assessments

An essential aspect of the 1990 Act is that services have to be provided in a cost-effective manner. Government policy is that care should be provided to people in their existing homes as far as possible where this is their preference, but that is only done on the basis that it is cost-effective. The cost of services may also be recoverable in whole or in part from the person receiving the service.

If the service required is residential care of some kind, the local authority is obliged to charge for the accommodation and the charge must be the exact cost of providing that accommodation. The actual payment made by the resident towards the cost of the accommodation depends on his means; the social services department will look at the total income of the resident (including any social security benefits) and also the total amount of the resident's capital. There will then be an assessment of how much the resident can afford to pay towards the total cost of the accommodation, subject to his being left with a weekly amount of at least the 'personal expense allowance' (which, in April 1994, was set at £13.10).

If the resident's capital (which may include the value of his home) exceeds £8,000, it will be assumed that the resident is able to meet the full cost.

The guidelines followed by local authorities in assessing the ability of residents to pay for residential care are those introduced by the Department of Health in the *Charging for Residential Accommodation Guide* (CRAG for short).

Income

All income is taken into account so, for retired people, that would include all pensions income. The local authority is entitled to take into account any income that the resident has deprived himself of in order to reduce his liability to pay for accommodation, together with certain notional income that would be available to the resident if it were claimed.

For many couples, their main income is the husband's occupational pension. The effect of this means-testing could be that the entire pension could be assessed as his with no allowance for the fact that his wife may also depend on it. This is a perfectly legal interpretation of the regulations although local authorities do have the discretion to increase the amount of the personal expense allowance. This would allow the husband to support his wife while he was living in residential or nursing accommodation.

Any payments made to a resident by his wife or former wife will also be treated as the income of the resident regardless of whether they are regular or one-off payments.

Capital

All capital between £3,000 and £8,000 is taken to produce a tariff income of £1 per week for each £250 or part of each £250 (eg capital of £3,250.00

would produce a tariff income of £1 per week; capital of £3,250.01 would produce a tariff income of £2 per week).

Any income earned by the capital (eg interest on a deposit account) is treated as capital from the date it is due.

One of the areas which can cause problems in the assessment is the value of the individual's home. If an individual going into care owns his own home, its value will be assessed as capital. Local authorities cannot force the sale of the house, but they can have a legal charge put on it. Consequently, when the house is eventually sold, they are in a position to claim some or all of the proceeds.

According to the CRAG guidelines, the value of the house has to be disregarded if a relative either aged over 60 or incapacitated lives in the property. Some local authorities nevertheless include the value of the house in the assessment but this is quite incorrect. Local authorities also have the discretion to disregard the value of the property if it is the sole residence of someone who has given up his own home to look after the individual.

It would also be incorrect for an elderly person to transfer ownership of his home to his children, so that its value cannot be eroded by care fees. If a local authority suspects that any assets have been disposed of with the intention of avoiding charges (and the general rule would be to include in this any assets disposed of up to six months before taking up residence), they can regard the disposal as never having taken place and claim some form of compensation both from the person who disposed of the assets and the people who received them.

15.3.2 The financial resources of relatives

A spouse with separately owned assets and savings could be asked to agree to contribute towards the cost of residential care or nursing home fees. He is entitled to refuse but could be taken to Court by the local authority to see what a reasonable contribution would be. The local authority are not entitled *automatically* to include the assets and savings of the spouse in the assessment.

Under most normal circumstances, other relatives should not be in any fear that their own savings or assets can be taken into account when assessing the needs of an elderly relative. However, although they are not obliged to contribute towards residential home fees (even if the elderly person is currently living with them), the final decision on what is best for the elderly person lies with the local authority. If the local authority decides that he is best left where he is (ie living with his relatives) then this decision will have been taken on the basis of what is best for the elderly person; the wishes of his relatives may not carry much weight.

They will have no choice other than to accept the decision; if they feel that they cannot cope with the situation then the only option they will have is to pay the full fees of private residential accommodation.

15.4 Sheltered housing

Sheltered housing used to be the sole preserve of local authority housing departments and housing associations. The objective was to provide low-cost accommodation for rent to those people who could not afford their own homes, but who needed an element of care. This area of provision still exists but the majority of sheltered housing is now provided by private builders. Along with this development has gone a change of name as sheltered housing is more likely to be referred to as retirement housing. The majority of this housing is now owner-occupied.

The usual format is grouped housing for elderly people who, while living their own independent lives in a self-contained home, may be vulnerable because of their age and require some degree of care supplied by a warden. Although the main appeal is to the older-retired, there are increasing numbers of younger-retired (ie age 55+) who see this form of housing attractive from the point of view of being relatively trouble-free.

Sheltered housing schemes are not regulated or controlled in any way; they cater exclusively for people who expect to be fairly independent and getting on with their lives. The warden is there to help, but will often play a part in the general administration of the scheme, and may even be referred to as the administrator or secretary. In some cases the warden has disappeared altogether and has been replaced by a continuously monitored alarm system.

15.4.1 The safeguards

Although there are no statutory safeguards surrounding sheltered housing as such, a number of the builders who specialise in this area do follow various guidelines laid down by their trade or marketing bodies. For example, builders and developers registered with the National House Building Council are expected to follow the NHBC Sheltered Housing Code (though this applies only to sheltered housing in England and Wales). Their definition of sheltered housing is accommodation that is exclusively for elderly people and which forms part of a scheme of grouped, self contained, accommodation provided with a package of estate management services. Under the NHBC rules, every first purchaser of a house has to be given an information pack giving full details of the commitment he is entering into and the services he is entitled to expect and the managing organisation of the scheme must enter into a management agreement which protects the rights of purchasers in the future.

As with any other form of voluntary code of practice, there is no guarantee that membership of a particular trade body or trade organisation means that you will have a trouble-free purchase. Some builders and developers decline to belong to any of these associations on the basis that their own individual standards more than meet the standards required by the trade organisations. When all is said and done, your assessment of a particular retirement housing development can only be by going and seeing for yourself, asking existing residents what they think about it and getting full details of the agreements you are expected to enter into.

15.4.2 The standards of management

The provision of shared amenities is usually paid for through a management fee. This will clearly vary from development to development and can only be assessed in terms of value for money like any other service. The most important aspects to be clear about (once you have decided that a particular scheme is suitable in all other respects) are to what extent you will be liable for charges (and how they will increase in the future) and to what extent you are restricted in the reselling of your property. All of this will be contained in the lease and the management agreement.

An organisation which is very active in the area of the management of sheltered schemes is the Association of Retirement Housing Managers. Members of the ARHM now manage the bulk of private sheltered housing. All their members subscribe to a framework of practice and, at the time of going to press, plans are well advanced to produce an ARHM Code of Practice which will develop and update the NHBC code. It is anticipated that the new code will have the approval of the Department of the Environment.

15.4.3 The problems of leasehold

One of the problems for many people with sheltered housing is that it brings with it (at least in England and Wales) the concept of leasehold property. After possibly many years of owning the freehold of their property (or of paying relatively small ground rents under a leasehold arrangement), they have become used to doing largely want they want with their property (when to paint it, how much to spend on the garden and so on). Moving into sheltered accommodation often means coping with a lease for the first time and this can occasionally cause problems for retired people who now find that, as far as their home is concerned, they are no longer free to make their own decisions. Despite the fact that they may have paid a capital sum for their property, they may find themselves having to pay quite high ground rents as well.

There are also, of course, the occasional stories of unscrupulous managing agents who can, and do, exact quite extortionate increases in service charges and management fees with little or no explanation of the increase. In *Hansard* of 18 January 1994, one such company (after levying increases of nearly 50 per cent) was quoted as saying of its tenants 'we do not speculate on their willingness to pay, they are bound to do so by the terms of their lease'.

Within that arrogant rejection of any responsibility towards leaseholders lies the first step in protecting your position. It is absolutely vital that you get a legal opinion on the terms and conditions of your lease and that you are fully aware of the costs you will be liable for both now and in the future.

Statutory rights

The statutory rights of leaseholders are contained in a series of Rent Acts, Housing Acts, Landlord and Tenant Acts and, most recently, in the Leasehold Reform, Housing and Urban Development Act of 1993. This legislation gives leaseholders and tenants the right to know who their landlord is, to be consulted about the appointment or employment of a managing agent and, in the event of bad management or actions in contravention of the terms of the lease, to request the Courts to allow compulsory acquisition. Qualifying long leaseholders also have the right either to extend their lease or, under certain conditions, to buy it outright. Under the 1993 Act, leaseholders and tenants have a statutory right to information on the composition of service charges and a right to consultation on major expenditure. The new Act also gives the Department of the Environment powers to approve codes of practice for retirement housing management such as the one proposed by ARHM.

However, the right to take legal action over a breach of a lease, and the right to insist on their statutory rights when trying to prise information out of a reluctant landlord, are not what most people look for in sheltered housing. What they want is a relatively trouble-free life and what they hope is that the costs will be fair now and that they will be kept fair in the future. In this area, the Sheltered Housing Advisory and Conciliation Service (SHACS) provides a meeting point for the resolution of problems between landlords (or managing agents) and tenants. There is no Ombudsman specifically for owner-occupied sheltered housing but there is an Ombudsman set up by the Housing Corporation for tenants of registered housing associations, some of which are covered by the Association of Retirement Housing Managers.

Also active in representing people in sheltered housing is the Federation of Residents Associations in Sheltered Housing (FRASH). This organisation acts as a representative body in trying to promote and protect the interests of its members and works closely with the Association of Retirement Housing Managers. FRASH is concerned with matters relating to retirement housing in England and Wales; the corresponding organisation in Scotland is the Sheltered Retirement Housing Owners Confederation (SRHOC) whose base is in Edinburgh.

All of this merely goes to show that sheltered housing is not automatically a way to a trouble-free existence. It is, of course, important to keep everything in perspective. Many sheltered housing schemes work extremely well with good relations between the residents and the managing agents. The most important steps to take are to decide whether the particular sheltered scheme suits you now and to get a full legal opinion on the terms of the lease and the management agreement to assess what changes could theoretically occur in the future.

15.5 Residential care homes and nursing homes

For the purposes of this chapter, residential care means managed accommodation providing a varying level of support for those people who are unable, or who no longer wish, to live independently.

Local authorities often run their own residential care homes with more and more running their own nursing homes. They are usually run by the local social services department (as distinct from locally supplied sheltered housing which is run by the housing department). Local authorities are also responsible for providing residential care for elderly people who, because of infirmity, are unable to live in their own homes. This is a requirement of Part III of the National Assistance Act 1948 and is referred to as Part III accommodation.

15.5.1 Private sector residential homes

The majority of available accommodation is run either privately or through voluntary agencies. The statutory safeguards to residential care are covered by the Registered Homes Act 1984. Any establishment which sets out to provide accommodation and personal care must be registered under the Act. The Act establishes standards of practice covering the care of people living in registered accommodation and also provides for the regular inspection of all registered homes. The responsibility for the implementation of the provisions of the Act lies with the local authorities (often at county level) and they will usually issue their own guidelines to anybody wishing to set up a residential home.

Registration under the Act offers a number of safeguards but no guarantees that a home will be run to a particularly high standard. Many homes now belong to one of the three major professional organisations each with its own monitoring system. The National Care Homes Association, the British Federation of Care Home Proprietors and the Registered Nursing Homes Association all set out to ensure the maintenance of high standards of care.

Residential care homes

These are normally registered by the local social services department who are then required to carry out an inspection at least once every twelve months (and who may also carry out unannounced visits). There are minimum standards laid down by the local authority, and such homes are expected to provide the same level of personal help that would be provided by a caring relative. The basic level of care would be assistance with toileting, feeding and dressing, together with three meals a day.

One weakness in the legislation surrounds those establishments which provide accommodation for less than four people. Although such establishments are now required to register under the Registered Homes (Amendment) Act 1991, the monitoring of them is entirely at the discretion of the local authority. In addition, there is no requirement for such establishments to meet either fire regulations or the requirements of the environmental health officer (both of which are mandatory for larger retirement care homes).

Nursing homes

Nursing homes have to be registered under the 1984 Act but are also registered and inspected by the district health authority. Nursing homes have to provide the same general level of service as a residential care home but must also provide the services of a qualified registered general nurse 24 hours a day.

Dual registered homes

These are homes which provide the concept of continuous care, providing the requirements of residential care for people who are not suffering from any sickness, illness or infirmity but also providing nursing home facilities for those who are. Increasing frailty, therefore, need not mean a move to a different home.

Dual registered homes tend to be few and far between. They have to be registered by both the local social services department and the district health authority which is perhaps an indication that we have some way to go in providing an all-embracing framework of legislation covering the standards of care in residential accommodation.

The work of the local authority

The local authority has the responsibility of ensuring that all residential care homes and nursing homes in its area are registered under the Residential Homes Act and regularly inspected. They will enter into contracts with those homes where they intend to place people assessed by them as being in need of residential care.

Residential homes do not necessarily have to restrict their contracts to their own local authority; they are perfectly entitled to contract with any local authority in the United Kingdom. There would be nothing unusual in an individual of limited means, having been assessed as being in need of residential care by his local authority, moving to another part of the country (perhaps to be near relatives) and going into suitable local residential accommodation, with the bills being paid by his original local authority. Provided the residential home can agree contractual terms with the original local authority, the system will work perfectly well (and it may often be the new local authority that handles the regular paperwork).

15.5.2 The choice of residential care

The choice of both residential care homes and nursing homes is very wide and, if the fees are being paid for out of private funds, you can go where you please. All three of the organisations referred to above offer advice on the kind of topics to be considered when selecting a home, but the ultimate choice will depend on the potential resident's current state of health, his personal preference and, of course, the financial resources available.

Personal preference will generally mean proximity to friends or relatives, peace and quiet (or, alternatively, closeness to shops and other centres of activity) and so on. However, if there is one regular source of dissatisfaction amongst people in residential care it is the loss of privacy and independence.

This aspect should, perhaps, be given quite a high priority when it comes to considering the final choice. Of course, privacy and independence are going to disappear with increasing frailty but there are degrees to which it has to be sacrificed.

If the local authority has carried out an assessment and decided that the individual should go into residential care, the local social services department will normally recommend a home—or a number of homes—which will suit the individual. There is no need to accept one of these; even if the local authority is meeting the full costs, the individual is free (indeed, he has the right) to go to any home that meets his needs subject, of course, to the approval of the social services department. If the alternative home is more expensive, the difference will have to be paid for by a third party or out of the individual's own remaining resources.

There is, of course, nothing to stop any individual entering a residential care or nursing home whenever he wishes. However, this will be as a private cost; if any help is required from the local authority, it must first assess the individual and decide what is the most appropriate solution for that individual (which may not necessarily involve residential care).

15.6   Long-term care insurance

Given the increasing cost of providing for care in old age, there have been a number of developments in the provision of long-term care insurance. In this context, long-term care is defined as the care required by those elderly people who have a progressive illness and who are assessed as being unable to carry out most everyday activities. The assessment is on the basis of the individual's inability to carry out a number of 'activities of daily living' (ADLs) which include bathing, eating, dressing and so on. The help provided can range from home help through to nursing home care; it may also cover respite care to give carers some breathing space.

There are two principal forms of insurance available:

(1)   Long-term regular premium plans taken out by people in pre-retirement to cover the future costs of long-term care.

(2)   Immediate cover to pay for immediate costs. This will typically be a lump sum investment to provide an income rather like an annuity.

The forms that the insurance takes vary from company to company. Some provide the cash out of which the costs of care are paid, others provide a level of care, not cash. Some insurers pay the costs of the residential care direct to the establishment and this has been confirmed by the Inland Revenue as not being regarded as taxable income in the hands of the insured person. Each company also has its own rules on the relationship between ADLs and benefits.

The principal difference between the two main approaches to providing long-term care is either regarding it as a true form of insurance (ie paying in advance with the risk that you may never need it) or paying for it when it is needed by depositing a lump sum with the insurer. The average stay in residential accommodation is about two and a half years which would mean, on average, a total bill of around £40,000 in today's terms. A typical premium for someone of about 50 years of age would tend to be in the region of £100 a month.

The flexibility offered by the plan is very important when it comes to making a choice. In general terms, the factors you should take into account are:

(1)   The plan should be flexible enough to cover the whole range of care from in-house to nursing home.

(2) It should cover an advice service as well as straightforward financial benefits.

(3) It should incorporate index-linking to maintain the real value of benefits.

(4) It should offer a facility to pay fees direct to the residential establishment so that the fees don't count as taxable income.

Overall, long-term care plans do provide a way of funding the costs of residential care and many do offer additional benefits. However, there is no getting away from the fact that the provision of care in old age is expensive and the cost of long-term care insurance reflects that. It is also important to remember that the level of care is based on assessed needs as laid out in the policy. Long-term regular premium plans are not a means of saving money for when you *prefer* to move into residential accommodation; they are insurance plans to provide the funds when you *need* to move into residential accommodation.

The increasing competition in this area has led to the fact that most of the companies offering long-term care insurance agree to meet certain minimum conditions. These include limits to the way existing medical conditions can be taken into consideration, the provision of home care benefits, unlimited years of cover, guaranteed renewability, protection against inflation and, perhaps most important of all, the dropping of exclusions for Alzheimer's disease, probably the biggest single cause of dementia.

It is also important to bear in mind that the costs of long-term care will not be met under private medical insurance. Private medical insurance is designed to cover the cost of medical treatment, it does not meet the needs of people who require help with the basic activities of daily life.

15.7 State benefits and residential care

15.7.1 Income support

People living in residential care, and of limited means, are entitled to claim income support in the usual way. However, the calculation of the resident's 'applicable amount' (ie his weekly assessed needs—see 14.1.4) depends on whether or not he first went into residential care before 1 April 1993 or on or after 1 April 1993.

Before 1 April 1993

Up until 1 April 1993, the applicable amount (see 14.1.4) for people living in a residential care or nursing home was a weekly accommodation allowance (and the cost of meals if charged separately) plus the weekly personal expense allowance. For 1994–95, the accommodation allowance ranges from £194 to £360 depending on the type of home and its location, and the extent of physical disability suffered by the individual.

Individuals who were living in a residential care home or nursing home on 31 March 1993 come under the 'preserved rights' rules. Under these rules, the maximum benefits will continue to be either the fees charged by the home or the higher amount of income support described above (whichever is the lower).

It would be possible for the resident to move to a different residential care home or nursing home and still qualify for preserved rights.

On or after 1 April 1993

Under the community care rules, the accommodation fees are paid for by the local authority. These fees are then reclaimable, either in whole or in part, from the resident. If the individual is of limited means, he will qualify for income support in the usual way (ie as though he were living at home) but the applicable amount will also include a 'residential allowance'. This is a standard weekly allowance throughout the country (set at £48 in April 1994) although there is an additional £5 paid for accommodation in the Greater London area.

15.7.2   Housing benefit

Individuals living in a residential care home or nursing home cannot normally claim housing benefit (see 14.3.1), although there are two circumstances when it can be paid:

(1)   If the resident was living in registered accommodation on 31 March 1993 and was obtaining housing benefit to meet the cost of fees, housing benefit will continue to be paid unless the resident moves to a different residential care or nursing home.

(2)   If the resident was living in registered accommodation on 29 October 1990 and was getting housing benefit to help meet the fees, housing benefit will continue to be paid provided the resident is not getting income support.

15.7.3   Disability living allowance

Residents living in registered residential care homes or nursing homes will always continue to be eligible for the mobility component of disability living allowance (see 14.5.1). If they qualify for the care component, this will generally be withdrawn 28 days after they move into residential accommodation. However, residents may continue to be eligible for continued payments provided they live in private accommodation paid for out of their own resources and are not receiving income support, housing benefit or any help from the local authority.

15.7.4 Attendance allowance

Attendance allowance (see 14.5.2) will generally be withdrawn 28 days after the claimant moves into residential accommodation. However, the resident will continue to be eligible for attendance allowance provided he is living in private accommodation paid for out of his own resources and not receiving any form of financial support from the State or the local authority.

15.8 Sources of help

The National House Building Council will be able to give you details of sheltered housing in your area, as will the Association of Retirement Housing Managers. Your local authority will also have details of sheltered housing schemes in the locality.

You will also find that your local authority will be able to give you details of the registered care homes and nursing homes in the area. The Citizens Advice Bureaux will also be able to help.

In addition, there are a number of other organisations up and down the country who could well be able to offer you assistance in your search for suitable accommodation.

Abbeyfield is a registered charity and is the name given to around 600 voluntary organisations throughout the United Kingdom to provide assisted living for older people. The aim is to provide a balance of privacy and caring support for those older people who would prefer not to live alone but who still retain a good deal of independence.

Each house is financially self-supporting with the cost being met by the charges paid by residents. For residents of limited means, help may be available from the local authority but only within the normal requirements of the Community Care Act.

The basic Abbeyfield house is not a residential care home as such, ie it will not be registered under the Registered Homes Act. The basis for this is that the level of care required by residents will not be as high as that required by a resident of a registered home. This sort of half-way house is called 'very sheltered' housing and, in Abbeyfield's case, it will usually mean live-in staff, an alarm system and two cooked meals a day. The absence of registration is no barrier to its availability to the local authorities. If very sheltered housing is appropriate to the needs of the individual, then local authorities may regard such homes as available resources under the provisions of the Residential Care (Accommodation) Act 1992.

For those residents who need a higher level of care, Abbeyfield have a number of 'extra care' homes which *are* registered and which provide 24-hour residential care. They also have a small number of nursing homes.

Age Concern is probably the best known of the organisations representing the interests of elderly people. They are a widely spread national organisation with branches throughout the United Kingdom. They offer not only practical help on an individual basis but have also established a formidable library of books, booklets and factsheets on many of the topics of relevance to older people. These are all available from their Information and Policy Department in London.

Information on the law and service provision in Scotland is available from Age Concern Scotland.

Counsel and Care is a registered charity which operates a free advice and information service on residential care in the Greater London area. They visit registered residential care and nursing homes on a regular basis and are able to suggest homes to people wishing to move into residential care and also to advise people on the suitability of homes after they have been assessed as requiring residential care.

For people outside the Greater London area, advice is available on appropriate sources of local information and what to look for when choosing a home.

Counsel and Care also undertake studies into the general provision of care for older people; copies of their reports are available from their London office.

The **Elderly Accommodation Counsel** is a charity which, in conjunction with the British Medical Association and the British Geriatric Society, has established a database of over 12,000 residential care and nursing homes throughout the United Kingdom. Information is held on the type of accommodation, the services offered, the level of fees etc and this forms the basis of a search facility available to the general public. By feeding in the parameters of the accommodation you are looking for, the Counsel will be able to offer you a list of names and addresses. There will normally be a fee for this service but it could well help you to narrow your search for a residential home to those in your area that meet your need.

The Counsel also maintains a database of sheltered housing for rent or for sale and is also building up a database of the services offered by various local authorities.

The National Care Homes Association is a national organisation of residential care home owners often with local ancillary associations. It advises its members on all aspects of retirement care and issues a code of practice which its members are expected to follow.

The Registered Nursing Homes Association deals specifically with the standards of care in nursing homes. Those who pass the initial inspection become one of the so-called 'Blue Cross' nursing homes and agree to maintain a high standard of care for their residents. Homes are inspected once every two years and the Association helps its members to maintain standards through advice and education.

The Relatives Association is a registered charity established by and for relatives and friends of older people in residential care, nursing homes and long-stay hospitals. Such people often face problems in coming to terms with this situation and the Association provides a forum for discussion and a centre of advice for helping relatives and friends make sure the quality of care in a residential home is as good as it can be. The Association is a relatively new organisation having been set up in 1992 under the auspices of Counsel and Care. It publishes its own Newsletter and provides a telephone advice line. Local branches are being formed in different parts of the country; the central office can put you in touch.

The Shaftesbury Housing Association was founded in 1970 and provides sheltered housing for the elderly. The Association operates mainly in the South and South-East of England and the majority of accommodation is for the frail elderly with full warden support.

Further information

Community Care Assessments by Richard Gordon (published by Longman) gives a good understanding of the legal framework behind assessments and explains the basis of means testing.

The **Centre for Policy on Ageing** publish a number of booklets on residential care and other issues facing the elderly.

Social Security leaflet IS 50 (Income support) explains how the payment of certain State benefits is affected by a move into residential accommodation.

16 Useful addresses

All telephone numbers change on 16 April 1995 (most with the addition of a 1 after the leading 0 of the area code, eg 0285 will become 01285.)

Abbeyfield Society
53 Victoria Street
St Albans
Herts
AL1 3UW
Tel: 0727 857536

Age Concern England
Astral House
1268 London Road
London
SW16 4ER
Tel: 081-679 8000

Age Concern Scotland
54A Fountainbridge
Edinburgh
EH3 9PT
Tel: 031-228 5656

Association of British Insurers
51 Gresham Street
London
EC2V 7HQ
Tel: 071-600 3333

Benefits Agency Distribution and Storage Centre
Manchester Road
Heywood
Lancashire
OL10 2PZ
Fax: 0706 622955

British Federation of Care Home Proprietors
852 Melton Road
Thurmaston
Leicestershire
LE4 8BN
Tel: 0533 640095 (0116 2640095 after 15 April 1995)

Carers National Association
20-25 Glasshouse Yard
London
EC1A 4JS
Tel: 071-490 8818 CarersLine: 071-490 8898

Centre for Policy on Ageing
25-31 Ironmongers Row
London
EC1V 3QP
Tel: 071-253 1787

Counsel and Care
Lower Ground Floor
Twyman House
16 Bonny Street
London
NW1 9PG
Tel: 071-485 1566

Court of Protection
Public Trust Office
Stewart House
24 Kingsway
London WC2B 6JX
Tel: 071-269 7358

Elderly Accommodation Counsel
46A Chiswick High Road
London
W4 1SZ
Tel: 081-995 8320

Federation of Residents Associations in Sheltered Housing
Secretary: D Johnson Esq MBE
Flat 23
Fernwood
Church Road
Upton
Wirral, Merseyside
L49 6PY
Tel: 051-678 7943

Financial Intermediaries Managers and Brokers Regulatory Association (FIMBRA)
Hertsmere House
Hertsmere Road
London
E14 4AB
Tel: 071-538 8860

Help the Aged
16-18 St James's Walk
London
EC1R 0BE
Tel: 071-253 0253 SeniorLine: 0800 289 404

The Inspector of Foreign Dividends
Lynwood Road
Thames Ditton
Surrey
KT7 0DP
Tel: 081-398 4242

(By the end of 1995, the office of the Inspector of Foreign Dividends will have completed a move to Nottingham but enquiries should go to Thames Ditton in the first place.)

Investment Management Regulatory Organisation (IMRO)
Broadwalk House
5 Appold Street
London
EC2A 2LL
Tel: 071-628 6022

The Law Society (England and Wales)
113 Chancery Lane
London
WC2A 1PL
Tel: 071-242 1222

The Law Society of Scotland
The Law Society's Hall
26 Drumsheugh Gardens
Edinburgh
EH3 7YR
Tel: 031-226 7411

Life Assurance and Unit Trust Regulatory Organisation (LAUTRO)
Centre Point
103 New Oxford Street
London
WC1A 1QH
Tel: 071-379 0444

Moneyfacts Publications
Laundry Loke
North Walsham
Norfolk
NR28 0BD
Tel: 0692 500765

The National Care Homes Association
5 Bloomsbury Place
London
WC1A 2QA
Tel: 071-436 1871

National House-Building Council
Buildmark House
Chiltern Avenue
Amersham
Bucks
HP6 5AP
Tel: 0494 434477

The Pension Schemes Registry
PO Box 1NN
Newcastle-upon-Tyne
NE99 1NN

Registered Nursing Homes Association
Calthorpe House
Hagley Road
Edgbaston
Birmingham
B16 8QY
Tel: 021-454 2511

The Relatives Association
5 Tavistock Place
London
WC1H 9SS
Tel: 071-916 6055

The Securities and Futures Authority (SFA)
Cottons Centre
Cottons Lane
London
SE1 2QB
Tel: 071-378 9000

The Securities and Investments Board (SIB)
Gavrelle House
2-14 Bunhill Row
London
EC1Y 8RA
Tel: 071-638 1240

The Shaftesbury Housing Association
2A Amity Grove
Raynes Park
London
SW20 0LJ
Tel: 081-946 6634

Sheltered Retirement Housing Owners Confederation
Box 321
Edinburgh
EH9 2QA

Appendix A

What goes into a will

Every will has slightly different wording, depending on personal circumstances and, to some extent, the particular style of the person drafting it. The notes explain the contents clause by clause.

The example follows a fairly typical sequence. First are the introductory clauses dealing with the appointment of executors and trustees together with a clause dealing with funeral arrangements. Next are the main provisions dealing with who is to receive money and other property from the estate and who are to be the guardians of any children. Finally, there are some administrative provisions. At the end are the signatures of the testator and witnesses.

The will is based on English law but the basic contents would be found, in a different form, in a will written under the laws of Scotland.

LAST WILL AND TESTAMENT

1   Revocation

> I James Rogers of 23 Acacia Villas Willstone Wiltshire revoke all former wills and testamentary dispositions and declare this to be my last Will ('my Will')

2   Appointment of Executors

> (a)   I appoint my wife Jennifer Rogers to be the Executor and Trustee of this my Will but if she shall be unable or unwilling to act for any reason then I appoint Malcolm Rogers of 17 High Street Willstone Wiltshire and William Smith of 23 The Street Upper Willstone Wiltshire to be the Executors and Trustees of my Will

> (b)   'my Executors' shall mean the executors or executor of my Will whether original or substituted

3   Funeral Directions

> I wish my body to be cremated and the ashes scattered in the grounds of the Willstone Crematorium

4   Definition of My Estate

> In my Will where the context so admits 'my Estate' shall mean:

> (a)   all my property of every kind wherever situate and

> (b)   all property of every kind wherever situate over which I have a general power of appointment and

> (c)   the money investments and property from time to time representing all such property

5   Administration of My Estate

> My Executors shall hold my Estate upon trust

> (a)   as to investments or property other than money in their absolute discretion to sell call in or convert all or any such investments or property into money with power to postpone such sale calling in and conversion and to permit the same to remain as invested and upon trust as to money with a like discretion to invest the same in their names or under their control in any of the investments authorised by my Will or by law with power at the like discretion from time to time to vary or transpose any such investments for others so authorised

Notes

Clause 1

This ensures that any earlier wills are revoked. Whilst the will says that it is the 'last will' this does not mean that it cannot be revoked at a later date.

Clause 2

This appoints the executors and the trustees. The executrix in this case is Jennifer, James Rogers' wife, but if she is dead or incapable of acting as executrix for some reason the executors will be his brother and a close friend.

Clause 3

This sets out James' wishes for his funeral.

Clauses 4 and 5

These are administrative clauses. Clause 4 states that the will is to apply to all of James Rogers' property. Clause 5 sets out the Executors' duties to gather in all the assets, pay all the debts and expenses and distribute the balance in accordance with the will.

Will—*contd*

    (b)   to pay my debts funeral testamentary and administration expenses

    (c)   to give effect to legacies

6   Pecuniary Legacy

I give free of inheritance tax One Hundred Pounds (£100.00) to each of my Executors provided that they accept their appointment as Executors

7   Appointment of Guardians

I APPOINT Malcolm Rogers and Sarah Rogers both of 17 High Street, Willstone, Wiltshire to be the guardians of my minor children

8   Gifts of Residue

SUBJECT as above my Executors shall hold my Estate

    (a)   for my wife Jennifer Rogers absolutely if she shall survive me by twenty eight days but if this residuary gift shall fail for any reason then

    (b)   for such of my children as shall survive me and attain the age of twenty one years and if more than one in equal shares absolutely provided that

    (c)   if any child shall fail to attain a vested interest leaving issue who shall survive me and attain the age of twenty one years then such issue shall take the share of my Estate which such child would otherwise have taken

    (d)   if there shall be more than one of such issue they shall take in equal shares per stirpes but so that no one shall take a share if their parent is alive and takes a share

Notes—*contd*

Clause 6

This clause makes a token gift called a 'pecuniary legacy' to the executors, if they accept their appointment.

Clause 7

This appoints the children's guardians. They are James' brother and sister-in-law. It is important to note that James has chosen people of near his own age to act rather than the grandparents. Also there is an independent joint trustee, William Smith, appointed under Clause 2 who is there to help James' brother look after the money matters. This is a useful safeguard to ensure that the interests of the children are fully protected.

Clause 8

This is probably the most important clause in the will as it deals with the bulk of James' assets, ie the residue of the estate after the gift to the executors. In the first instance the residue will pass to Jennifer but the gift is conditional on her surviving for 28 days. Making the gift conditional in this way can have inheritance tax advantages, particularly if one spouse dies shortly after the other, perhaps as a result of the same accident. The 28 day period could be extended up to a maximum of 6 months but 28 days is long enough to cope with most situations without being so long that there is an undue delay in the administration of the estate.

The remainder of the clause deals with what happens in the event of Jennifer not surviving the 28 day period. If this does happen the estate will be held in trust for Jane and Michael, James' two children, until they attain the age of 21. In the event that either Jane or Michael dies before they reach 21, the result will depend on whether they have any children living at their death. If they have a living child at that time (ie if there are any grandchildren), that child will take the share that his parent would have received had he or she attained the age of 21 (this is what 'per stirpes' means, ie the share passes down through one branch of the family tree). If there are no grandchildren, the half share in the estate will pass to whichever of Jane and Michael survives the other.

Will—*contd*

9   Executor's Powers

MY Executors shall in addition and without prejudice to all statutory powers have the powers and immunities set out in the Schedule provided that they shall not exercise any of their powers so as to conflict with the beneficial provisions of my Will

Testimonium and Attestation

SIGNED by me on the   day of   19   as and
for my last will and testament comprising 3 pages

_ _ _ _ _ _ _ _ _ _ _ _ _ _ _ _ _ _ _ _

Signature of testator

SIGNED by the testator in our presence and then by us all in his

                    Witness 1   Witness 2

Signature:

Full name:

Address:

Occupation:

Notes—*contd*

Clause 9

Clause 9 gives the Executors some additional powers to enable them to administer the estate more easily and to ensure that the children are adequately provided for. For convenience these are contained in a separate schedule (not reproduced).

For the most part these clauses are standard and would include as a minimum:

(a) a power of investment so that the Executors are able to take advantage of the wide range of investment opportunities that exist.

(b) a power of 'maintenance and advancement' which allows the executors to pay out money to look after the children before they attain the age of 21, at which point they become entitled to the money absolutely. This is needed to ensure that, for example, the children's school fees can continue to be paid. There would also be other powers depending on the complexity of the will.

Attestation Clause

This is the part of the will where James and the two witnesses have signed. The rules for witnessing wills are quite complicated and must be rigidly adhered to for the will to be valid. This is covered in more detail in 10.5.4.

Index